Advance Praise for …..

One good sea story does not always lead to another. It is truly remarkable that Gary Slaughter should have managed to provide 60 good sea stories in chronological sequence describing the life of a young man from the Mid -West through his halcyon youth to that of a highly trained expert in Anti -Submarine Warfare (ASW). That these events took place in a decade of change throughout the naval establishment provides the opportunity to share a multitude of situations that will be of interest not only to the military reader but to all that have an interest in history and autobiographical writing.
CAPT Earl H. Russell, USN (Ret.)

… Award-winning author Gary Slaughter's memoir chronicles rivet ing first-hand experience as a Cold War Naval officer.
VNN Veterans News Now

A great read! Slaughter takes us on a cruise which starts with the evolution of a Michigan farm boy into a commissioned Naval Officer and continues into one of the most dangerous periods in U.S. history - the Cuban Missile Crisis. Slaughter, as a young destroyer officer on the *USS Cony,* must communicate with an exhausted Russian submarine commander who is on the verge of making a huge mistake, which would start the Third World War. Slaughter's many vignettes give a vivid glimpse of life at sea on a destroyer.
CAPT Paul Goorjian, USNR (Ret.)

… each of these 60 incredible stories shows new insights into everyday life on the Cold War frontline.
VT Veterans Today

I wish I had read Gary Slaughter's *Sea Stories* when I was in high school, contemplating military service. His memoirs are an encyclopedia of events in his naval career that are humorous, empathic, heroic, and tragic. It would have been an eye-opener on what could lay ahead, with some valuable wisdom for maneuvering in confused seas
LT Les Westerman, USNR (Ret.)

During the Cuban Missile Crisis in 1962, U.S. Navy Ensign Gary Slaughter helped defuse a possible confrontation between his destroyer and a Soviet submarine armed with a nuclear-tipped torpedo. The Owosso native's skillful handling of what could have prompted World War III was featured in two documentary films, including *The Man Who Saved the World* by the PBS and *The Silent War* by BBC.
Argus-Press

By the mid-1950s, radio, movies, and TV exposed small -town kids to the world beyond their parents' lives. The military was then the common escape route, though college was an option for those who qualified and could pay - no guaranteed student loans in 1957. Slaughter and many of us found we could combine the two with the NROTC program. And bo y does he show how quickly those college and Navy adventures can lead to extraordinary responsibility for a young officer, as Gary becomes a player in an historical nuclear standoff, classified as "Top Secret" so he can't tell us about it until forty years later.
LT Karl (Chuck) Nuechterlein, USN (Ret.)

..... Sea Stories: A Memoir of a Naval Officer (1956-1967)

Shedding light on some of the most infamous conflicts in United States history during the Cold War, Gary Slaughter shares his recollections of his direct involvement in *Sea Stories: A Memoir of a Naval Officer (1956-1967)*, a gripping collection of vignettes fusing the optimism, morality, and patriotism of the era with hard facts and grim realities of naval warfare. Taken as a collection of short stories or altogether, *Sea Stories* is sure to capture attention of historians everywhere.
Foreword Reviews, **Pallas Gates McCorquodale**

... his writing style is easygoing...highly readable. An enjoyable account of Navy life.
Kirkus

The book is made up of ... vignettes recounting episodes from his life serving on destroyers during the Cold War. All these encounters are given equal billing to an extraordinary event during the Cuban missile crisis when our hero had to face up to an emotional captain of a Soviet submarine armed with nuclear weapons. This is heady stuff and one of those lost stories of the Cold War well worth knowing. These vignettes add up to a very real story that is neither gung-ho or shallow. The book has comedy, tragedy, and drama in equal measure.
War History Online, **Mark Barnes**

Gary Slaughter's sharing of the details of his emerging from college and enjoying seven years as a junior officer aboard two US Navy destroyers, is amazing in his recapture of so many interesting details. There is much to be learned and treasured by young men heading into a life of adventure, on the high seas and in marriage.....that I want to recommend it to young NROTC graduates and Surface Warfare Officers of the future. Revealed in his book are moments in history which could have reshaped the modern world we live in.
RADM J. C. Breast, USN (Ret.)

... A former naval officer recalls how nuclear Armagedodon almost started at sea in October 1962.
Task & Purpose

Slaughter's memoir offers stories about his 11 years in the Navy, some humorous, some more somber, but these stories are real and give the readers a first-hand look at the immense amount of hard work and dedication it takes to be a U.S.naval officer. It is clear that Slaughter has used the same dedication in writing these stories that will educate and inspire all who read it.
Belle Meade Living, **Emily Grant**

Gary Slaughter's memoir is a reminder of a far simpler time when the request of a crest fallen adversary for cigarettes and bread could be fulfilled on the spot without reference to a phalanx of State Department and Pentagon lawyers.
CDR Andrew Bradick USN (Ret.)

Also by Gary Slaughter

Cottonwood Summer '45
Cottonwood Spring
Cottonwood Winter: A Christmas Story
Cottonwood Fall
Cottonwood Summer

SEA STORIES

A Memoir of a Naval Officer
(1956 - 1967)

This book is a memoir, reflecting the author's present recollections of experiences over time. Some names have been changed, some events have been compressed, and some dialogue has been recreated. Because this is a book of memory and memory has its own story to tell, the author has done his best to tell a truthful story. The author recognizes that his memories of the events described may differ from those of his Navy comrades.

ISBN: 978-0-9744206-6-0

Copyright © 2016 by Gary Slaughter Corporation. All rights reserved.

Copyedit and Layout: Publish & Launch
Cover design: Damonza.com
Cover photo: Roger Rieman

Library of Congress Control Number: 2016942720

Publisher's Cataloging-in-Publication Data
Slaughter, Gary, 1939-
Sea stories: a memoir of a naval officer (1956-1967) / Gary Slaughter.
    pages cm.
Includes bibliographic references.
    ISBN: 978-0-9744206-6-0
    1. Cold War (1945-1989). 2. Cuban Missile Crisis, 1962. 3. United States Naval Academy -- Alumni and alumnae -- Biography. 4. United States. Navy -- Maneuvers -- History -- 20th century. 5. United States. Navy -- Officers -- Biography. 6. Slaughter, Gary, 1939 -- Biography. 7. Bulkeley, John Duncan, 1911-1996. I. Title.
    V63.S62 A3 2016
    359.0092; B
                        2016942720

Published by Fletcher House
PO Box 59504
Nashville, TN 37205

Sea Stories: Memoir of a Naval Officer (1956-1967) was written to honor the hundreds of Navy friends and shipmates with whom I served during my eleven years of naval service. I am particularly grateful for those of you with whom I have shared even closer friendships over the course of the decades since we served together.

This book is dedicated to my wife Joanne for her untiring energy and encouragement during the writing of Sea Stories, as well as my five Cottonwood novels. Without her loyal support and active involvement, I would have never accomplished this body of work.

VIGNETTES

SEA STORIES

A Memoir of a Naval Officer
(1956 - 1967)

GARY SLAUGHTER

Prologue

Nashville, Tennessee
Spring 2016

At the height of the Cuban Missile Crisis on October 27, 1962, called *Black Saturday* by the White House, I found myself staring eye to eye with the Captain of a Soviet submarine at a distance of only 200 feet. His name was Vitali Savitsky, and he was an angry and desperate man. I was a 22-year-old US Navy Ensign and the only person in our squadron of eight anti-submarine destroyers who had the skill to communicate with Savitsky.

Sea Stories: Memoir of a Naval Officer (1956-1967) describes my role in dissuading Savitsky from unleashing the nuclear weapons of the Soviet Union and America, which most certainly would have destroyed the world. This dramatic event is vividly depicted in one of the 60 vignettes comprising this book that spans the dozen years of my naval service during the Cold War.

Becoming a naval officer was the best thing that had ever happened to me, but this was not something I dreamed of as a boy. In fact, just the opposite was true.

Growing up in Owosso, Michigan during World War II, like all of my friends, I never imagined myself as a Navy man. I declare this with the authority of a boy who spent a great deal of his childhood watching war movies. On weekends, for only 22 cents, we reveled in at least four patriotic movies about brave American soldiers, marines, or pilots kicking the stuffing out of our enemies.

Not that we had anything against the Navy. As far as we were concerned the Navy didn't do any real fighting. The only Navy movie I recall seeing was *The Fighting Sullivans*, which was released in 1944, and all except a few minutes of that story was set in a small American town far from the frontlines.

After high school, boys had three choices. We could join the military (preferably the Army), we could go to work in a

General Motors factory, or we could work with our fathers in whatever trade they practiced. This was particularly true of boys growing up on farms. Of course, my father was highly keen on my becoming his assistant in his sewing-machine repair business, which was definitely not the career for me.

Since I knew that going to college would be financially difficult for me, I laid down a two-part plan to achieve my goal. First, if I got exceptionally good grades, I could qualify for a college scholarship. Second, if I gave up high-school sports, I could work a part-time job to earn money for college.

After school, on weekends, and in the summer of 1955 and 1956, I worked as gardener for the Woodard family. When Mrs. Dolly Woodard discovered my academic standing and my desire to attend college, she tried to convince me to attend the US Naval Academy. She assured me that her neighbor, Congressman Alvin Bentley, would certainly give me that appointment. By the fall of my senior year, I had saved $1,200, which would only pay for about three semesters at Michigan. I needed to find another source of college money. And I did.

Coincidentally, Lynn Siebold, the sister of my good friend Betsy, was to be married at her family home in Owosso. Lynn had attended Smith College, and her fiancé, Cliff Watts, had recently graduated from Harvard. I was invited to the wedding. Much to my surprise, it was a military wedding that included six newly-commissioned and smartly dressed Navy Ensigns. These young officers had all come from humble backgrounds like mine, and they had been bright enough to win NROTC scholarships to Harvard.

In conversations, they told me about the Holloway Plan that provided full scholarships to 40 universities around the country, including my first choice, Michigan. When they learned that I was near the top of my high-school class they urged me to apply for a Navy scholarship.

I applied in the fall of 1956, and Congressman Alvin Bentley, a Michigan man, offered me the choice of an appointment to the US Naval Academy or to the Regular NROTC program at Michigan. Of course, I chose Michigan.

Naively, I thought that, after completing the application for the NROTC scholarship, providing a transcript of my high school grades to date (nearly all A's), and a recommendation by Congressman Bentley, I would automatically be named the recipient of the prized scholarship. However, the Navy had more requirements.

At 7 am on a Thursday morning in March 1957, I reported to the Naval Hospital at Fort Wayne, located in the city of Detroit, Michigan. Because of the distance between Owosso and Fort Wayne, Dad and I left at 4 am to arrive by 7 am, hitting Detroit during the morning rush hour. Along with hundreds of applicants, I was subjected to a rigorous physical examination. Then we went to the training facility to take the Scholastic Aptitude Test (SAT). These tests ensured that I met the Navy's high physical and mental standards. While not daunting, they consumed most of the day.

As we were about to depart, the Chief Petty Officer, who had administered the SAT, found us and delivered good news. "Son, I have been administering that SAT for years, and I am happy to report that your test scores were the highest I have ever seen." He patted me on the back and said, "Well done, Son." Then he shook my father's hand and congratulated him on my excellent test performance.

The drive back to Owosso was far more relaxing than our trip earlier that day. Most important, after meeting the Navy's standards and then some, I was officially named the scholarship winner, and the *Owosso Argus Press* announced this news, accompanied by my photo, on its front page. What a proud moment for my family and me. I sent my thanks and a copy of the article to Cliff and Lynn Watts.

I immediately fell in love with the Navy, a love affair that has never ceased. My experiences were so rich, positive, and varied that my memory is filled with the wonderful and some-times unusual people, places, and experiences I had in the Navy.

Most important, the officers I served with share my feelings. We stay in constant contact with each other and spend time together at our reunions, where we relate sea story after sea story.

In this book, I share my rich collection of stories in the hope that you will enjoy them as much as I enjoyed remembering and recording them.

Captain Mothersill

NROTC - University of Michigan
Spring 1958

During the second semester of NROTC classroom training, my friend Jim Miller and I endured an unpleasant experience. Like me, Jim was a Regular NROTC scholarship holder. We were both committed to studying hard, not only in NROTC classes but in our other classes as well, because we needed high grades to retain our substantial scholarships.

Also, we knew that if we ranked as one of the top three in our class during our junior year, we would be assigned to a plum 1st Class Midshipman Cruise in the Mediterranean. However, in our freshman year, a serious situation reared its ugly head in the form of Bill Taylor, a bully and a cheat. Taylor was a large, muscular fellow with a shock of red hair. Although I don't think he earned a football scholarship, he was physically impressive enough to make the team, which caused his head to swell. He made Jim and me uncomfortable when he threatened the eligibility of our coveted scholarships.

While Taylor may have worked very hard in the weight room, there was no evidence that he did a lick of homework for the NROTC class. Nevertheless, he was smart enough to ascertain the identities of two bright students. Acting quickly on this knowledge, he took a seat in the row directly behind Jim and me. Taylor was tall enough to look over our shoulders and would read what we wrote on our exam papers. When we realized that he was copying our answers, we hunched over our desks to prevent him from seeing what we were writing. When we did so, he grabbed our arms with his massive paws and squeezed them until we were forced to sit up. By using this technique on a regular basis, he raised his test scores dramatically.

Jim and I weren't sure exactly what to do. If we told our instructor the truth, would he believe us? Besides, if we spilled the beans and Taylor found out, he would make our lives miserable. He would probably use us as tackling dummies. In the midst of our turmoil, a hero came to our rescue.

Among other things, Lieutenant DeMartini was a well-liked and highly respected NROTC freshmen instructor, a Frenchman from New Orleans and, to the admiration of many of our peers, a top-notch naval aviator. The first thing he said to Jim and me was, "I've been observing your interaction with Midshipman Taylor over the past few days. He's dead wrong. Still I don't blame you for not speaking up. Nobody likes to rat out another fellow, especially when we're supposed to be building mutual trust and character within this corps of midshipmen here in North Hall. "

I don't know about Jim, but I was relieved to know that someone in authority was aware of our predicament. Still, I was extremely curious about what would happen next.

The Lieutenant told us, "Because I don't want you fellows to be snitches, this is what I have decided to do. After we're finished here, I plan to tell Captain Mothersill about this entire situation. I'll tell him that I've observed a serious case of cheating and that when you two resisted, Taylor bullied you into helping him by physically threatening you. I'll ask the Captain not to mention your names to anyone, especially Taylor. I'll take the heat on this, and let's see if Taylor tries to strong-arm me. One last thing: Knowing the Captain, I'm certain he'll want to talk to you after he hears my story."

We thanked Lieutenant DeMartini profusely and shook his hand. As he was leaving the room, I asked, "Lieutenant, what do you think will happen to Taylor?"

His answer stunned me. "If I have my way, he's gone from NROTC, from the football team, and from the University of Michigan. And I bet that Captain Mothersill will agree."

With that, he left the room to confer with the Commanding Officer.

Before leaving the building, Jim and I agreed not to discuss this with anyone. On my way to the SAE house, I fantasized about ratting out Taylor to some of my fraternity brothers who were heavy weights, including Brother Jim Orwig, who was Michigan's football team captain. But I kept my mouth shut.

The next morning, Jim and I met at the entrance to North Hall, where Captain Mothersill's secretary was standing outside his office door. She stopped us and said that the Captain would like to see us. To our surprise, the conversation took an unexpected turn.

Captain Mothersill was a soft-spoken, handsome man with broad shoulders and a narrow waist. His black hair, streaked with gray, gave him the distinguished look of a movie actor, and his piercing blue eyes kept our attention.

We each shook the Captain's hand and took our chairs in front of his desk. To put us at ease, he came around his desk and sat in a leather side chair near us, forming an intimate circle. I remember thinking that it was quite cozy.

"Men, Lieutenant DeMartini has related his observations of Midshipman Taylor's behavior with respect to you two," he said. "I'll make this short and sweet. That type of bullying is absolutely immoral and flies in the face of naval ethics and tradition. There is no room in this man's Navy for a person of that low moral character. You see, I believe that what binds this country together is just the opposite – High Moral Character. I think we must demonstrate this character in our relationships with those countries who are our allies, those who serve us in the American government, and those who guide their flocks in the churches of this country. I am personally committed to this belief system and pride myself as being morally pure.

"Now don't get me wrong. When I was a young fellow like you boys, I used to sit those pretty girls on my lap and turn their knobs like radios. Those were the days before I found my way. Now I'm very active in an organization called *Moral Re-Armament*. It was founded during the war in 1942. As a matter of fact, each summer we hold our annual conference on Mackinaw Island, where we discuss what we call *Initiatives for Change*. Hundreds of people attend and share their high ideals with all of us."

Jim and I were speechless. The best we could muster was a nod and an occasional, "Well, I'll be."

"Good!" said the Captain. "That's enough of my pontificating. Here's a *Moral Re-Armament* brochure for each of you. I hope you'll read it carefully. Then if you want to join, make an appointment with me, and I'll sign you up. It'll be the best thing to happen in your life."

He stood, and we stood. As we were on our way out the door, he added, "And don't you worry another second about that immoral lout Taylor."

Neither of us ever saw Midshipman Taylor again, which was a great relief to us both.

Years later, when my wife and I were visiting Mackinaw Island, I saw a large hunched-over man with an unusually large crop of reddish-gray hair. He was dressed in work clothes and was raking leaves from around the Moral Re-Armament Meeting Hall. For a moment, I wondered. But no, it couldn't be.

My Head

USS Valley Forge – Norfolk, Virginia
Summer 1958

During my freshman year, I was enrolled at the University of Michigan as a Regular NROTC student. At Michigan, the NROTC unit consisted of four classes, each having about 60 to 70 students, both Regular and Contract NROTC. We regulars were the scholarship holders. Winning a Regular NROTC appointment was an honor and was financially rewarding as well. The Navy paid for our tuition, books, and fees. Plus, we received a monthly stipend of $50 during the school year, which, back in those days, more than covered our room and board. During our three summer cruises, we were paid about $150 per month plus room and board. We were also given an allowance to purchase our uniforms at a great discount. By my calculation, the Regular NROTC appointment allowed me to pocket a small profit at the end of each school year. In addition, the cruises didn't last all summer, and I could work as a carpenter's assistant for a few weeks each year.

Our NROTC class of midshipmen learned the basic skills and knowledge required of a US naval officer. We met for one hour on Monday, Wednesday, and Friday. For this class, we could wear civvies, provided our shoes were shined and our hair was cut military style. For the entire year, we studied US Naval History and Introduction to Naval Life. Our classes were taught by career Navy officers.

On Thursdays, we were bused to a park. There, wearing our Service Dress Blue uniforms, we drilled for two hours. We learned to march in a precise synchronized manner, to bark responses to the upper-class midshipmen who led our drill sessions, and to handle our rifles in drill-team fashion. Our rifles were Springfield '03s, meaning they were introduced in 1903 and used in World War I. These bolt-action rifles had a five-round clip filled with .30-03 cartridges. I should say they *could* be filled with cartridges, but we drilled with unloaded rifles. They were also designed to carry attached bayonets. However, we midshipman weren't allowed to have such dangerous devices when we drilled.

During the summer of 1958, all Michigan Regular NROTC students were required to participate in an eight-week summer cruise. In preparation for the 3rd Class Midshipman Cruise, each of us was issued a sea bag. This heavy canvas sack, when flattened on the deck, measured approximately two feet by four feet. Its top was secured by a heavy length of nylon rope (*line* in naval terms) threaded through six large brass grommets fitted into the double-thick canvas strip encircling the bag's opening. A heavy canvas handle was sewn on its side for toting the bag when it was filled with our work uniforms and other clothing. We were also issued stencils with our full name, *G.L. Slaughter,* and initials, *GLS,* which were used to mark every piece of our clothing to differentiate it from the clothing of other midshipmen. We were also issued laundry bags in which our dirty clothing would be washed by the ship's laundry.

I'm proud to say that I still have my stenciled sea bag. It hangs on a hook near my work bench. Every now and then it comes in handy. Its only flaw is that its canvas handle is stenciled with a *KWN* because of a joke played on me by my college roommate and best friend, who was also a Regular NROTC midshipman, Karl William Nuechterlein or Chuck for short.

Our Regular NROTC class assembled at Willow Run Airport near Ann Arbor. Each midshipman wore the Service Dress Khaki uniform. We were flown to the Naval Air Station (NAS) Norfolk on a Military Air Transport Service (MATS) airliner. From there, we were bused to the Naval Operation Base (NOB) piers where the *USS Valley Forge* (CVS 45), or the *Happy Valley*, as she was affectionately nicknamed, awaited us. She was the flagship of Task Group Alpha, an Anti-Submarine Warfare (ASW) unit composed of an aircraft carrier, its helicopters and fixed-wing ASW aircraft, and a squadron of eight ASW destroyers.

Here we would spend the summer learning about life in the US Navy – from the bottom up. We would also observe ASW operations of Task Group Alpha.

Carrying our sea bags, we boarded the ship, going up the gangway and then down into a large compartment equipped with small lockers and nearly 100 four-level, tie-up beds. These were aluminum frames into which sheets of sturdy canvas were tied to serve as our mattresses. We were soon joined by our compartment mates, a class of Regular midshipman from the University of Missouri, with whom we would spend the next eight weeks. Our Missouri counterparts and we became good friends. During the time I served in the Navy, I often bumped into a Missouri compartment mate, and we would savor a brief reunion, reminiscing about our summer together on the *Happy Valley.*

Once we were settled in, we changed into our neatly stenciled work uniforms consisting of blue dungaree trousers, light-blue chambray shirts, black work shoes, and a white sailor cap. To identify us as midshipmen, a narrow band of dark blue material was sewn to our hats' brims.

Our daily routine was simple. Our mornings were spent learning what it was like to be an ordinary seaman. Each of us was assigned a *cleaning station* for which we were responsible. We mopped, scrubbed, and polished our stations to perfection. Mine was a small head (bathroom) located just outside the Wardroom, the officers' dining room and lounging area. By small, I mean the dimensions of this compartment were about five feet by five feet. The head was equipped with one commode, a small sink, and a mirror. Since there was no stall in the compartment, the officer using my head had to lock the door for privacy. Its unique attribute was that entire compartment, including all the equipment, was constructed of stainless steel. Even the deck plates were stainless steel, cross-hatched to prevent slipping on the otherwise slick surface.

This cleaning assignment introduced me to a magic potion that dominated an average seaman's life. *Brasso!* That summer I learned to use this magical liquid to make my head sparkle. I spent hours shining that stainless steel, using *Brasso*-soaked cloths to remove the dullness and clean dry towels to bring the surfaces to a sparkling shine. Officers muttered and complained when they saw my *Head Closed for Cleaning* sign hanging on the door handle. They rattled and sometimes knocked on the locked door. How could I help it if it took me four hours to do a perfect cleaning job each day? Today I am still an aficionado of *Brasso*. I use it to polish the brass fixtures of the sink in our powder room. As I shine away, I am always reminded of *My Head*.

After mornings at our cleaning stations, we spent afternoons touring various functions aboard the ship, including repair shops, engineering spaces, gun mounts, and the aircraft residing in its hangar deck. And every week or so, we changed into Service Dress Khaki uniforms and traveled to other naval locations in the Norfolk area. We visited the mine school in Yorktown, where we learned about the art of sweeping mines, and also attended lectures at Little Creek, a nearby amphibious base.

On one occasion, we attended a lecture by a Marine General who strutted officiously to the center of the stage to address us. While he was rather short for a Marine, he stood straight and tall, an apparent attempt to impress us with his toughness. I am sure that he, having been promoted to General in the Marine Corps, had a distinguished record of military service. Unfortunately the poor man suffered from a distinct speech deficiency.

"All wight, you men, woosen up!" He sounded exactly like Elmer Fudd.

We all bit our tongues to avoid laughing out loud, and all 70 of us squirmed in our seats in an effort to dissipate our repressed laughter. A mandatory quality of a naval officer is self-control. On that occasion, we all perfected that discipline.

Unexpected New Career - Anti-Submarine Warfare

USS Valley Forge – Norfolk, Virginia
Summer 1958

When we reported aboard the *USS Valley Forge* for our 3rd Class Midshipmen Cruise, none of us knew that the Task Group Alpha Commander would be Admiral John S. "Jimmy" Thach. In 1941, he led a squadron of Navy fighters, the F4F *Wildcats*, and developed a tactic for defeating the Japanese Mitsubishi *Zero*. The *Zero's* extraordinary climb and maneuverability had been a big advantage in one-on-one encounters with any American fighter of that era.

Thach devised his famous tactic, *The Thach Weave*, during one intense dogfight. A *Zero* had pulled up behind a *Wildcat* in Thatch's squadron. Lieutenant Commander Thach radioed the doomed pilot to continue in a so-called scissors pattern, the first phase of which would cause the endangered aircraft to pass under Thach's *Wildcat*. Then both Americans would circle out and return on collision courses with each other to confront the unwary *Zero* pilot with two undesirable choices. If he continued following his prey, he would fly right into Thach's concentrated fire. If he broke off, he would subject himself to the combined fire of both Americans. There was no way out. When executed correctly, *The Thach Weave* was a deadly trap that neutralized the *Zero's* superior performance capabilities. This gave the F4F *Wildcat* a tremendous advantage over the *Zero*.

When we reported aboard, we also didn't know that the *Happy Valley* was the flagship for Task Group Alpha, the first integrated Anti-Submarine Warfare fighting unit assembled during the Cold War. What amazed me most was the sheer number of ASW platforms comprising Task Group Alpha, and, more significant, how the majority of these platforms provided the ability to detect, track, and destroy Soviet submarines. The

Valley Forge itself was made up of or had immediate access to the following ASW platforms:

- a fully equipped and trained squadron of eight highly capable *Fletcher Class* ASW destroyers
- two submarines completely weaponized for offensive action against the enemy and also highly skilled in Soviet tactics, enabling them to act the role of a Soviet submarine during our ASW exercises
- a full squadron of ASW fixed-wing aircraft, specifically the Grumman S2F *Tracker*
- a full squadron of ASW helicopters, specifically Sikorsky HSS-1 *Seabat*
- a detachment of airborne early warning (AEW), modified Douglas A-1 *Skyraiders*
- a detachment of land based Lockheed P-2 *Neptunes*

Task Group Alpha 1959

Tools that the Task Group Alpha platforms could employ to detect and/or track Soviet submarines as early as 1958 were impressive:

- radar
- sonar
- *Julie* (small explosives that create echoes detected and located by sonobuoys)
- *Sniffer* (sensitive smoke detectors that caught the emissions of snorkeling submarines)
- sonobuoy arrays, dispersed by helicopters
- dipping sonars, lowered from helicopters
- aircraft deployed MAD (magnetic anomaly detection) of submarines moving through magnetic fields of the earth)
- Infra-Red (IR) sensors
- high altitude sighting by blimps and patrol aircraft
- SOSUS, our top secret network of sophisticated underwater hydrophones stretching along the coast of North America

The array of weapons that Task Group Alpha platforms could employ to destroy a Soviet submarine in 1958 included:

- bombs
- torpedoes, heat or metal seeking
- torpedoes, wire-guided
- depth charges
- mines
- *Hedge Hogs*
- *Weapon Alpha*
- *Harpoon* missiles
- 5"/54 guns
- 5"/38 guns
- 40mm guns
- K-guns
- under-wing rockets

These weapons did not include tactical nuclear devices that were under development in 1958 and are still deployed today.

Given the increasing threat from evermore numerous and capable Soviet submarines, including nuclear-powered boats, I concluded at a young age that the battle for supremacy over the Soviet Union would be fought on and, more significant, under the surface of the ocean. Therefore, I committed to be a part of this struggle. Fortunately, for the remainder of my Navy career, the following assignments enabled me to follow this course successfully:

- Third Class Midshipman: *USS Valley Forge* (CVS 45), Task Group Alpha: Summer Cruise, Western Atlantic, 1958
- 1st Class Midshipman: *USS Valley Forge* (CVS 45), Task Group Alpha: Summer Cruise, Mediterranean, 1960
- Ensign: Electronics and Communications Officer School (six months)
- Ensign: *USS Cony* (DDE 508), Task Group Alpha
- Ensign: Electronics Material Officer
- Ensign: Communications and Cryptosecurity Officer
- Ensign: ECM Officers School
- Ensign: ASW Air Controller School; Crypto Operators School
- Ensign: Gunfire Support School
- Ensign: JOOD/Translator, Cuban Missile Crisis; Surfaced Soviet Foxtrot Submarine *(B-59)*
- Ensign: OOD, Sea and Anchor Detail
- Ensign: OOD, Condition 1ASW
- Lieutenant (jg): US Naval Destroyer School
- Lieutenant: *USS Blandy* (DD 943), Task Group Alpha
- Lieutenant: Engineering Officer
- Lieutenant: OOD, Sea and Anchor Detail
- Lieutenant: OOD, Condition 1ASW
- Lieutenant: Aide and Office Administrator to the President of the US Navy Board of Inspection and Survey (INSURV), Washington, DC

I am proud to have devoted eleven years of my life to serving the US Navy and my country. I am particularly proud to have been considered qualified to serve as the Officer of the Deck (OOD) during ASW exercises and combat situations, both as an Ensign on my first ASW destroyer and as a Lieutenant on my second. I believe that, while performing those positions, I contributed to improving the tactics and methods used against the potential enemy.

Midshipman Crisis Cruise

USS Valley Forge – Norfolk, Virginia
Summer 1958

In the fall of 1957, we began our NROTC training with 40 Regulars in our class. Because the attrition rate of Regulars was not insignificant, we had about 35 Regulars in the program when we began our 3rd Class Midshipmen Cruise. Academic problems and other factors caused this reduction in class size. At that time, there was no penalty for resigning from the program, even in your senior year. That rule changed after our class, and, from that time on, those Regular scholarship holders who resigned before being commissioned still owed the Navy time, which they would serve as enlisted men.

On our summer cruise in 1958, with midshipmen from the University of Missouri, we were crammed together in a relatively small sleeping compartment. Because we needed storage space for our wide range of dress and working midshipman uniforms, we faced a serious challenge.

It was the height of summer in Norfolk, Virginia. Since the *Valley Forge* had been built and commissioned during World War II, we did not enjoy the luxury of air-conditioning. Compared to living conditions aboard Navy warships today, the *Happy Valley* was a virtual inferno. In some respects, this challenging environment created a bonding experience for the 70 of us trapped in that oven. In an odd way, these difficult living conditions deepened our mutual respect and friendship.

When we were in Norfolk that summer, there was very little to do for after-hours recreation. On weekends, it was no small task to get away from the ship and find a place of relaxation and fun. Because most of us were from Michigan or Missouri, we had never seen the ocean, so going to the beach became our highest priority. But getting to a beach wasn't easy.

In order to leave the ship on liberty, we were required to wear our Service Dress Khaki uniforms. This uniform consisted of a tight-fitting blouse (suit coat) over a non-breathing khaki shirt with a black tie whose knot was pressed tightly to our throats by a Spiffy, a wire and spring device inserted under the collar. In addition to a pair of non-breathing khaki trousers, we wore black socks and heavy brown Oxford-like shoes. Finally we wore a non-breathing khaki covered combination cap resembling that of a police officer. By the time we travelled from our compartment to the quarterdeck to leave the ship, we were drenched in perspiration.

Since none of us had cars and our meager midshipman pay ruled out the use of taxis, we relied on city or county buses. Our choices in beaches boiled down to two. Ocean View featured an amusement park with a roller coaster, open-air bars that served 18-year-olds draft 3.2 beer, a locker rental area that allowed us to swap our stifling uniforms for bathing suits, and beaches teeming with hot-and-cold-running Norfolk girls. The other choice was Virginia Beach, featuring pure white sand, miles of wide, unpopulated beaches, wild body-surfing, and no girls to distract us.

Travel by bus was time-consuming. After we left the ship, we walked a mile to the city bus stop located just outside the main gate. There we caught a bus that transported us via Granby Street to the main bus terminal located in downtown Norfolk. Then we waited for a local bus to take us to Ocean View, or we could wait for a county bus to take us out to the wilds of Virginia Beach. If we were lucky, one-way travel time to Ocean View was about an hour and a half. Virginia Beach added another hour to the trip, but it was worth the time, because our final destinations were so fascinating. Besides, as we travelled along Norfolk's streets, we were entertained by the assortment of signs that homeowners placed in their front lawns. Typically the signs read *Dogs and Sailors - Keep Off the Grass.*

Back in 1958, there also were reflections of Norfolk's stubborn resistance to desegregation. During our time there, we became used to seeing two sets of restrooms and water fountains – one for *Whites Only* and the other for *Colored Only*. Because we Michiganders had never seen such signs, they seemed strange to us, yet they were perfectly normal to our Southern-born shipmates, both black and white.

(Some years later, at Great Lakes where I attended the Electronics Officers' School, my Bachelor Officers Quarters (BOQ) roommate was a fellow Ensign from New York City named Al Garcia. By nationality, Al was Puerto Rican. Ethnically, he was obviously a black man. Coming from Owosso, Michigan, a so-called Sundown Town, I wondered why Al's being black never bothered me. I concluded that color simply didn't matter, and that's remained my attitude during my entire life.)

After returning to the ship from our third visit to the beach, we were informed that the *Valley Forge* would soon depart for an at-sea period to participate in ASW exercises as the flagship of Task Group Alpha. Our partners would be Desron 28, a squadron of ASW destroyers, including the *USS Cony* (DDE 508) on which I would serve some years later.

Our first experience at sea was exciting for all of us midshipmen. We loved watching night air operations from perches in the superstructure above the main deck. The electrifying sights and sounds of S2F *Tracker* ASW airplanes and ASW helicopters taking off and landing was exhilarating. And seeing submarine search operations carried out by the fast-moving destroyers cutting through the sea at 35 knots or more took my breath away. Our excitement was heightened by knowing that there were real American submarines down there, dodging detection by employing the evasive tactics used by their Soviet counterparts.

Without warning, the exercises were terminated, and Task Group Alpha headed back to Norfolk. We knew something was up. Within a short time after tying up at the NOB pier, the ship's crew was informed that President Eisenhower had declared a national emergency, later known as the *1958 Lebanon Crisis.*

Lebanon, a friendly ally of the United States, was on the brink of civil war. The regime under President Camille Chamoun feared being overthrown by pro-Soviet insurgent forces opposed to his administration. When he requested our military assistance, we responded immediately by launching *Operation Blue Bat.*

Soviet Premier Nikita Khrushchev threatened the use of nuclear weapons in the event of US intervention, but we ignored his threat. With help of the friendly Lebanese military, American forces secured and occupied the Beirut International Airport and the port of Beirut. Task Group Alpha, led by the *Valley Forge*, was an integral part of the American forces responding to the call.

Prior to the ship's deployment, our contingent of 70 midshipmen was enlisted to assist in preparing the *Valley Forge* for an extended operation in the Eastern Mediterranean. We worked as stevedores, restocking the ship's supply of arms and ammunition, fuel, and food and dry stores. Working day and night, we unloaded dozens of trucks filled with supplies for the long voyage and engagement with an enemy supported by the Soviet Union.

Within days, Task Group Alpha was ready to assume a leadership role in *Operation Blue Bat.* We midshipmen were exhausted but prepared to join the operation and do our part in winning this battle. Unfortunately, we were excused from the fray. Our 3rd Class Midshipmen Cruise came to an abrupt end, and we were issued orders to return home.

Naturally we had mixed emotions. I was disappointed and a bit embarrassed by being asked to step away. The bad news was that we would miss an exciting adventure involving actual engagement with the enemy. We would also miss our Missouri partners. The good news was that we would be home with our friends and family nearly a month earlier than planned.

Five years later during the Cuban Missile Crisis, as a part of Task Group Alpha, I would be presented with an opportunity to take on the Soviets in a very personal way.

Firearms

NROTC – University of Michigan
Winter 1959

During my time in the Navy, some of my fellow midshipmen and officers confided that not only were they incompetent in the use of firearms, but they also had an aversion to them. In some cases, I sensed that this aversion amounted to a near phobic fear. Through the years, I have not mentioned this phenomenon to anyone, respecting those who trusted me enough to confess having this mindset, or perhaps I should say condition. When hearing a colleague express this idea, I was always struck by the irony of the situation. He chose to perform a job for our country in the *armed services* while declaring his abhorrence of *arms*.

Another question continually comes to my mind: How did I become a person with a completely opposite viewpoint on the subject of firearms? Today this question is prompted by two stimuli: first, when I recall the past comments of gun-shy Navy colleagues, and second, when I listen to current advocates of gun control. Our NROTC training classes were designed to turn us into officers and gentlemen. One of the lessons we learned was that three topics were forbidden in Wardroom conversation: sex, religion, and politics. Since I consider gun control to be a political subject, as an officer and gentleman, I will refrain from discussing that subject here.

What I will say is that my familiarity and comfort with handling, firing, and caring for firearms resulted directly from my family background. Every male family member was a hunter and a gun owner. I cannot remember exactly how old I was when I first fired a gun. I do know that it happened on my grandparents' farm, where I spent my summers as a boy during the war, so I was probably four or five years old.

One summer, my grandfather gave me his old .22 caliber, single-shot rifle, but he provided me with very little instruction.

Instead, he bought me my own box of .22 short cartridges and sent me to his woods. There I pretended to stalk and bag a wide variety of game, including squirrels, rabbits, and pheasants though I knew I couldn't actually bag the game until hunting season, which began in October each year.

I developed my shooting skills by targeting discarded tin cans that my grandparents deposited in the corner of the woods. My favorite targets were empty *Prince Albert* tobacco cans. (My grandfather was a whiz at rolling his own.) I became adept at plugging holes in those cans at greater and greater distances as my shooting skill improved. Regular practice taught me how to use the rifle effectively. I also learned the damage it could do to my targets. The point is that I learned how to use that rifle safely on my own. To me, it was just common sense.

At the end of the summer, I returned home to Owosso, only ten miles away. Sadly, I had to leave my rifle at the farm, because it was against the law to discharge a rifle or shotgun within the city limits, with one exception. When the clock struck midnight to welcome in the New Year, every rifle and shotgun in town roared in celebration.

Shortly after school started, my birthday arrived and with it, the surprise of my life. I was presented with a brand-new Red Ryder Air Rifle and hundreds of BBs packaged in red cardboard cylinders. Since it was legal to fire a BB gun in town, I spent every waking minute perfecting my aim. It required a good eye, and I soon learned to follow the predictable arc of the BB as it sailed through the air. This enabled me to guide the BB to the desired target. After a few hundred practice shots, I could hit a small target at 100 feet or more.

When hunting season began, Dad and I headed for the farm. Here my uncles and grandfather introduced me to a wide array of firearms including shotguns, rifles, and pistols. They even taught me how to shoot skeet. Seeing how good a shot I was, they invited me to join them on their hunts for pheasants, the most desirable game that inhabited my grandfather's farm. While the adult men all had fancy shotguns for the hunt, I carried my old .22 single-shot rifle, hoping for just the right opportunity to bag my first pheasant.

I got my wish on the first day. Uncle Clarence flushed a cock pheasant near the edge of the woods. When the bird startled him, his aim was not as perfect as it should have been. He only winged the pheasant, which strangely enough, flew to a tree limb about 20 feet above the ground.

My uncle shouted, "Gary, he's yours."

I raised my .22 and with my one shot I bagged my first pheasant. At the cheers of the men, my cheeks burned with pride.

Before the end of my first hunting season, I was presented with a more suitable firearm. All the men chipped in and bought me my own shotgun. It was a 410 single-shot model, and it was beautiful and all mine. I practiced shooting skeet with my new shotgun and became as good a shot as any of them. I could shoot a pheasant in the air, which was my proudest accomplishment. Luckily, at an early age, I became skilled and enamored with firearms.

Some years later, prior to our 2nd Class Midshipman Cruise, we were all required to qualify in the use of the .45 automatic handguns. None of us had ever fired this heavy, somewhat cumbersome weapon. Despite its size and weight, it was widely used in the Navy. (After all, naval officers often had to lead shore-patrol details, and this was the weapon they were required to carry.) We traveled by bus to the army shooting range on the outskirts of Ann Arbor. On the trip over, no one said a word. I could see that many of my classmates were nervous about this requirement. Because of my familiarity and comfort with a variety of firearms, I was calm and confident.

I couldn't have done better. Despite my unfamiliarity with the weapon, my score was the highest in our class. When we arrived back at North Hall, I was informed that I would be captain of the pistol team and would represent Michigan at the competition in Corpus Christi. My opponents would be the best shots from the NROTC units who also were spending their 2nd Class Cruises there. Unfortunately, we were not given much opportunity to practice prior to our departure. While I didn't come in first in the competition, I did come in a respectable third, which pleased my fellow Michigan middies to no end.

When I was commissioned, I felt fortunate to be able to use firearms capably. On my first ship, the *USS Cony*, firearms were an obsession. Our Master at Arms maintained a virtual arsenal, and Commander Morgan, the *Cony's* Captain, was a firearms fanatic. When we were at sea, he took advantage of any opportunity to conduct target practice with the ship's vast array of personal weapons. We officers were under great pressure to participate in target practice and become familiar with every variety of weapons available. Large tin cans were tossed into the water and sunk by a barrage of small-arms fire from .45 automatics, M-1 rifles, and Captain Morgan's favorite, tommy guns.

I was thankful to be familiar with the .45 automatic pistol. Because of my familiarity with this weapon, I was constantly called upon to serve as Shore Patrol Officer. When I was Communications Officer, twice each month a Master at Arms and I were required to strap on the .45 hand pistol to carry out my duties as Registered Publications Custodian. We did so for both collecting our consignment of classified material from the Registered Publication Office and for making a burn run of classified materials that were outdated and needed to be disposed of in the secure furnace on the base.

I learned at a very young age to be comfortable with firearms on the farm, and when I was in the Navy I learned to depend on them for my own safety and the safety of others. Appreciation of their value has stayed with me all my life. Today I own a .38 special handgun, my original Red Ryder air rifle, and the last shotgun I used to hunt at the farm, a single-barrel 20-gauge shotgun.

2nd Class Midshipman Cruise

Corpus Christi, Texas – Coronado, California
Summer 1959

Our 2nd Class Midshipman Cruise was divided into two different components. The first part was a three-week exposure to Naval Air at the Naval Air Station (NAS) Corpus Christi, Texas, where it was hot and humid. The objective was to stimulate our interest in aviation and to participate in all forms of naval flying.

Perhaps for good reason, naval aviators are a laid-back group. So we spent about 80% of our time cleaning and maintaining the large ramshackle barracks or playing sports all afternoon with other NROTC midshipmen from a half-dozen colleges. At the end of a hard day's *work*, drinking cases of cold beer in the huge middy beer tent, erected in the center of the parade field was an enjoyable way to pass the evening.

The academic portion of the curriculum boiled down to the bare essentials. Each midshipman was given a single ride in one of three types of naval aircraft:

- a two-seater jet fighter (F-4B *Phantom*) (most popular)
- an amphibious motor-driven seaplane (P5M) (least popular)
- a helicopter, one of the various types that populated the air station (despised)

Each day, all midshipmen from one college were given their rides. The type of aircraft each midshipman was assigned was determined by the luck of the draw or, more accurately, by the bounce of the ball. Each of us 30 midshipman from Michigan was given a card numbered from 1 to 30, corresponding to the numbers of 30 balls inside a bingo cage.

My college fraternity brother Chuck and our mutual friend Greg had both planned to choose the Naval Air option when they were commissioned. Naturally, they were eager to win one of the jet-fighter rides. Because I planned to take a regular commission in hopes of being assigned to an ASW ship, I couldn't have cared less about a jet-airplane ride.

The first ball drawn was the number of the class nerd. Twenty-nine groans roared across the room. True to form, he grinned foolishly. As luck would have it, the second ball drawn was Chuck's number. Cheers went up all around, because we all knew how much this meant to him.

Since Greg was a bit superstitious, he chose to stand as far away from the bingo cage as possible. I joined him in the far corner of the room. As the third ball was drawn, we both stared at our cards. When #28 was announced, I gasped. That was *my* number! I quickly snatched Greg's card from his hand and replaced it with my lucky #28. He looked at me with his trade-mark wide grin. I smiled back at him and nodded my head. To cinch the deal, I yelled, "Greg's the winner. He's #28!"

Once again, cheers roared. We all knew how important this was to Greg, and I was particularly proud of the role I had played. My role remained secret until recently. At Chuck's fiftieth wedding anniversary, Greg went public and dramatically acknowledged his gratitude by planting a kiss on my cheek!

Then, my number, formerly Greg's, was drawn. I had won the last spot on the P5M seaplane, which was an interesting ride, because the pilot both took off and landed on the water. When airborne, we each took the wheel and *drove* the airplane in a lazy circle or two over the bay. That was the first and last time I ever *drove* an airplane.

Finally, each of us made a bombing run on a wooden float in the middle of the bay. As the pilot steered the seaplane directly over the float, we each dropped a five-pound sack of flour out of the open hatch toward the float. Out of ten bombs dropped, none hit the target. None even came close. It was a good thing that most of us had planned to choose the sea-duty option.

For our exemplary behavior during the stay, young Texas beauties from the area assembled in the NAS Officers Club and treated us to a scrumptious genuine Texas dinner followed by an elegant formal dance. We were attired in our dress-white uniforms, while the young ladies sparkled in their formal gowns. Going back to our thin mattresses in our barracks was a bit of a let-down after such royal treatment. Nonetheless, we all enjoyed Texas-sweet dreams.

The second part of our cruise was a three-week stay with the United States Marine Corps in Coronado, California, where it was hot and arid. Some of the same midshipmen with whom we'd shared the Corpus Christi experience joined us on the sandy beach. Here we lived in Quonset huts adjacent to those occupied by obsessively compulsive young men going through the rigors of Underwater Demolition Team (UDT) training. Their training was accompanied by an unusual amount of grunting and shouting. Some years later these men would be known as SEALS.

During this phase of our training, our primary occupation was preparing for our final exam, the nighttime invasion of Camp Pendleton. Oh, boy! We could hardly wait. Our instructors for this exercise were a trio of young, smallish but muscular, tattooed, cocky Marine Staff Sergeants. Despite the dry climate, our instructors seemed to do an excessive amount of spitting. The first thing they taught us was how to field-strip our butts. The nonsmokers among us found the subject a bit irrelevant. Generally I thought it was a strange first lesson. What did I know about combat leadership?

We were divided into two battalions of invaders. I was in the one that would invade from the sea. We had to climb down wide rope ladders attached to the railing of a troop-transport ship to our destination, a wildly rocking landing craft some 40 feet below. These craft were about the size of the swimming pool in the park where I learned how to swim.

Before starting our descent, we blackened our faces with grease paint to fool the enemy. This greasy stuff made the exercise harder. Because our hands were thoroughly lubricated, grasping the rope was nearly impossible. Our expert leaders assured us that most of this would wash off in the surf as we waded through the choppy waves to reach the beach. Why hadn't we thought of that?

Before our descent, we were each handed one of our drill-field favorites, a Springfield '03 bolt-action rifle and three rounds of blank ammunition to place in our otherwise empty bandolier. The rifle and shells added about ten pounds to our twenty-pound backpacks filled with essentials like first-aid kits, extra socks, K-rations, and a second canteen of water. I assumed this extra ration of water would be necessary when we, too, began to spit excessively. Until that moment, I never realized how heavy and long a Springfield rifle was. Climbing down that rope ladder would be a real challenge. No doubt about it.

The other battalion was loaded into helicopters poised on the decks of helicopter carriers that had been converted from former aircraft carriers after World War II. Those middies were to fly *quietly* over the heads of the dug-in enemy so the enemy wouldn't know they were there. Then they'd land behind the enemy, surprising them with their stealth and skill. For some reason, they were not required to wear the black grease paint. Perhaps this had something to do with the position of the moon.

Our knowledgeable marine instructors informed us that these two clever methods of attack were called *Frontal Assault* and *Vertical Envelopment*. Knowing we had these two tricky maneuvers in our arsenal must have sent shivers up the backs of the bad guys waiting for us in their sandy foxholes along the beach.

Our Staff Sergeant mentors gave us a few tips before we plunged down the ropes. First, the invasion was scheduled to begin at midnight and would last until shortly after dawn. During that time, we were likely to become tired, especially if we had to endure long periods of silent waiting, which was also likely. However, we must never be tempted to sit down let alone lie down, because the landing site was heavily infested with scorpions and rattlesnakes, both of whom loved to snuggle up to warm bodies lying in their territories.

After that good news, I noticed my fellow Frontal Assaulters taking long slugs of water from their first canteens. I decided to join them, and the nervous spitting began. I felt sorry for our enemies lying among the scorpions and rattle-snakes in their foxholes.

With the exception of one heavy midshipman, we all managed to navigate our way down the rope ladder and drop into our bouncing landing craft. The chubby middy beat us to the landing craft by losing his grip and falling seaward. Luckily, his bandolier snagged a belaying pin sticking out of the rail of the landing craft, and he was immediately dragged aboard by two marines who manned the machine guns mounted on the bow of our craft.

Once we were all aboard, the landing craft slowly chugged shoreward. Somehow we managed to make it to within about 200 feet of the sandy beach before the skipper dropped the *front door*, and our sergeant ordered us to exit into the four-foot deep water. It must have taken us 15 minutes to waddle to shore. As directed, we headed straight toward the ridge of hills that would provide us a vantage point to pick off unsuspecting enemies. On this ridge, we spent the remaining four hours of the exercise. Though I thought I would tire soon, scorpion and rattlesnake images pretty much kept me marching in place the entire night.

When we did see flashes of gun fire from a hillside about a mile away, we asked if we should shoot back. We were wisely advised that those shots could very well be friendly fire. The smart aleck in me thought, "If we are all using blank ammunition, isn't it all friendly fire?"

We made it back to our Quonset huts at about ten the next morning. Since it was Sunday, we were allowed to sack in until supper time, if we desired. And we did desire.

The next Saturday was another formal dinner-dance held in the Pavilion of the San Diego Zoo. The young women were bronzed beauties. I struck up a conversation with a strikingly beautiful young woman, who then introduced me to her mother, a member of the event's organizing committee. They invited me to join them for a tour of the San Diego area the next day. Naturally, I accepted immediately. We arranged to meet on the front steps of the Hotel del Coronado at 11:00 am.

The next day, I wore my summer whites with long trousers, not shorts, to the hotel. At precisely 11 am, the young lady pulled up in a sporty red convertible. A *Cooper.* I didn't recognize that make of car. Being from Michigan, the only cars I'd ever seen were made by the Big Three automakers. The young lady drove through downtown San Diego, which was exotic but practically deserted. Then we snaked our way to her parents' oceanside home in La Jolla, where we ate lunch and swam in their pool. As the sun began to set, the young lady drove me back to Coronado Island in time for my curfew.

For years after that day, I dreamt of living in La Jolla, but since then, I have not even visited, let alone lived there. Still, now and then I have to admit that I wonder what happened to that bright, beautiful young lady, and every time I see a Mini-Cooper convertible, I think of her.

Matamoros

2nd Class Midshipman Cruise – Matamoros, Mexico
Summer 1959

During the Naval Air phase of our 2nd Class Midshipman Cruise, five of us rented a station wagon and drove from NAS Corpus Christi to Brownsville, Texas. We covered the 120-mile trip in a little over two hours. At Brownsville, we crossed the Rio Grande River and found ourselves in Matamoros, Mexico. After checking in at our hotel, we decided to explore the city.

It was Saturday, and the city square had become a huge open-air marketplace, where you could purchase anything from vegetables to furniture. We were sophisticated enough to know you never paid the asking price for any item. Bargaining was necessary before any purchase. In fact, we learned that not squabbling over the price was considered an insult to the seller.

Being a 2nd Class Midshipman wasn't a high-paying position. Just the cost of the rental car, hotel room, and meals had depleted almost our entire travel budget, and none of us was in the market for anything in particular. Still, I was eager to learn how this bartering process worked, so I decided to haggle with a man selling lavishly decorated, pale-yellow leather saddles.

I pretended to window shop by walking through his display, caressing first one saddle then another. My travel mates, who instinctively sensed what I was doing, smiled slightly and followed me around the saddle display. Finally, the owner approached and asked in broken English if I was in the market for a saddle. I shrugged my shoulders, playing hard to get.

The owner picked up the pace of his sales pitch, inviting me to sit on a saddle displayed on a low platform beside his old cash register. I turned to my four companions for their advice. They nodded their heads, encouraging me to sample the goods so to speak. For the first time in my life, I climbed onto a saddle. I was pleasantly surprised by how soft the leather felt.

"How much?" I asked. "Dollaros, por favor?" (I took French as my foreign language at Michigan, and I didn't know a word of Spanish, but I thought I remembered Gabby Hayes using that phrase in a Roy Rogers' movie I had once seen.)

"$500," the salesman replied with barely an accent.

I shook my head and stepped down from the saddle.

"$300," the salesman countered.

"No. Gracias," I said, drawing on Gabby once again.

"Please, Sir. Make me an offer," the salesman pleaded, again in nearly perfect English.

I was beginning to feel uncomfortable. My four friends, sensing the tension in the air, turned and walked away. Some friends!

"I'm sorry, Sir," I finally confessed. "I've wasted your time. Please forgive me."

He slapped me on the back. "That's okay, I knew you weren't serious."

We shook hands and said, "Adios!"

"Hey! Wait up, guys," I yelled to my friends. They stopped, and I joined them.

"Where's the saddle?" Chuck asked.

I gave him a dirty look and changed the subject. "Where are we going to eat dinner? I'm getting hungry."

"Lieutenant Mathews suggested the *El Capitan*," Jim said. "He's been there a number of times with his wife." Lieutenant Matthews was the liaison officer who ensured that our needs were met while we were in Corpus Christi.

"Where is it?" I asked.

"Right there," Jim pointed across the square to a warm brick building with the restaurant's name emblazoned in gold letters across the front.

We wandered over to check out the menu, printed in both English and Spanish. What we read was hard to believe. "Look at that four-course dinner!" I said. "An appetizer followed by a steamed lobster. Then a filet mignon. And look at those dessert choices."

"You think that's good. Look at the price. Eight dollars!" said Jim.

"That's unbelievable!" said Pat. "And this is supposed to be the best restaurant in town. Wow!"

"Hey, with this price we can afford to order a bottle of wine," I suggested.

"Why not two bottles?" asked Chuck.

"Let's get a table," said Greg. "Right now."

When we entered the dining room, nearly all the tables were empty. I found it hard to believe that there weren't more people. In one corner, sat four young men who, we guessed, were Navy-types because of their short hair.

They finished before we did and wandered over to our table, where they introduced themselves as Navy pilots.

One of them asked, "What do you boys have on tap for this evening?"

We shrugged our shoulders as we polished off the last of our lobsters.

"Well, you can't visit Matamoros without taking in *Boys' Town*," he said.

"What's *Boys' Town?*" we asked.

"Let's put it this way," he said. "You've never seen anything like it anywhere."

"Where is it?" I asked.

"Only about ten miles outside of town." He wrote down some simple directions, handed them to me, and said, "Check it out." With that, the four aviators wished us luck and left the dining room.

"Whata ya think?" I asked the others.

Their collective answer was generally, "What do we have to lose?"

"Pat, you don't seem very enthusiastic about the idea," I observed.

"Oh, no. I want to go, but I'm a bit tired, what with the wine and all this food."

Our waiter had told us we might get a bit of rain that evening, so we stopped at our hotel rooms to grab our jackets.

(Before the night was over, we would learn the Mexican definition of a bit of rain.)

As we entered the town, we noticed the words *Boys' Town* sprawled across a billboard. We also noticed was that there were no electric lights. Every building was illuminated by candle or lantern. The town itself was not that large, roughly eight square blocks, I estimated. Each block was encircled by a four-foot wide, wooden boardwalk about a foot and a half above the ground, and on each corner of these blocks stood a large saloon with the sound of live music blaring from its windows.

Between the saloons stood dozens and dozens of small shanties with just enough floor space to accommodate a double bed. They were built on the ground so that when the door of the shanty was open, those walking on the boardwalk could look down on the bed and the woman posing sexily against the doorframe. Each tiny shanty was lighted by a single candle. There was no doubt in our minds what the shanties were used for.

We parked the station wagon in front of one of the nicer looking saloons and went inside. The layout reminded me of saloons depicted in old cowboy movies: high ceilings over the center of the building, a large bar with no stools, and three or four dozen card/drinking tables, each seating four or five people. A stairway led to a narrow balcony circling the perimeter of the building. Off this balcony, at least four dozen *sleeping* rooms could be accessed through wooden doors constructed of the same dark-stained wood as the balcony railing. On the wall opposite the main entrance stood a large stage where a five-piece band played loud, bawdy music.

The most significant feature of the saloon was the dozens of very young Mexican senoritas who moved from table to table soliciting business in a most aggressive fashion. Without exception, they were absolutely beautiful. To me, each bore a remarkable resemblance to Natalie Wood. The waitresses were older and tended to our drink orders with efficiency and grace. We all settled on draft beer, the least expensive drink. Since it wasn't that cheap, we sipped slowly and took in the scenery.

Pat excused himself, saying he had to find a *head*. None of us thought anything of it, until his absence had extended to about 40 minutes. Then we didn't know whether we should be concerned or look the other way. None of us took any action. I was relieved when he returned to our table and ordered a cold beer.

Pat was soaking wet, and his feet and lower legs were covered with a thick coat of mud. Evidently it was raining outside, but the band was so loud, we hadn't heard the storm. I thought about Pat claiming that he was sleepy after the wine and four-course meal. Perhaps he went somewhere and caught a little nap. I hoped that was all he caught.

After watching the stage show and the circling solicitors for about an hour, Chuck said he'd seen all he needed to see. The rest of us agreed, paid our tab, and headed for our station wagon. By the time we got there, we were all soaking wet and covered with mud, just like Pat. And we had thought this was the desert.

We returned to Corpus Christi about midday on Sunday. On the drive home, no one mentioned any aspect of *Boys' Town*. That self-censorship has continued for nearly 60 years. I suppose now, my old midshipmen friends can accuse me of letting the cat out of the bag. That is, those who are still with us and whose minds are agile enough to have recollections of our memorable trip to Matamoros.

The JO Bunkroom

USS Valley Forge – Naples, Italy
Summer 1960

Near the end of our junior year, we Regular NROTC midshipmen eagerly awaited news of our class standing, because the desirability of assignments for our 1st Class Midshipman Cruise depended solely on where we ranked. Past experience told us that if we were one of the top three in our class, we would be assigned to the best summer cruise available. Based on my test scores, I knew I was close. Still, I was a bit nervous the night before our orders for the summer were to be disclosed.

First thing the next morning, our entire class assembled in the main auditorium. Three years earlier, there had been 40 of us Regular NROTC scholarship holders. Through attrition, that number now stood at 25. Our Commanding Officer, Captain Mothersill, stood in the center of the stage surrounded by members of his faculty, all of whom were Navy or Marine, both officers and enlisted.

The Captain stepped to the front of the stage, and the room fell silent. "This is a very important day for you, Gentlemen," he said. "When you leave Ann Arbor for your summer cruises, you will all be 1st Class Midshipmen. And at this time next year, you will be commissioned officers, Ensigns in the Navy or Second Lieutenants in the Marine Corps. While that seems like a long time from now, it will fly by faster than you can imagine. This will depend greatly on how hard you work on learning all you can from this upcoming 1st Class Midshipman Cruise.

"I know you're all eager to see your orders Following a long-standing tradition here at Michigan, I will announce the names of the top three men in your class. Please give them a nice round of applause. Then all your orders will be distributed. The top three men in your class are James Miller, Richard Siemen, and Gary Slaughter."

Our classmates burst into applause and cheered. We three were certainly good students and well-liked and respected by our classmates. I knew both Dick and Jim well. We had shared two summer cruises and countless hours of NROTC classroom time over the past three years. Jim and I were particularly close friends, because both of us were business majors. During our senior year, we planned to be roommates.

We three formed a circle to examine our orders. What we saw shocked us. We had spent our 3rd Class cruise on the *USS Valley Forge* (CVS 45) out of Norfolk, Virginia. This summer, we would spend our 1st Class cruise on the *Valley Forge* once again, but in Naples, Italy.

USS Valley Forge (August 1958)

We flew from Willow Run Airport near Ann Arbor. Our Military Air Transport Service (MATS) flight was on an old, slow, converted cargo airplane. Although we flew the great circle route, the shortest and quickest way, we were in the air for about 24 hours, not counting an overnight stop in Morocco.

Our route included stops at the following military bases:

- Willow Run, Michigan
- Argentia, Newfoundland
- Lajes, Azores
- Port Lyautey, Morocco
- Rome, Italy
- Naples, Italy

Needless to say, the trip was long and taxing. Because the noisy engines prevented us from conversing, it was also boring. By the time we reached Naples, we were like zombies.

We were met in the Naples airport by a bus that took us and our sea bags and hanging bags to the *Valley Forge*. When we pulled up to the gangway, I looked up to admire her enormous size, reviewing all I remembered about her. She looked about the same. What had changed was that Task Group Alpha was now commanded by Admiral Allen E. Shinn, with whom I would develop a special relationship over that summer of 1960.

We were escorted to our new quarters, a former Chief Petty Officer's compartment that had been converted to accommodate eighteen 1st Class Midshipmen. Fifteen of them were from the Naval Academy, and were, to a man, the loudest and most obnoxious soon-to-be officers and gentlemen that I had ever encountered. Without the discipline of the Academy, they were simply out of control. The three of us looked at each other, shook our heads, and carried our gear to a corner of the compartment that was the farthest from the riotous behavior.

"ATTENTION ON DECK!" exploded outside our compartment. Suddenly there was silence, and all the rowdy Academy types snapped to attention. The source of the booming sound marched through the hatchway and entered the compartment. He stood about six-four, and his chest was covered with a square yard of medals and ribbons. Most impressive, he carried a swagger stick, which he constantly used to swat his left hand.

This was no ordinary officer. This was a MARINE officer with extensive combat experience.

"MY NAME IS WARD. CAPTAIN JOHN WARD, UNITED STATES MARINE CORPS. DON'T FORGET IT!"

His eyes darted around the compartment, before spotting the three of us standing at attention, surrounded by our gear. "You men must be the three from Michigan. You're head and shoulders above this gang of monkeys. I know that, because your commanding officer and I served together on this very ship during the war more than 15 years ago. He's a good man. I assume you are as well. Welcome aboard."

Then he turned his attention to the fifteen academy types and gave them a simple order, "Have this compartment ready for inspection in 20 minutes, or you won't see a minute's worth of liberty for the rest of this cruise. Got it?" He turned back to us. "You three Michigan men! I've reserved your bunks and lockers over there in that far corner. I'd make it a practice to stay clear of these monkeys. They have a contagious and fatal disease called **DIS-ORDER.** But we'll cure that before summer's over."

The three of us were flabbergasted. We'd never observed an officer take on a group of *monkeys* like Captain Ward did that day. After he left the compartment, everything was quiet for about five minutes. Then the ruckus picked up again.

"Those guys are incorrigible," Jim observed quietly. Dick and I nodded in agreement.

Once our gear was stowed away, we decided to tour the ship for old time's sake. We'd been told we'd be taking our meals in the Wardroom, so we were welcome there. I wanted to see my old cleaning station. Since examining my spit-shined head didn't inspire much enthusiasm from the other two, I simply peeked in the door for a quick glimpse.

It was standard procedure for the *Valley Forge* to invite locals from our ports of call to come aboard for personal tours conducted by us three midshipmen from Michigan. We were chosen because of our demeanor, and I for one spoke French fairly well. Jim and Dick made up for their lack of language skill with friendliness and wide smiles. Visiting hours lasted for three hours every day. Naples could accommodate us alongside the pier. For the other ports we visited, we anchored out, and visitors were shuttled back and forth by a dozen or so liberty boats.

On my first day as tour guide, my initial visitors were an attractive middle-aged American lady, accompanied by her daughter, whom I guessed to be about 19. They were both well-dressed and very pleasant. I introduced myself, and the mother nodded but did not mention her name. She simply said, "Pleased to meet you, Mr. Slaughter. We look forward to your tour."

The visitors had to climb the ladder (stairs) to the quarterdeck located on the hanger deck. In this cavernous area, the carrier's aircraft were stored and maintained by the men from the various repair shops that lined the perimeter of the hangar deck. This deck was just beneath the flight deck, where airplanes were launched by giant, steam-powered catapults. Aircraft were moved between the hangar and flight decks by huge elevators with doors about 25 feet high and 40 feet wide. The platform on which the aircraft rested was also 40 feet by 40 feet to accommodate the giant fixed-wing and helicopter aircraft.

After showing my guests the hanger deck and explaining its features in far more detail than they probably wanted to know, I escorted them up the aircraft elevator to the flight deck. There I showed them the catapults and the tie-down mechanisms to hold the aircraft stable while the ship turned into the wind for easier takeoffs.

The bridge was located in the forward side of the starboard superstructure, a multi-layered edifice that loomed over the flight deck. The ship was operated from the bridge, where I showed my guests both the helm (steering wheel) and the lee helm (the engine-order telegraph) used to signal main engineering the desired engine turns or revolutions needed to reach the desired speed. These orders were delivered by the Officer of the Deck (OOD), who was solely in charge of the ship's movement through the water. I also showed them the radar sets and compasses positioned conveniently around the bridge for easy access by the OOD.

By the time I finished my tour, it was nearly time for lunch. I assumed the women would want to depart to their favorite Naples restaurant on shore. The mother surprised me by saying, "We're having lunch in the Wardroom. Would you care to join us?"

"Yes, Ma'am, I'd be delighted. That's where I have my meals as well."

The daughter looked pleased by her mother's invitation as well as my acceptance. I quickly deduced that the women must be related to a *Valley Forge* officer, but I was polite enough not to ask his name.

When we entered the Wardroom, every officer seated at the large array of white cloth-covered tables stood at attention. The woman led us to the head table, and after we sat, the dozens of officers took their seats. I thought this was quite a welcome for two women whose names I didn't know. I did know the gentleman standing behind his chair at the head of our table. He walked toward me and introduced himself as *Shinn*. Of course, he was Admiral Allen M. Shinn, Commanding Officer of Task Group Alpha.

"I'm Midshipman Slaughter, Sir. Very pleased to meet you, Sir."

Admiral Shinn said, "I see that you have already met my wife and daughter Mary."

"Yes, Sir," I said, pleasantly surprised to finally learn who my tour mates were. "We just completed a tour of the ship."

Standing behind the Admiral was Captain Ward, whom I had met a few days earlier. I greeted him, "Good afternoon, Captain Ward." Seeing him at the Admiral's table indicated that he was a member of the Admiral's staff.

"Good afternoon, Midshipman Slaughter, said Captain Ward. "I was just telling Admiral Shinn about you and your two Michigan comrades. You'll be glad to hear I gave you good reports."

"Good news, indeed," repeated the Admiral. "Let's get on with lunch, shall we?"

After we were served, Mrs. Shinn offered a suggestion to her husband. "Allen, we were thinking about inviting Mr. Slaughter to join us for our trip to Amalfi this afternoon. Mary and he have a good deal in common."

"Splendid idea!" said the Admiral. "We'd be delighted to have you along. What do you think, Mary?"

Mary was grinning from ear to ear. All she could do was nod. I joined her in both, delighted to be included in their plans. I really was attracted to Mary, and her mother was exceedingly charming.

As lunch progressed, I overheard Admiral Shinn ask Captain Ward, "What's happening with your Academy boys, John?"

"I sent them out of town on the Welfare and Recreation bus tour of Rome. The Olympics are in full flare there, Admiral. While I think some positive distraction would do them good, you never know with that bunch."

I had forgotten that the 1960 Olympic Games were being held in Rome. However, since my responsibilities on the *Valley Forge* were far more important to me than the Olympics, I had no compelling desire to attend them.

"Well, I hope they behave themselves," the Admiral said. "All I'd need would be an international incident caused by that crew. Did you send someone to keep an eye on them?"

"The Welfare and Rec officer is handling that assignment personally," said Captain Ward. "Hopefully, he'll keep them between the fences."

The Admiral nodded his head, then turned to us and announced, "What say we freshen up and head for Amalfi in about 30 minutes?"

Captain Ward said, "I'll make sure the driver and car is all set for you, Sir."

The tour was amazing. I had never seen more spectacular scenery, and Mary was charming, as I had expected. In fact, the whole family was very welcoming. All through the trip, the Admiral attempted to convince me to select naval aviation as my Navy career choice after I was commissioned. Truthfully, I'd never considered the aviation option, but I still had time to make that choice if it felt right for me. After the tour ended, while I never saw Mary or her mother again, I thought of them often.

The sun was setting as we pulled up to the pier. From a distance, I saw Captain Ward pacing nervously back and forth on the dock. He seemed very upset. "Glad you're back, Admiral. I hope you all had a nice trip. I –" He stopped abruptly.

"What's happened, John?" asked the Admiral.

"Well, truth is that all of those Academy idiots are in jail in Rome," said the Captain. "Our shore-patrol boys are trying to convince the Roman police to turn them over to us."

The Admiral was livid. "Damn! John! What have they done now?"

"Last night, after far too much vino, they decided to shinny up a couple of dozen street lights around the Olympic stadium and steal the Olympic flags," said the Captain. "You know the flag: five interlocking rings. Anyway, by the time they were arrested by a hoard of policemen, they had removed close to two dozen flags and stuffed them in their pants under their uniforms."

"That's the last straw!" said the Admiral. "When the Shore Patrol boys have those middies in custody, tell the Shore Patrol to call us. Let's talk to our legal folks in Washington and determine what charges to file against them. Then I want them shipped back home, brought before a Court-Martial, and tossed out of the Navy. Got that?"

"Exactly what I had in mind, Sir," said the Captain.

Within a week, the unruly Academy types were indeed on their way home, facing a General Court Martial and sure expulsion from the Navy. Jim, Dick, and I rattled around in our spacious compartment, which seemed unusually quiet and calm without the Academy loudmouths filling the air with noise.

To compensate us for our nominal isolation, the Admiral asked the ship's captain to move the three of us in with his cadre of aviation junior officers, who were quartered in what was lovingly called the JO (junior officer) Bunkroom. This large, open sleeping compartment with bunk beds was located on the far frontier of Officers' Country, way up in the ship's forecastle, right beneath the catapults.

Our new bunkmates were young aviators, all commissioned officers, mostly Lieutenants (jg) and a few senior Ensigns who had been commissioned after completing the Navy's Air Cadet (NavCad) program, years later made famous by the Richard Gere movie, *An Officer and a Gentleman*. As mere midshipmen, we were by far the most junior men in the bunkroom.

In the JO Bunkroom, competition was fierce between the fixed-wing aviators and the helicopter jocks, as they were known. Each considered the other to be inferior, and they argued constantly. They couldn't agree on anything except that we junior men and non-aviators were fair game for constant hazing. And haze they did. We caught it from both sides. By sentencing us to the JO Bunkroom, the Admiral ensured that I would choose any option other than naval aviation. Even the Marine Corps began to look good to me.

In the end, I settled on being a Navy Line Officer serving aboard ASW destroyers, which were a critical component of Task Group Alpha. During stormy weather, from the bridge of my destroyer, I often watched the *Happy Valley* crash into one gigantic wave after another. Each wave would lift its bow 100 feet or more and then, in passing, thrust the bow downward again to await the next wave. For hours on end, the mammoth ship would endure this pounding. Despite the undeniable rigors of destroyer life, I always considered myself fortunate not to be among those young aviators who, for their own safety, were required to ride out storms ignominiously strapped to their bunks in the JO Bunkroom.

Five for Seven Man

Midshipman Cruise aboard USS Valley Forge
Summer 1960

In the summer of 1960, I was ordered once again to serve my 1st Class Midshipman Cruise on the *USS Valley Forge* (CVS 45). I had served my 3rd Class Midshipman cruise on the *Happy Valley* as well. However, being a 1st Class Midshipman this time, I was afforded the privileges of an officer. I bunked in Officers' Country and took my meals in the Wardroom.

Much to my surprise and delight I knew one of the Steward's Mates, an affable 2nd Class Petty Officer named Stokes, who was a curious character. Stokes was still aboard, fulfilling his duty by serving meals in the Wardroom. When our eyes met, his face lighted up with a broad grin. As he served my meal, he whispered, "I don't suppose you miss cleaning that head, do you Midshipman Slaughter?"

I must admit I was flattered that he remembered me. As I described previously, during my 3rd Class Cruise, I was assigned duties typically performed by enlisted men. My cleaning station had been an officers' head near the Wardroom. As a result, I became acquainted with a number of Steward's Mates, who were required to spend their days tending to the needs of the ship's officers. They served their officers by cleaning their staterooms, making their beds, shining their shoes, handling their laundry and dry cleaning, and preparing and serving their meals in the Wardroom. Stokes had been one of these Steward's mates. We'd nothing approaching a friendship, but we had seen each other daily and had exchanged greetings.

Stokes was an African-American man, small in stature with graying, short black hair. He had a pleasant disposition and prided himself by initiating a friendly greeting to everyone he met. In short, he was a very popular shipmate among officers and enlisted men alike. No one was certain of his age, and he was the only sailor still aboard the ship who was a *plank owner*, meaning that he had been aboard the *Happy Valley* since her launching on July 8, 1945.

His sole plank-owner status may have contributed to another peculiar aspect of Stokes' persona. Since coming aboard near the end of World War II, Stokes had never left the ship. And I do mean *never*. Being an aircraft carrier, the ship provided all the services a seaman might require to maintain a satisfactory lifestyle. Stokes' commitment to staying aboard perpetually, while a bit odd, was quite understandable.

Stokes had another peculiarity that fascinated the entire crew and created consternation on the part of the ship's Paymaster. Since reporting aboard, Stokes had never drawn any pay. Payday after payday, he simply let it ride. What he was owed by Uncle Sam had been accumulating in his payroll account since 1945. Speculating about how much the Navy owed Stokes after all those years was the subject of conjecture and conversation throughout the ship. Pay records were not public documents, and the Paymasters who served during the years of Stokes' tenure refused to reveal the number to anyone.

How could anyone live aboard ship without at least some small amount of cash for personal items like a tooth brushes or shaving supplies? How could he afford to purchase new shoes or uniforms when his wore out? The Navy didn't supply these items at no cost to sailors. The answer was simple. Stokes was also a businessman who made a good wage being the ship's only *Five for Seven Man*. In short, he was in the business of making small loans to sailors who came up short before payday. Stokes would make loans in five-dollar denominations. Then, on payday, he demanded the five-dollar loan be repaid with seven dollars.

Most reasonable people would say that this was a usurious rate of interest, and they would be right. Since young, gullible sailors were broke and itching to go on liberty, they didn't seem to mind. Not only were Stokes' services in demand, he also had a huge market. The *Valley Forge's* personnel complement was 3,448 officers and men. So Stokes did a land-office business in short-term loans. He conducted his business under the watchful eyes of the ship's command, which took the attitude that if Stokes didn't provide the service, someone else would. Because Stokes was well-liked and trusted by all, his *Five for Seven* franchise aboard the *Valley Forge* was a virtual monopoly.

No one was certain how much profit Stokes pocketed every two weeks after payday. No one, that is, except the Postal Clerk who was sworn to secrecy by the oath of office all postal clerks take before assuming that position. After each payday, Stokes would take his profit to the ship's post office and purchase a money order, which he dropped into an envelope and mailed to an unknown person. Though some speculated it was his mother, Stokes was no spring chicken, so she would have been pretty old by this time. Perhaps it was a brother or sister. No one knew except the secretive Postal Clerk.

Of course, Stokes retained a small portion of his profits for his personal needs like toothbrushes or new shoes. He also needed to maintain a large cache of five-dollar bills as working capital to make loans to his customers. But most of his profits were accumulating ashore somewhere just as all of his pay was accumulating aboard ship in his payroll account. To any rational thinker, Stokes was a wealthy man.

Because I had served two midshipman cruises on the *Valley Forge* and, after I was commissioned, operated with her on destroyers as a part of the ASW task forces she led, I felt a special connection with the *Happy Valley*. When she was decommissioned in 1970 and sold for scrap shortly thereafter, I was saddened. And I couldn't help wonder whatever happened to Stokes and his accumulated wealth.

La Portuguesa

Communications School – Newport, Rhode Island
Summer 1961

On June 17, 1961, I received my commission as Ensign in the United States Navy. My orders were to report to the US Naval Communications Officers School in Newport, Rhode Island. Unfortunately, the class did not start until mid-July. I could either stay at the University of Michigan and burn some of my allocated 30 days of annual leave or travel to Newport and report early without knowing what the Navy would do with me for nearly a month.

Ensign Slaughter's Commissioning Photo (June 1961)

Eager to begin my Navy career, I left Michigan in my red Karman Ghia and drove 24 straight hours to Newport via Canada without stopping to sleep. I called the school and received instructions to check into the Bachelor Officers Quarters (BOQ) on the base and report to the school by telephone once a week. What an opportunity to explore Newport!

Having seen the movie *High Society,* starring Bing Crosby and Grace Kelly, I had an image of Newport in my mind. The next few days were spent driving around scenic Newport, including Ocean Drive, and observing the stately mansions that dotted the coast. By the weekend, I had tired of typical tourist activities and decided to check out the Newport night life. I donned my madras sports coat and tan slacks and headed downtown.

Though I had heard that *The Moorings* was a popular night spot, popular was an understatement. The open-air bar was jammed with young Navy officers and Officer Candidate School students. Noise from the crowd drowned out the music from a small band perched on the stage above the dance floor. A throng of at least 200 Navy men surrounded a small circle of about two dozen pretty young women.

This scene was too much for a BMOC from Michigan, so I decided to call it a night and headed back to my car. As I crossed the street, I saw two beautiful young women walking toward me. Their bright smiles were most friendly.

One of them asked, "Aren't you heading the wrong way? *The Moorings* is the place to be."

I quickly described the scene, and both women wrinkled their noses. The most striking of the two suggested an alternate plan. "There's a small restaurant around the corner. We could order a glass of wine. Would you like to join us?"

After introducing ourselves, we headed for what turned out to be a delightful evening of wine and conversation. I learned that the women lived in nearby Fall River, Massachusetts. Both were school teachers who preferred to spend their nightlife away from the view of their town elders.

As the night wore on, we decided that it was time to part. We agreed to meet again in Newport some Saturday evening in that same small restaurant.

As I drove back to the base, I couldn't shake my memory of the striking woman with dark eyes and black hair. There was something especially exotic about her. Strangely, I could remember her name, Maria Silva, but not that of the other woman. I wondered if I would ever see her again.

That night back in the BOQ, I had trouble sleeping, because I was thinking about Maria Silva. At last a plan emerged. In the morning, I would drive to Fall River, look her up in the phone book, and ask her to join me for lunch. With that in mind, I quickly fell asleep.

The next day when I arrived in Fall River, I located a telephone booth and opened the phone book. When I turned to *Silva*, I couldn't believe my eyes. There must have been over 300 Silvas listed, and not one of them was a *Maria*. With a heavy heart, I returned to my car and headed back to Newport.

Later that day, I confessed to one of my fellow officers what had happened. He was a big, friendly Irishman from Boston who immediately broke into laughter and slapped me on the back. "This part of the country is heavily populated by the Portuguese. You just happened to choose the most common Portuguese family name. Silva! Silva!" He broke into laughter, and I joined him to ease the pain I was feeling in my heart.

Before writing this vignette, I checked the current Fall River white pages. Today there are 940 listings of the name *Silva* in the telephone book. And there was still not a single *Maria Silva* listed. If only.

My Dental Friends

Communications School – Newport, Rhode Island
Summer 1961

While waiting for communications school classes to begin, I was living in the Bachelor Officers Quarters (BOQ) on the base. There I became friends with a pair of dental students from the University of Washington who lived next door to me and were attending a six-week Navy orientation program at the Officers Candidate School. After another year of dental school, they would be commissioned as Lieutenants and serve three years as Navy dentists. Like the Regular NROTC program, the Navy was footing the bill for their entire dental-school education.

My dental friends had reported to Newport in civilian attire and were issued a full range of officers' uniforms, sporting the rank of Lieutenant (jg). I was just an Ensign at the time even though I'd had more than four years of Navy service as a midshipman and officer, all served wearing the same uniforms that now baffled and frustrated my new friends. Out of pity and friendship, I offered to instruct them in the finer points of dressing as a naval officer. This was no easy task and they were extremely grateful for my assistance.

I quickly learned that I had taken my extensive knowledge of preparation, wear, and maintenance of uniforms for granted. My friends didn't know the first thing about this skill. So I started from top down, beginning with the assembly of the officer's combination cap, composed of a white cover, a gold chin strap that was seldom worn as such, and a band and a bill depicting the general category of rank by the amount of gold affixed to these components. I assembled one of the caps as a model. Even with considerable coaching on my part, it took them about an hour to accomplish what I had done in five minutes.

I then shifted focus to the midsection, starting with belt and buckle and finishing with the decorational sword, sheath, and belt. This last item sparked mock sword play on their parts, which was to be expected from first-time sword owners.

Finally, I focused on the shoes. After I demonstrated my skill at spit-shining one of their black dress shoes, they took a stab at it with incredibly less success and considerably more time than I. I didn't reveal to my friends that all us midshipmen from the University of Michigan had bunked next to a compartment of spit-shining experts during our 3rd Class Cruise on the *Valley Forge*. These experts were the ship's company of Marines who had little to do all day except shine their shoes and belt buckles and press stiff creases in their uniform trousers. They had been proud and eager to share their expertise with us.

In the end, my friends were fully dressed and ready to make their debut as bona-fide Navy officers by walking to the officers' mess for dinner. During the meal, I capped off their training by instructing them on basic table manners, which for some reason were completely foreign to them. Presumably table manners were not in the dental-school curriculum.

After dinner, we left the officers' mess and were walking towards the BOQ when I realized that both dentists were uncovered, meaning that they had forgotten to retrieve their combination caps from the shelf near the mess entrance. I informed them sternly that a naval officer is never outdoors without his cap squarely on his head. Over the next few days, this basic rule was forgotten frequently, causing one or the other of the men to run back for his cap.

After we three became immersed in our own classroom training, our social interaction subsided considerably, with one pleasant exception. Before they returned to Washington, my friends were determined to see Cape Cod. Because neither had a car, the three of us crammed into my Karmann-Ghia one weekend and drove from Newport to Provincetown, Massachusetts, located on the far eastern tip of the cape. On our way home, we stopped at Hyannis to see the Kennedy compound and peeked through the wrought iron fence at the residence and boat dock. Wouldn't you know? We saw nary a Kennedy.

Soon thereafter, my friends completed their six-week Newport stints and said goodbye. They headed back to dental school in Seattle, and I soon set off for Great Lakes to attend Electronics Officers School. It had been an enjoyable relationship for all concerned. But, as with so many short-term Navy friendships, we never heard from each other again.

La Catolica

Communications School – Newport, Rhode Island
Summer 1961

My classes finally began at Communications Officers' School. The school lasted eight weeks, after which I would depart for the Naval Station Mayport, Florida. There I would be stationed on the *USS Power* (DD-839), presumably filling the role of Communications Officer. I couldn't have been happier heading into a summer in beautiful Newport followed by the fall and winter in sunny Florida.

There were about 60 officers in my class, most of us newly minted Ensigns. In his introductory remarks, the school's Commanding Officer announced that the dozen or so students with the highest test scores would be selected to attend advanced training in Great Lakes, Illinois at the US Electronics Officers' School. That course would last an additional 12 weeks.

The plan was sounding better and better. Summer in Newport, fall in Great Lakes, just a short drive to Michigan football games, then off to sunny Florida. I couldn't have asked for more.

I thought I had it made. Perhaps I was a bit cocky, but I did know radios. I had inherited an old console radio from a friend of the family when I was in fifth grade. Because it didn't work, I took that as a challenge. I read everything I could about radio-equipment operation and repair, disassembled my radio, and replaced the old components with new ones. It worked like a charm. My family was impressed to say the least.

My cockiness wore off quickly after I studied the Communications School curriculum, which, among other subjects, included cryptography, cryptosecurity, facsimile equipment, Morse code, signal flag communications, and the handling and disposal of registered publications. It was not going to be as easy as I thought. Still, I rationalized I had been a good student in high school and college. I'd even been a member of two college honorary societies. So I rolled up my sleeves and went to work.

By about halfway through the eight weeks, I was doing nothing but studying. While I'd produced excellent test scores, I was beginning to burn out. I longed for another form of social interaction, especially with the opposite sex. Having experienced a fine social life at Michigan, I concluded that my standards were higher than what I had observed in Newport to date. From my first, and last, experience with the Newport bar scene, I knew that was not the place to find female companionship. This called for some creativity on my part. I thought about joining a church or the main Officers Club on the base. These choices had their drawbacks, not the least of which was that I would be leaving Newport in less than two months. There would be hardly any time to get to know anyone. In the final analysis, I fell back on my customary practice for resolving complex issues. I decided to take a walk on the beach. And Newport was just the place.

One Friday after class, I slipped into some casual civvies with tennis shoes for beach walking. Newport had three beaches to choose from. The longest and most deserted was 3rd Beach, which was the farthest from downtown Newport. I chuckled to myself when I observed that the western end of 3rd Beach was located at the corner of Purgatory and Paradise Roads. What perfect descriptors of my social conflict at the time.

I parked in the nearly empty parking area and walked briskly toward the distant Sakonnet River that formed the eastern watery side of the Island of Newport. The beach was nearly deserted. There were only a few couples with little children, as well as two young boys trying their hand at body surfing in the long, languid waves that slapped soundlessly onto shore.

In the distance, someone was sitting on a beach blanket with a stack of books, reading. Curiously, I was working out my thoughts by walking, and the reader was sitting quietly augmenting thoughts with words in books.

I waved at the family with two young girls playing in the surf and continued my trek eastward. When I came to within a quarter of a mile of the reader, I could plainly see that she was an attractive woman, probably in her early twenties. My curiosity was heightened by this chance meeting, even though I was skeptical about what this new encounter might offer.

As I approached the woman's blanket and piles of textbooks, she smiled at me as though we were old friends. She was indeed gorgeous with brilliant blue eyes and lustrous wavy blond hair. A few brown freckles dotted her lightly tanned skin. Although she hadn't risen, it wasn't difficult to note that she had a stunning figure from top to bottom.

"Good afternoon. You appear to be concentrating on something important. I was just taking a walk to give myself a much-needed break from my studies. My name is Gary Slaughter. I'm a student at the Communications Officers School on the base." I held out my hand to shake hers.

She took my hand and popped to her feet and declared warmly, "I'm so very pleased to meet you. My name is Mary McGinnis. I'm a graduate student at Providence College. I hope to teach at the graduate level after I earn my master's degree. Currently I'm preparing to student-teach high-school English Literature in the fall. I'm doing some reviewing. It's been years since my last course on English Literature. I'm ready for a break. Do you have time to sit down for a minute? I'd love to know how you ended up in Newport's communications school. I understand some of the men find it a rather difficult curriculum."

We sat on Mary's blanket for what must have been another hour and a half. I learned that she was an only child and that her father was very protective. (A warning signal sounded.) She assured me that she was so busy with school she hardly had time for a social life. Naturally, she was Irish Catholic like so many women in Newport. But her church followed the Dominican Order, in which she found comfort, because it was less strict than other Catholic denominations.

I began to feel that Mary was confiding all this to give me fair warning. If our relationship passed beyond the casual level, it might be more difficult than I had anticipated. I took it in stride, shrugging off her veiled warning as if it didn't bother me in the least. To be honest, I wondered if it would be possible for us to have a normal dating relationship, let alone a friendship.

By the time I told Mary about my family, my religious background, and my schooling, the sun was beginning to set. At this point, I had no love interest in my life. In fact, prior to meeting Mary McGinnis, I had been relieved to think of the freedom that being unattached afforded me. Yet I felt slightly uncomfortable realizing how difficult it might be for me to establish a lasting and meaningful relationship because of the unsettled nature of a Navy career.

Mary picked up her books and blanket, and I helped her carry them to the parking lot. When we arrived at her car, a beat-up Nash Rambler, I took a chance. "If you don't have dinner plans, perhaps you could suggest a nice place where we could enjoy a meal and continue our conversation."

I thought I detected a bit of hesitation, which disappeared quickly. Mary nodded and suggested we take her car. She knew just the place.

I gathered my wallet and shoes from my car, and we drove about ten miles up-island to a quaint seafood restaurant that advertised lobster, oysters, clams, and several varieties of fresh fish. The current menu, posted on a large blackboard that nearly covered the front porch, convinced me that the fare would be local and extremely fresh.

We enjoyed a delicious meal and even a bottle of chardonnay. Our conversation continued to grow more comfortable, and I would say just short of intimate, especially for the short time we'd known each other. I was thoroughly enjoying myself, and I daresay so was she.

After dinner, Mary drove me back to my car. As we sat looking out on the water, she did something completely unexpected. She leaned over and kissed me full on the lips. I was totally taken by surprise. Then she reached over my lap and opened my car door. "I have to be going. My father will be home shortly."

"When can we see each other again?" I asked.

"Let me try to work something out," she said. "I'll call you tomorrow."

I gave her my number at the BOQ and shook her hand.

Mary kissed me again. "My father is a very difficult man. If he had his choice, I would never see you again. I hope you can understand, Gary."

I stood in the parking lot watching her tail lights fade into the darkness. My only thought was, "Is this what I bargained for?"

I had difficulty sleeping that night. I tossed and turned, wondering what would happen next. In fact, I wasn't sure what I wanted to happen next. "Perhaps this is too hard," I thought. "On the other hand, Mary is a very charming and intelligent young woman."

On Saturday, I waited for Mary's call in my room until it was nearly last call for dinner. Just as I slipped on my Service Dress Blue blouse, my phone rang. Mary quickly apologized for not calling earlier and just as quickly gave me my instructions. Tomorrow I was to park my car in the lot outside the main gate, where she would pick me up about 1 pm.

"Where are we heading?" I asked helplessly.

"We're going to Providence so I can introduce you to my grandmother – my father's mother. She's the only person on earth who can convince my father that it's okay for us to see each other."

"Wow! She must be a very powerful woman."

"You don't know the half of it. Here's the thing: You've got to dress in your most formal uniform. You know, the white tieless jacket with gold buttons, your white dress shoes, your shoulder boards, the white combination cap with gold trim, and above all, wear your sword. You got that? Don't forget your sword. That's very important. And make sure your shoes are shiny white. "

I had never ever worn this full formal uniform except at Change of Command and Graduation Ceremonies. Perhaps Mary hoped that some form of *Change of Command* would happen.

The next day, we pulled up in front of a modest bungalow in South Providence. Though it didn't seem like a proper residence for the Dowager Queen, I figured, "Mary knows best."

We entered the front door without knocking. Mary seated me in a huge overstuffed chair against the front wall of the tiny room. A similar chair stood opposite me against the rear wall. Mary advised me to rise when her grandmother entered the room. Then she left to inform her that we had arrived.

When Grandmother McGinnis entered the room, I rose. She was dressed to a tee. My Dowager Queen descriptor had been more accurate than I had anticipated. She thumped into her chair and then motioned me to sit opposite her.

Mary shrank down onto a small tapestry covered bench against the wall between us two principal negotiators. "Grandmother, I should like to introduce Ensign Gary Slaughter, United States Navy. He is an officer studying naval communications in Newport. Soon he will be assigned to an important position aboard a Navy ship stationed in Mayport, Florida."

Grandmother waved her hand in Mary's direction as if to say, "That'll be enough details." She then paused a minute and asked, "Slaughter? What kind of a name is Slaughter?"

I said, "Slaughter is an English name, Madam."

Grandmother looked at me for about two full seconds and said, "It was nice to meet you, Mr. Slaughter." She then lifted herself out of her chair and promptly left the room.

Naturally, Mary and I were in shock. We had known it wasn't going to be easy, but neither of us anticipated a summary verdict with so little presentation of evidence or deliberation.

We drove back to Newport without saying a word. When we arrived in the parking lot, Mary reached over and opened my door. I took the hint and, without saying a word, got out of her car. That was the last time I ever saw Mary McGinnis.

In Love Again!

Great Lakes, Illinois – Highland Park, Illinois
Fall 1961

Unlike most of my Navy friends and fraternity brothers, I graduated from college and started my post-college career without being married. In fact, when I left Ann Arbor for Newport, I knew of no one who had the faintest interest in being my wife.

This was not always the case. During my junior and senior years, there were two attractive young women whom I believed would have been happy to be my bride. Yet, when I left college, neither of them wanted anything to do with me. I wondered why, but the truth was I couldn't bring myself to choose one and let the other go. I got exactly what I deserved. They both had fired me!

When I attempted to change my ways in Newport, I had been abandoned by Maria Silva, who disappeared into the Fall River phone book. Then I had been rejected by Mary McGinnis, or perhaps I should say by her grandmother. Needless to say, I was discouraged.

Everything changed when I learned that I was one of a dozen officers selected to attend Electronics Officers School in Great Lakes. I saw this as a sign. Susan Parker and I had dated off and on since my junior year at the University of Michigan. She was from Highland Park, Illinois, just down the road from Great Lakes. Ann Arbor was an easy drive from Great Lakes, and Susan would be starting her junior year at Michigan sometime during the weeks following my arrival at Great Lakes. Until then, chances were that she would be at home. This would give us an opportunity to meet and renew our relationship. Perhaps my future wife might be Susan Parker.

I had learned from an instructor at the Communications Officers School that the Electronics School gave exams on Fridays, which allowed students to enjoy their weekends without homework or study. I imagined myself heading for Michigan football games and parties at the SAE house on weekends with Susan. I could even stay at the SAE house at no cost.

All these factors presented a perfect opportunity for me to risk proposing reconciliation with Susan. I sat down immediately and wrote her a long letter, apologizing for my past hurtful behavior and suggesting we try to rebuild our relationship. I dropped the letter in the mailbox and crossed my fingers.

While I waited for Susan's response, I allowed my mind to travel back to the time when I had first met her at an SAE party in the apartment of one of my fraternity brothers. She was sitting on the knee of my SAE *little brother*, a new pledge that I had volunteered to mentor during the months before his initiation as a full-fledged SAE. My first impression was that Susan was absolutely gorgeous. One of her most alluring features was her beautiful blue eyes. She had rich chestnut-brown hair, a flawless complexion, and a marvelous figure. But her most appealing feature was her laugh. She laughed easily and often, which made her attractive to everyone she met.

That evening, I learned that Susan was a fine dancer. We jitterbugged as if we'd been dance partners for years. I would learn later that she was a talented athlete and could readily thump me in tennis and golf. For cappers, she was a member of Michifish, the most popular synchronized-swimming team in the Big-Ten. Most of all, she was adored by all her friends, making her a shoe-in for membership in the most desirable sorority on the campus, *Kappa Kappa Gamma*.

When I pulled into the Parkers' driveway, Susan's mother Virginia was arriving home from shopping. I was startled when she stepped out of the car. She was very attractive and dressed elegantly. While I wasn't certain of her age, I believed she was in her late forties, though she appeared to be about the age of her daughter. I was immediately smitten, especially when she greeted me warmly. It was the beginning of a mutual admiration that spanned several decades.

Virginia told me that Susan was doing some last-minute shopping and that her father Carl had driven her to the mall.

When they arrived home, Carl greeted me like a long lost son. Susan hugged me and kissed me on the lips. It was an especially warm and pleasant introduction to Highland Park and the Parker family.

That fall, when I stayed at Great Lakes during the weekends, Susan's family took me into their home and into their hearts. During my four months at Great Lakes, I saw them frequently, even when Susan was at Michigan studying hard to accumulate credits to graduate early so we could marry. I also became close to Margaret and Bill Gooch, Susan's aunt and uncle who lived nearby. They, too, immediately treated me like a member of the family.

I also met Susan's sister Kathy and her husband, Steve Groves, who had been an NROTC scholarship holder at the University of Illinois. Because Steve was a graduate engineer, he had opted to serve his active duty in the Civil Engineering Corps or Sea Bees as they were once called. He was stationed at Crane Ammunition Depot in southern Indiana. The evening we met he had arrived in Highland Park dressed in the same uniform as mine, Service Dress Blues. His stripes indicated that he was a Lieutenant (jg), and I was a mere Ensign. Steve also stood about five inches taller than I, making him a fitting partner for Kathy, who was about my height. Coincidentally, Steve's widowed mother was Susan's house mother at the *Kappa Kappa Gamma* sorority at Michigan.

Carl, Susan's father, had graduated from nearby Northwestern University before joining Commonwealth Edison's management team. When the Michigan football team came to Evanston to take on Northwestern, the Parkers and Gooches invited me to the game. Susan was back in Ann Arbor that weekend, studying for an important exam, so I gladly accepted. Back in those days, Northwestern was the doormat of the Big Ten. Of course Michigan gave them quite a beating. I felt privileged to join Susan's family for the traditional football weekend. After the game, we had a marvelous dinner at the Gooch's home.

One of the most memorable occasions of my stint in Great Lakes was in the fall of 1961, when the Parkers invited those of my classmates who were not going home for the holiday to join them for Thanksgiving dinner at their home. Five of us took them up on their offer. Dressed in our Service Dress Blue uniforms and bearing bottles of wine, we were an impressive set of holiday guests. The only missing element was Susan who, once again, remained in Ann Arbor to study for an important mid-term exam. Yes, while we missed her, we all still had a whale of a time. The Parkers were magnificent hosts, and, for weeks, my classmates did not stop talking about the festive occasion. At one point that fall, I pondered who I was falling in love with: Susan or her family. What a pleasant dilemma!

Sigma Alpha Epsilon House, University of Michigan

Because electronics school students had weekly exams on Friday, our weekends were free. Often I traveled with a fellow classmate back to Michigan. Ralph Smaltz had a sister in Detroit and a shiny new red Corvette, which was much more suitable for a five-hour drive to the Detroit-Ann Arbor area than my stodgy Karmann-Ghia. He went home every weekend, and I usually joined him every other weekend. Sharing the driving made the trip easier on both of us. Ralph would drop me off in Ann Arbor to see Susan and pick me up on his way back to Great Lakes on Sunday night. Susan lived at the *Kappa Kappa Gamma* sorority house, and I stayed at my old fraternity, the *Sigma Alpha Epsilon* house, where there was always a party every Saturday night. Over the course of my 12 weeks at Great Lakes, I was with Susan at least every other weekend. Our time together cemented my relationship with both Susan and her family. I can honestly say it was one of the most enjoyable periods of my life. I have the Navy to thank for bringing us back together.

Cryptosecurity

Electronics School – Great Lakes, Illinois
Fall 1961

The fleet was in the process of implementing a revolutionary new technology designed to improve the speed, accuracy, and security of transmitting classified messages. This new technology was online cryptography. The components of this top-secret methodology included specialized radio equipment, card readers, and key cards. These cards fell into a number of operational categories and, depending on the security classification involved, were only used for a short period of time.

A major security concern was ensuring that new cards were transported, stored, used, and then ultimately destroyed following a rigid, safe procedure. This was defined by the rules created, maintained, and promulgated by the Registered Publication System (RPS) Headquarters in Washington. RPS offices located at each naval base around the world provided ships with these new online key cards, which came bundled in packages containing one card for each day of the month. Because ships often were away from port at month's end, additional packages of cards were issued to ensure a ship had a three months' supply. These packages, along with all other classified documentation, were stored in a huge safe in the stateroom of the RPS Custodian.

The RPS Custodian was the ship's officer responsible for pickup, transportation, distribution, and destruction of all RPS materials, including online key cards. When the RPS custodian picked up materials at the RPS Office or transported them to special protected furnaces on each base for complete destruction, he had to be accompanied by a petty officer, who usually had a Master at Arms rating. Both men were armed with .45 automatic pistols. We graduates from Communications Officers School were drilled in RPS procedure thoroughly enough to qualify us to assume the role of RPS Custodian when we reported to our new ships.

Of the 60 graduates from the communications school, 12 of us were selected to attend the US Electronics Officers School at Great Lakes, Illinois. My friend Art Sommers and I were among them. During this 12-week school, we studied electronics theory, advanced communications, radar, fire control, and sonar equipment. Even though I'd had two semesters of physics at the University of Michigan, this school was not easy for me. Most of us students spent as many hours studying our textbooks and handouts as we did listening to lectures and conducting lab experiments during our eight-hour class days.

U.S. NAVAL SCHOOL ELECTRONICS OFFICERS (COMMUNICATIONS/ ELECTRONICS COURSE) CLASS 2C-62 US NTC, GREAT LAKES, ILL. 12 DEC, 1961

One man among us never took a note and never spent a minute doing homework and passed our weekly examinations with perfect scores. That person was Art, an electronics genius. Before joining the Navy, Art had worked as a computer designer for a prestigious computer company. While some classmates were envious of his abilities, I appreciated his knowledge and was grateful for our friendship.

When the school ended, everyone received orders to different destroyers in homeports on the east and west coasts. We all wondered whether we were destined to be the Communications Officer or the Electronics Material Officer on our new ships, because we were qualified to fill either role. The yeoman at the electronics school thoughtfully provided us with a list of our classmates and the ships to which we would shortly report for duty. I was pleased to see that Art and I were headed to ships in Norfolk, which would enhance our chances of seeing each other and continuing our friendship. However Art's destroyer was heading to the Mediterranean for a six-month deployment, and my ship, the *USS Cony*, was heading to Portsmouth Naval Shipyard for a six-month overhaul followed by a six-week stint at Guantanamo Bay for Refresher Training. So I gave up any hope of seeing my friend in the near future.

Some months later, after returning to Norfolk, I joined a shipmate for a before-dinner drink at the Des-Sub Pub, near the destroyer piers. As I entered the pub, my old friend Art was just leaving. We shook hands vigorously and agreed to meet the next evening for drinks and dinner at the NOB Officers Club. I would pick him up in my Ghia.

The next evening, I arrived at Art's ship and told the OOD whom I was to meet. He directed me to Art's stateroom. I knocked on the door, and Art asked me to enter. When I stepped inside, I saw his RPS safe wide open and classified material covering every surface of the room.

"What's going on, Art?" I asked.

"I was putting a burn together, and I seem to be missing a couple packs of unopened key cards we didn't need. They have to be here someplace. Let me put this stuff back in my safe, and then we can be on our way."

"God, Art. Why don't we both look for them so you'll have peace of mind and a relaxing dinner?"

"Naw, Gary. I'll find them when I get back – or tomorrow. I don't have to go to the furnace for a couple of days."

Though I didn't really want to agree, I said, "If that's the way you want it."

We put all the materials we could find into the safe, locked it up, and headed for dinner.

It was great seeing Art, but I must admit I was very concerned about his missing key cards. From our Comm School training, we both knew the consequences of losing Top Secret material. Since that threat didn't seem to bother Art, I relaxed and had a marvelous time catching up with all that had happened since we'd seen each other.

After dinner, Art reluctantly agreed to let me help search for the missing cards. We took off our coats and he turned to the huge safe. Placing his left hand on top, he began to turn the combination lock. Then he abruptly stopped. Grinning, he pulled down his hand, and there they were. Two packages of cards.

"I told you they were here someplace!"

I rolled my eyes and said, "Oh, Art. That was a close call!"

"Naaaaa!" he said in a Bugs Bunny voice. "You got to unlax, Gary."

Chicago Surprise

Electronics School – Great Lakes, Illinois
Fall 1961

In the fall of 1961, while I was stationed at Great Lakes, through correspondence with my college roommate, Chuck Nuechterlein, I learned that his sister Suzy was enrolled at Concordia University in River Forrest, Illinois, a western suburb of Chicago.

During our four years at the University of Michigan, Chuck and I had developed a close, lifelong friendship which was predictable because we had so much in common. First, we both came from small Michigan towns. Frankenmuth, Chuck's hometown, was only about 35 miles from Owosso, where I grew up. When we were home from college, we spent our time primarily in Frankenmuth where I got to know Chuck's family, including his younger sister Kay, or Suzy as she was called by her family.

Second, we both went to Michigan on Regular NROTC scholarships. Our NROTC schooling placed us together for three one-hour classes and one two-hour field drill each week for four years. In addition, in 1958, we spent eight weeks together on our 3rd Class Midshipman Cruise and seven weeks, in the summer of 1959, on our 2nd Class *Cruise*.

Third, we both pledged the same fraternity, *Sigma Alpha Epsilon* (SAE). During our sophomore and junior years, we were roommates in the fraternity house. For our senior year, we moved out of the house to make room for new fraternity brothers. With two fellow SAEs, we rented an apartment not far from the fraternity. Chuck and I were the cooks, and the other two apartment mates bought and assembled the ingredients and cleaned up after meals. Chuck and I considered ourselves fortunate that we knew how to cook.

Because Chuck had chosen naval aviation and I had chosen the surface Navy, we saw very little of each other after we became commissioned naval officers. We did have a short visit in Jacksonville, Florida, where Chuck was stationed to complete a phase of his aviation training. My ship, the *USS Cony*, had pulled into Mayport, near Jacksonville, for repairs of damage caused by Hurricane Ella.

While at Great Lakes, on a Sunday afternoon, I decided to pay Suzy Nuechterlein a surprise visit at Concordia. This was a long shot, because I wasn't exactly sure where on campus she lived or even whether she was there that weekend. Despite the odds stacked against the success of this venture, I told myself, "The hell with it. Let's give it a shot!"

To maximize the impression I hoped to make, I packaged myself as a handsome young naval officer instead of some college guy in Ivy League civvies. I put on my best Service Dress Blue uniform complete with the white-covered combination cap and smartly spit-shined black shoes. Before leaving my room, I glanced at myself in the long mirror mounted on the back of my door. I looked like Richard Gere in the movie, *An Officer and a Gentleman*. I really did look good.

I hopped into my Karmann-Ghia and headed south. It took me well over an hour to reach River Forest, but I quickly found Concordia University. Since the college wasn't quite as big as Michigan, I had no difficulty locating the Women's Dorm. I parked my car and walked to the front door. Seeing no sign restricting Gentlemen Visitors, I opened the door and walked in. A young woman, whom I assumed to be a student, looked up from behind a reception desk, smiled brightly, and asked, "How may I help you, Sir?"

"I'm looking for a friend whose name is Kay Nuechterlein. Or she may go by Suzy, her family nickname."

"Oh, we call her Kay. She's not here at the moment. When our dining room is closed on Sunday evenings, we students eat at local restaurants. She just left for dinner with a couple of her friends."

That was not good news. Suzy could be at any number of restaurants I had noticed as I had driven through town. "Would you happen to know where they went?"

"Oh, that's easy. They always go across the street to Ken's. You can see it as you leave the dorm. It's less than a block away. "

I shook the young woman's hand. "You've been very helpful. Thank you so much."

As I ambled toward Ken's, I thought, "If all the girls are as pretty as that receptionist, this must be quite a school."

As I opened the door and stepped into Ken's, I saw Suzy sitting in a booth with two other young women. They were facing me, and Suzy had her back to me. I didn't hesitate, but walked straight to the booth, shoved in beside Suzy, leaned over, and gave her a big kiss on the cheek. The screams of the three women filled the restaurant. I broke into laughter.

When Suzy regained her composure, she hugged me like a mother bear. "Gary! What are you doing here? How did you find me? What a surprise!"

I grinned from ear to ear and so did the two women across the table.

Suzy stumbled through the introductions, then turned and kissed me on the cheek. It was my turn to blush. "I am so glad to see you!"

I joined the three friends for dinner, and I chattered with Suzy about her family's latest news. I told her about my Newport stint and about Great Lakes. Finally, the conversation slowed to an occasional, "Oh, my! I can't believe this." I glanced at my watch. It was approaching nine o'clock. While I didn't want to end our visit, I had a long drive ahead of me and a full day of classes starting bright and early the next morning.

Despite protests from Suzy and her friends, I picked up the tab, and we all headed for Ken who was standing behind his cash register. We were his last customers, but he wasn't at all annoyed by our lingering. He seemed to sense that this had been a special reunion. I told him to keep the change. He thanked me, smiled, and shook my hand.

The three women walked me to my Ghia. This time each of them hugged me and kissed my cheek as I climbed into my car.

"Wow!" I thought. "Hugged and kissed by three attractive women in one night."

I waved as I left the parking lot and headed north. It had been one of the most enjoyable evenings I could remember. I laughed and thought, "Wait 'til Chuck hears about this!"

Junior Ensign

USS Cony – Norfolk, Virginia
December 1961

When I reported aboard the *USS Cony* in December 1961, I had four and a half years of naval experience under my belt. Even still, I was totally unprepared for the challenge of being the junior-most officer in the *Cony* Wardroom. The closest I had come to experiencing the treatment this status brought me had been when I was a pledge in the SAE fraternity during my freshman year at Michigan. Being the junior officer and a gentleman was far more demeaning than being a lowly SAE pledge.

One of the most undesirable responsibilities of the Junior Ensign was to operate the movie projector in the Wardroom, usually every evening after dinner. It's not that the movie projector was difficult to operate but that it brought back old memories. In high school, we had a projectionist club which operated the classroom projectors. The members of this club were considered to be the school's most pitiful losers. They were ridiculed behind their backs some of the time and to their faces most of the time. As a result, when I set up the projector in the Wardroom, I automatically felt demeaned.

In my case, those who harassed me most were junior officers who had recently gone through what I was being forced to endure. Andy Bradick, a fellow Ensign who had about six month's seniority on me, was absolutely the worst offender. To make matters worse, he and I were the only two unmarried *Cony* officers. We both lived aboard ship, which gave him around-the-clock hazing opportunities. While I wouldn't say I hated him exactly, but it was close at times, although later we became best friends. (He even served as an usher in my wedding some 14 months after I reported aboard, and we're still good friends.)

Much of the harassment revolved around the in-port watch schedule. The Senior Watch Officer demanded that the

Junior Ensign have duty every holiday, including Thanksgiving, Christmas, New Year's Eve, and New Year's Day. The Junior Ensign would also have duty on the days the ship arrived in port to allow married officers to return home to their families. Then Andy, my fellow bachelor officer, moved off the ship into a house rented by a number of naval officers, officially known as a snake ranch. So it became my obligation to cover the watches usually assigned to Andy.

Shortly after I reported aboard, Commander Bill Morgan became Captain of the *Cony*. After a stint in the shipyard, we were scheduled to return to sea when Captain Morgan realized that he had a shortage of underway OOD's. He took a risk with Ensign Dave Dean and me, directing the Senior Watch Officer to assign us both to the same underway watch, during which one of us would act as OOD and the other acted as the Junior OOD. On our following watch, we would swap jobs. Captain Morgan justified having less than qualified OODs on watch during this rotation period by saying, "What one doesn't know, the other will know. It's a safe proposition." Using this clever, somewhat chancy rotation approach, both of us soon became qualified OODs and gambling on us, Captain Morgan produced two OODs in a relatively short period of time.

Meanwhile, as the junior-most officer, I was treated by those senior to me as if I were a speck of dust. I endured constant hazing, put-downs, and ridicule for six months. Mercifully, I was relieved of my role as punching bag by the arrival of an Ensign who was junior to me. That new Ensign was George Taft, who had been a year behind me in NROTC at Michigan.

After I was relieved as the Junior Ensign, I soon became qualified as an underway OOD and an in-port Command Duty Officer (CDO). Since the other CDOs were married, I continued take CDO duty on holidays and on the days we pulled in from sea. By that time, I was used to it and didn't mind doing a favor for my married fellow officers.

The Captain's Blouse

USS Cony – Portsmouth, Virginia
Winter 1962

I reported aboard the *Cony* just before Christmas. During the following weeks, we prepared to enter the Portsmouth Naval Shipyard for a regular shipyard overhaul, which normally occurred approximately every three years. The scheduled overhaul was especially important to the Communications and Electronics officers, because we were scheduled to receive a major upgrade in equipment, including the addition of highly sophisticated single sideband (SSB) communications and on-line coding and decoding equipment.

During the shipyard overhaul, Andy Bradick, the ASW officer, was sent to a special four-month ASW training school in Key West, Florida. That left Captain Morgan and me as the only two *Cony* officers living in the Bachelor Officer Quarters in the shipyard. Because he was a Full Commander, his room was about three times the size of mine, and it was equipped with a refrigerator in which he kept cocktail supplies. Each night prior to dinner, he invited me to his room to share a drink or two. He really enjoyed his cocktails. Unfortunately, he sometimes overindulged.

One evening as usual, Captain Morgan and I met for cocktails in his room, which I'm sure we followed with wine at dinner. Then we went to the Officers Club bar where there were more drinks. The bar was crowded and quite noisy. We sat at a table and our Service Dress Blue coats were hung on the back of our chairs. Technically, while these coats were called blouses, I was always uncomfortable with that term because it didn't sound masculine.

On this uniform, an officer's rank is only shown on the sleeve of the coat. With the coat off, all officers wore clean white shirts and a black tie with no indication of rank. Aside from my age, no one in the room could determine my rank. When I went to the bar to purchase a package of cigarettes, I accidentally bumped the arm of an officer. I could see by the coat he wore that he was a Lieutenant Commander. I could also see that he'd had one too many drinks. He chewed me out royally. Everyone in the bar heard his loud dressing-down, including Captain Morgan. I wasn't bothered. I apologized to the man and returned to our table.

Captain Morgan was outraged. He immediately ordered me to put on his coat, which sported the stripes of a full commander on the sleeves.

I was only an Ensign and did as I was commanded. "Now what, Sir?" I asked.

"Go back to the bar and really chew him out!" ordered Captain Morgan.

I did so with great exuberance, and the Lieutenant Commander apologized to me. When I returned to the table, I slipped off the coat and rehung it on the back of the Captain's chair.

The next day, I realized I had made a grievous error. Impersonating an officer of a superior rank was technically a chargeable offence as spelled out in the Uniform Code of Military Justice. I was so worried I decided to tell Lieutenant Rowsey, the Operations Officer, what I had done and ask his advice. He was infuriated both with me and with Captain Morgan for ordering me to commit an unlawful act. I felt embarrassed, ashamed, and stupid to boot.

This occasion nearly landed me in deep trouble with Lieutenant Jim Rowsey, who was not only my boss but also my state-roommate. Even though I said his name was Jim, I always called him Lieutenant Rowsey or Mr. Rowsey. While I don't think he ever asked me to address him in that formal manner, he clearly communicated non-verbally that this was his choice. Because I respected him so much, I honored his preference. It's only been in recent years that we have been on a first-name basis.

While Lieutenant Rowsey and I never talked about that incident again, I assumed he said nothing to Captain Morgan.

Nevertheless, I carried the memory around in my head for decades. Recently, I mentioned this incident to Jim, and he told me that honestly he had no recollection of it. I had felt guilty for over 50 years, and he had forgotten all about it. I rationalized that a prolonged dose of guilt was just what I deserved.

Captain Morgan retired from the Navy at the rank of Full Captain. He then went on to enjoy a successful career as a real estate agent. I believe his success had something to do with the fact that about 40 years ago, well before his retirement, he swore off alcohol altogether.

Gitmo Diversions

USS Cony – Guantanamo Bay, Cuba
Spring 1962

During my naval career, I spent a total of 20 weeks at Guantanamo Bay. I probably covered every square inch of the 45-acre base as a confined tourist. Some men with whom I served had spent time at Gitmo before Castro locked the gates to Cuba. They speak of their Cuban visits with mixed feelings because of the honky-tonk atmosphere just outside the gates. Since those gates were always closed to me, I don't know what I missed.

On my Gitmo visits, my fellow officers and I had no difficulty finding ways to entertain ourselves because of the varied activities the base offered. First and foremost for many was the Officers Club, which served excellent food and a variety of drinks, many of which were exotic Caribbean rum concoctions. One of those, a tasty Anejo Punch, was a popular staple of the Gitmo Officers Club. The only trouble was that it was impossible to drink just one. The first tasted like an alcoholic beverage. The rest went down like a new flavor of Kool-Aid. After a day confined at GQ in the closed spaces of the ship where temperatures hovered above 100 degrees, one's thirst was not quenched by a single Anejo Punch. I observed shipmates who were not satiated until they had crossed into the double digits on their Anejo scorecards. In Spanish, Anejo means *aged*, which is how these double-digit dabblers felt when they stepped down from their bar stools.

At Gitmo, there was only one taxicab. Despite the tiny size of their fleet, the taxi company used a radio dispatch system. The dispatcher imitated the formality of US naval ships. His call sign was *Peso,* and the taxi's was *Cab Number One.*

His call would go out, "*Peso* calling *Cab Number One. Over.*"

The cabbie would answer, "Peso, this is *Cab Number One. Over.*"

"*Cab Number One*, pick up two officers on the porch of the O-Club. Their destination is Pier One. Over."

"Roger, *Peso.* Over and out."

Long after leaving Guantanamo Bay, we Wardroom dwellers imitated this exchange.

One Sunday, my boss, Lieutenant Rowsey, suggested we go to the beach for a swim. This was the first time I had heard of a beach at Guantanamo Bay, and a swim sounded great to me, so I readily agreed. The Lieutenant assured me it was a fine beach covered with a variety of shells, and the water was clear as glass. Then he added, "There are two things I have to warn you about."

My ears perked up. "What are they?"

"There are Cuban army guards posted on the hill beside the beach. They carry sub-machine guns, and their job is to keep swimmers from crossing the line into Cuban waters."

"What if someone drifts across the line?" I asked.

"They shoot"

"Ye gads! What a restful place to take a swim! I can hardly wait to hear your second warning."

"It's only sharks. Sharks infest the water a few yards from shore. Keep your eyes open!"

"Sounds like we're going to enjoy a simply perfect afternoon of relaxation. Given these warnings, do many people use this beach?"

"Saturday afternoon with weather like this, the beach will be packed. Let's get an early start so we can find a spot to put down our blanket. Or rather *your* blanket." He had obviously remembered that I was the Junior Ensign, and he was a full Lieutenant. "I've got a friend, Joe Collins, who lives near the beach. We can borrow some snorkeling gear from him."

I had momentarily forgotten that the Lieutenant's first job after he had been commissioned was here at Guantanamo Bay. He had served as boat officer in charge of the sundry small craft that people used to commute across the waters inside the boundaries of the base. He had taken advantage of his position to explore the entire area, including the nearby Cuban waters, which were open at that time before Castro toppled Battista on some pretext and closed the gates. Because Cuban civilians were essential to the workings of Gitmo, they were given an opportunity to stay. If that was their decision, they could never return to their homes outside the gates on Cuban soil. The vast majority chose to stay and brought their families onto the base with them. Special housing was built to accommodate this large number of newcomers.

Lieutenant Rowsey and I took the base taxi to his friend Joe's house and borrowed two sets of snorkeling gear. As we headed back to the cab, Joe stopped us. "Look. The taxi's busy on Saturdays back at the base. Let him go and use my jeep. I'm working on a project in the garage that'll keep me busy all day and into the night."

We immediately accepted Joe's offer. That avoided the problem of getting back to the ship from the beach.

When we parked the jeep, we observed that there weren't many people at the beach. "That's funny," said the Lieutenant. "Usually on a Saturday this place is packed. Oh well! Let's go for a swim."

As we followed the path leading to the beach, I saw a Cuban soldier standing on a hilltop not more than 50 feet from our path. He was armed with a sub-machine gun just as Lieutenant Rowsey had predicted. Being a friendly guy from Michigan, I smiled and waved at him. It must have caught him off guard, because he waved back and grinned. Then he apparently came to his senses and turned his back to me. I made him aware of my presence by whistling one of my favorite tunes, *The Star Spangled Banner*. I stopped after one verse to give the poor guy a break.

Because I hadn't snorkeled much in my life, I practiced in shallow water near shore to ensure that I remembered what to do. Lieutenant Rowsey swam farther out into the bay. He was a very competent swimmer and put his snorkel to good use. I dove under the water and followed him out toward deeper water. The reef was covered with shells and brilliantly colored coral. I had never seen so many different fish and crabs and tiny sea horses.

I was lost in the beauty of my surroundings until I realized that Lieutenant Rowsey was swimming madly for the beach.

He was so determined to get to shore that he zipped by me without even looking. I couldn't shout at him or even wave to get his attention. Then I saw the reason for his hasty retreat, and my back stiffened. About 20 feet behind him was a huge shark, swimming as fast as the Lieutenant. The shark was at least ten feet long, and even though I was no shark expert, I was sure it was a Great White.

I turned and swam as fast as I could toward shore. It seemed to take forever, but that was just my fear at work. I was relieved when I came upon a coral reef positioned between me and the shoreline. The tide was out, and the reef was covered with only about four inches of water. I stood and ran toward the beach, which was about a hundred feet away. My swim fins enabled me to avoid cutting my feet on the sharp coral.

When I reached the shore, Lieutenant Rowsey was waiting to pull me from the water. I was so exhausted and out of wind that at first I couldn't speak. For some reason, a great chill overcame me. The Lieutenant wrapped his towel around my shivering shoulders as we made our way to the jeep. We hopped in without saying a word and headed back to Joe's house.

Finally, the Lieutenant broke the silence. "Well, how did you enjoy your swim, Ensign Slaughter?" he asked.

"I'll let you know after I get my heart out of my throat."

We both laughed, which helped relieve the tension. "Next time, let's use a glass-bottom boat."

We both laughed louder and longer than necessary, indicating how nervous we still were.

Joe was surprised to see us back so soon. When he heard our story, he completely understood. "I think you fellows could use a good stiff drink. How about some Anejo on the rocks?"

He didn't have to twist our arms. After a couple of settling drinks, we said we should be getting back to the base. Joe kindly offered to drive us, and we took him up on his offer.

"Where to?" he asked.

"To the bowling alley, please," the Lieutenant said. This surprised me. I had no idea that he was a bowler. I knew I wasn't much good at bowling, so I hoped he wouldn't embarrass me.

As it turned out, it was just the opposite. I rolled about 110, a record high for me, while the Lieutenant was unable to keep the ball out of the gutter. His score was less than half of mine.

"Must be the Anejo," I offered as consolation. "Next time we'll both do better." (For the record, there was no next time. I was pretty sure I knew the reason.)

Lieutenant Rowsey asked, "Where to next, Ensign?"

"What about some tennis?" I asked.

"Deal! Let's go back to the ship and get some gear."

Since I had seen the Lieutenant's gear in our stateroom, I knew it was a bit old, but I was game to try. He had rackets and balls for both of us. Actually, I was a fair player, because there were about a half dozen courts in my hometown, and I had played there often in the summer.

We took the base taxi to the O-Club tennis facility, which was maintained extremely well. Most of the courts were in use and the players seemed quite skilled. At least, they were above my level. Since the Lieutenant didn't comment, I assumed he was pretty good himself. Again, as it turned out, he was less skilled at the game than I. After I had readily won two straight sets, he suggested that we change into our uniforms, head for the bar, and perhaps have a bit of dinner after a couple of drinks. That sounded like a good idea to me. I wasn't eager to best him in another athletic competition – at least not today.

As if he had read my mind, he said, "You ought to try golfing tomorrow. Right after breakfast."

"What about you?"

"Oh, golfing is my nemesis. I'm a terrible golfer. But I bet you're good at it."

By the time we finished dinner it was nearly 2200 hours (ten o'clock) in the evening. At that hour, *Cony* was no longer tied up at the pier but was stationed in the upper reaches of the bay for a night of surveillance duty. We took a taxi from the Officers Club to the pier and boarded a motor whale boat that returned us to the ship.

Huge sixty-foot square mooring structures had been sunk into the bay near the Gitmo northern boundary. The moorings had been constructed from long oak rails that reminded me of super-size railroad ties. After these enormous structures were firmly set, they had been filled with soil and topped with grass. Smaller ships like ours would tie up to the huge cast-iron rings that had been sunk into the soil and set firmly in poured concrete jackets around the perimeter of these structures. Or we could simply drop our anchor on the structures with the flukes pointed downstream, and they would dig themselves into the soil to hold us in place.

(In the early 1900s, the mooring structures had been used by old battleships that came to Gitmo for the winter to avoid the ice and cold weather of their northern homeports like Boston and New York. The US Navy used Gitmo as an opportunity to continue training under more favorable weather conditions.)

In 1962, to be on the safe side, we lit off both our surface and air-search radars even before we were securely tied up. The radar men and gun crews were placed on watch to scan the northern skies for waves of Cuban fighters and bombers sweeping down to surprise the unaware Americans stationed at Gitmo.

Weather permitting, we held ship's parties for the crew on these mammoth structures. Food was prepared on grills on the fantail, and from a locked compartment below deck, hundreds of bottles of export beer were brought out and iced-down on the mooring structure. There they could be consumed without violating the prohibition against serving alcohol aboard ship. Technically, when standing on the mooring structure, you were ashore. Sailors would fill their paper plates on the fantail and then step out onto the mooring structure to enjoy a picnic of hotdogs, hamburgers, potato chips, and ice-cold beer. We repeated this party several times during our Gitmo stays.

On Sunday, Bill Poteat and I decided to play golf. We grabbed a motor whale-boat ride into the Officers Club, which was a short walk from the Guantanamo Bay Country Club. Bill carried his shiny new steel-shanked clubs, which I understood he used skillfully on the course. On the other hand, I had never played golf before. Oh, I knew the game all right. I had spent a summer in high school as a caddy at the Owosso Country Club.

And just before this cruise, I had been the recipient of a bag of ancient, wooden-shaft clubs from an Owosso neighbor who had retired from the game. He knew that I had been one of the hottest baseball and softball hitters in Owosso and had concluded that I would be a terrific golfer. What he didn't know was that I batted left-handed. Unfortunately, his gift was a set of right-handed clubs.

When I told Bill my problem, he shrugged it off and advised, "Just give it a shot. I bet you'll do okay." So I agreed to try.

When we reached the caddy shack/golf equipment store, only one man was in attendance. We were surprised to be the only golfers at the course that morning. "Where is everybody?" we asked.

The attendee's answer was short and sweet. "The course hasn't been watered for a year. It's bone dry and the greens are in terrible shape. Fast as hell. And the sand traps can't be accessed. Also there are a number of excavations that will impede walking on the course. Don't get me wrong, you can use the course at your own risk."

"What risk?" Bill asked.

The man explained that the golf course lay in a valley that would have been an ideal route for Castro's army to invade Guantanamo Bay from the mountains. Bunkers had been constructed and mines were laid in the sand traps.

"That doesn't seem like a big deal. Let's go for it." said Bill. "What have we got to lose?"

I nearly told him, but I thought it would be a bit macabre to mention arms and legs flying through the air.

Despite my difficulty in hitting with right-handed clubs, I soon settled in and began enjoying the game. We played 18 holes. While I forgot what Bill's score was that morning, I shot a 55. The fairways were as hard as concrete. When you'd hit a drive, the ball would roll about a thousand yards after it landed. It didn't take us long to finish the 18 holes.

On the way back to the ship, Bill said, "If anyone asks, let's tell them our scores, but don't mention the condition of the fairways. Okay?"

That was good enough for me. After all, it was the best golf score I'd ever had. Come to think of it, it was the first and last score that I ever had.

After I returned from Gitmo in the spring of 1962, my wife and I threw a party in our small apartment for some of my *Cony* shipmates. I thought it would be appropriate to serve Anejo Punch. At my local liquor store, I was informed that, while Anejo rum was not commonly carried, it could be special ordered. Instead, I decided to go to Norfolk's Spanish-speaking neighborhood, where I had no trouble purchasing as much as I wanted of this amazing elixir.

Our male guests were excited that Anejo Punch was our featured cocktail that evening. Their wives were not as pleased as they drove home with husbands who refused to stop singing *Yellow Bird*. Our wives simply didn't appreciate the fact that this ditty had become the theme song of our Cuban trip.

Suggestible Twosome

USS Cony – Portsmouth, Virginia
Summer 1962

In January of 1962, the *USS Cony* underwent a routine shipyard overhaul at the Portsmouth Naval Shipyard, just up the James River from Norfolk. The overhaul was scheduled to last six months, but we were delayed a few weeks because of difficulties installing our new sonar dome. During this period, I lived in the BOQ in the shipyard, where I had a sheltered parking spot for my Karmann-Ghia sports coupe, which I treated with great care.

After our overhaul was finally completed, we made preparations to travel to Guantanamo Bay Naval Base (Gitmo) in Cuba for an intensive six-week period of Refresher Training. Because we would be gone for at least eight weeks, I put my car in a storage garage not far from the Norfolk Naval Operating Base (NOB). If I was at sea for more than a week or so, I routinely stored my car rather than leave it on the pier, where it would collect soot and saltwater from the nearby destroyer and submarine activities at the Des-Sub Base.

Upon our arrival back in Norfolk after completion of our Refresher Training, I decided to retrieve my car. At the time, I was the only officer on the ship who wasn't on duty, which meant there was no one to give me a lift. When I was halfway to the front gate to catch a taxi, a horn honked behind me. I turned around to see a pickup truck with a driver and a passenger I recognized. They were members of the deck force, and both, for reasons not known to me, still held the lowly rate of seaman.

Scott, the driver, was accompanied by Bushby, who rolled down his window and greeted me, "Hey, Mr. Slaughter! Where 'ya headed?"

I explained that I was taking a taxi to pick up my car at a storage garage near NOB.

"Heck, we're on our way to NOB to get some parts for the chief," said Bushby. "Why don't cha hop in?" He shoved over, I hopped in, and off we went.

There was a reason behind their friendly and generous manner. When we first became acquainted, we'd learned that all three of us were Michiganders. They were from the Detroit area, and I was from Owosso, located about ninety miles to the northwest. And we were all great fans of Detroit major league sports teams including the Red Wings, the Lions, and the Tigers. Because none of us cared that much for basketball, we seldom chatted about the Pistons. Back in those days, when you were stationed aboard a Navy ship, it was difficult to keep up with your favorite sports teams, so we shared any little piece of news that we heard.

Scott pulled up to the garage, and I opened the passenger door. Jokingly, I admonished him and Bushby, "I know you two haven't been home in a long time. I haven't either. Just don't get any bright ideas about driving this truck to Detroit. You hear me?"

They laughed at such a suggestion, and the last words I heard as I hopped out of the truck were, "Gee, Mr. Slaughter. You don't think we'd do something that dumb, do you?"

"No. I don't really think you'd do that. You're both good guys. Thanks again for the ride."

They waved at me as they drove off toward NOB.

I didn't think about Scott and Bushby until several days later when I learned they were Absent without Leave (AWOL), and the pickup was missing. You can imagine what went through my mind. First of all, I knew I couldn't keep my exchange with them from the First Lieutenant, their boss, nor from the Operations Officer, my boss. I related my story to Lieutenant Rowsey first. Then he asked the Gunnery Officer and the First Lieutenant to join us in the Wardroom.

I told everyone exactly what had happened and admitted how bad I felt about joking around with the two runaways about such a serious matter. Everyone assured me that I couldn't possibly be blamed for the acts of these two foolish seamen. I was relieved, to say the least.

The Gunnery Officer suggested that we inform Captain Morgan and the Executive Officer about my conversation with Scott and Bushby. When I told my story to the CO and the XO, they took the same position, reassuring me that I was not responsible for the acts of two loose cannons.

Weeks passed without a single word on Scott and Bushby's whereabouts, after about three months, the local Shore Patrol headquarters sent Captain Morgan a message reporting that the case had been turned over to the Federal Bureau of Investigation. The FBI was calling their crime *Desertion* which carried a far more serious punishment than AWOL. After several months I forgot about Scott and Bushby, having decided we would never know what had happened to them.

Then the FBI turned the two deserters over to the shore-patrol headquarters in Norfolk. Scott and Bushby were incarcerated in the brig to await their trial, and Captain Morgan immediately convened a Special Court Martial. The Commanding Officer of our sister ship, the *USS Conway* (DDE 507), agreed to act as Military Judge, and Captain Morgan named the Gunnery Officer as the Defense Counsel. Much to my amazement, he named me as Trial Counsel (Prosecutor) and selected three other *Cony* officers to form the Panel of Court Members (Jury).

The Court Martial was accomplished quickly with little defense offered by the defendants. Within two days, Scott and Bushby were found guilty of desertion and theft of naval property, the pickup truck, which had been confiscated by the FBI at the time of the arrest.

After a half day of discussion about appropriate punishment, each of the two was sentenced to a year's confinement in a federal prison, which we learned later was Leavenworth Prison in Leavenworth, Kansas. As the pair of handcuffed prisoners were being escorted out of the Court Room, both turned to me and said simultaneously, "Sorry, Mr. Slaughter. Really sorry."

I was sorry as well. After all, now who could I possibly talk to about Detroit's sport teams?

The Cuban Missile Crisis - Preparation

USS Cony – ASW Exercises
Summer 1962

USS Cony, my first ship as a commissioned officer, was a *Fletcher* class destroyer with a distinguished war record that included surviving two Japanese bomb hits in 1943. Later, as the Cold War heated up, *Cony* was converted into an Anti-Submarine Warfare (ASW) destroyer. After reporting aboard, I was selected to attend ASW Air-Controller School, because of my experience serving aboard the *USS Valley Forge*, the flagship of Task Group Alpha.

After Air-Controller School, and back on *Cony*, I served as a qualified ASW Air-Controller. Using radio communications, I directed coordinated search and attack operations employing several types of aircraft including the land-based *Neptune* (P2V), the carrier-based, fixed-wing *Tracker* (S2F), and various carrier-based helicopters. Within months, I was assigned as the 1JS talker during Condition 1ASW, a watch configured to carry out simulated or actual submarine search and attack operations. As the 1JS talker, I acted as the chief communicator between the bridge, Combat Information Center (CIC) and Sonar, as well as the weapons stations.

Prior to reporting to *Cony*, I had attended the Naval Communications Officers School where I had been trained to communicate with Soviet warships, by employing the Cyrillic alphabet transliteration table, International Signals Book, and Morse code.

In learning these skills, I was uniquely qualified to perform my job as an ASW specialist during the Cold War.

And I'm proud to say that my performance during my first few months on *Cony* enabled me to become a fully qualified OOD(F), Officer of the Deck, Fleet (at-sea operations) prior to my first promotion from Ensign to Lieutenant (jg).

My ASW background and training really paid off!

USS Cony change of command from Captain Bill Morgan to Captain Thomas Brennan (June 1963)

USS Cony officers during Cuban Missile Crisis (October 1962)

Cony Car Friends

USS Cony – Norfolk, Virginia
Summer 1962

Two of my *Cony* shipmates were old friends from my hometown, Owosso, Michigan: Melvin Tattersoll, the Ship's Cook, and Tony Oswald, Third Class Gunner's Mate. I was the only one of us who owned a car, my snazzy red Karmann-Ghia, which I had acquired in the fall of my senior year at the University of Michigan. Only seniors were allowed to own cars, presumably because of the scarcity of parking space.

Upon completion of our extensive overhaul in June 1962, we headed for Gitmo for six weeks of Refresher Training. At the suggestion of a shipmate, I left my car at a convenient storage garage. While this was a little expensive, leaving my car parked on the pier for eight weeks would not have been a prudent choice.

On our arrival back in Norfolk, I retrieved my car from storage and again parked it on the pier. Then we received word that *Cony* would be deployed to the Mediterranean as a member of Task Group Alpha.

I was suddenly in conflict. The good news was that we'd be going to the Med for four to six months. I'd been there on the *Valley Forge* for my 1st Class cruise and had had a wonderful time, touring all the beautiful and interesting sites. The bad news was what to do with my car? I could store it in Norfolk, but that would mean incurring a rather large expense for an Ensign who only earned $269.80 per month, consisting of a taxable salary of $222.30 plus a non-taxable Basic Allowance for Subsistence (BAS) of $47.50. Then it struck me! Melvin Tattersoll was being discharged from the Navy prior to our planned Med deployment. So I went to talk with him.

"Melvin, how are you getting home after you're dis-charged?" I asked.

He shrugged his shoulders, "Hitchhike, I guess."

"I have a better idea. How would you like to drive my Karmann-Ghia home? I'll furnish the gas money."

"Are you serious?" asked Melvin. "That would be great!"

The next day, I said goodbye to Melvin and my Ghia and called my folks to let them know that Melvin and the car were on the way. My father assured me that he would store it in the horse barn at my grandfather's farm. On July 28, 1962, I went to bed at peace with the world.

The very next day, my peace evaporated. Our Med deployment had been cancelled. Instead Task Group Alpha spent the next several weeks going in and out of port to conduct ASW exercises in the Virginia Capes Operating Area. And each time we returned, I was stuck without my car. I plotted ways to retrieve it, but before I could, the Cuban Missile Crisis intervened, and I was again relieved that my car was safely stowed away at the farm.

Our attention turned to Cuba on October 14, 1962, when Task Group Alpha was assigned to provide the ASW screen for PHIB-RIG-LEX-62. This huge amphibious task force was formed to conduct a mock invasion of Puerto Rico. While we didn't know it at the time, this task force was designed to shake up Fidel Castro and to send a message to the Soviets to stay out of Cuba.

We were just off the southern tip of Florida when Hurricane Ella threatened the task force. The massive exercise was cancelled, and all the ships were ordered to return to their homeports. Before our squadron made it back to Norfolk, Ella caught up with us. Since the *Cony* and others sustained damages, the squadron pulled into the Naval Operations Base in Mayport, Florida for repairs.

The following is from a letter to my fiancée, Susan Parker, dated October 20.

Right now we're about 500 miles east of Key West. This cruise has been long and extremely grueling. The seas have been constantly heavy (15 to 20 feet) because of Hurricane Ella. There's no real way to rest when you are battered so much. We went south when Ella was moving north. Now we're going to turn and follow it back up north, keeping us bouncing for the whole period. This time out at sea has really been rewarding for me. I think I am in contention for being made a Fleet Officer of the Deck. It depends on how good the replacements for Mr. Rowsey and Paul Goorjian are.

After the repairs were completed, we headed for Norfolk. However, President Kennedy's October 22, 1962 television broadcast changed everything. He announced that, because the Soviets had deployed troops and nuclear missiles to Cuba, he was ordering a Quarantine of Cuba to prevent further missiles and other arms from being delivered to Castro. Task Group Alpha was ordered to take up station in the Bermuda Triangle as a part of the Quarantine.

The Cuban Missile Crisis - Prelude

USS Cony - Western Atlantic Ocean
Fall 1962

October 2012 marked the 50th anniversary of the Cuban Missile Crisis, which brought the United States and the Soviet Union to the brink of nuclear destruction. Just how close we came to an exchange of nuclear weapons was not revealed until the 2002 publication of Peter Huchthausen's book entitled *October Fury*. This gripping history describes the formerly top-secret facts about a near catastrophic confrontation that occurred on October 27, 1962 between an American destroyer, *USS Cony*, and a Soviet Foxtrot-class submarine, *B-59*. Unknown to *Cony*, *B-59* was armed with a deadly nuclear-tipped torpedo.

The crisis with Cuba had been building for some time. In 1960, two years earlier, President John F. Kennedy had concluded that Castro's Cuba was a Soviet client-state working to subvert Latin America. After much debate within his administration, Kennedy authorized a clandestine invasion of Cuba at the Bay of Pigs. The invasion force of 1,400 Cuban exiles was called Brigade 2506. The brigade was funded, organized, and trained by the CIA. Their training began on Useppa, a small deserted island on the southwest coast of Florida not far from Fort Meyers. Subsequently, the brigade transferred to a CIA Base in Guatemala, where they made final preparations for the invasion.

Under the operational control of the CIA, the *Cony* was one of a squadron of eight destroyers, each with a CIA agent assigned to monitor its activities. To hide its identity as an American war ship, each destroyer painted out its hull number and the ship's name on its stern. We were not required to lower our American flag, but rather to smudge it with dirt to prevent identification from a distance. The destroyers were to provide gunfire support for the invasion, and *Cony* also provided Lieutenant Rowsey, our Operations Officer and a qualified air controller. Rowsey was to direct the attacks of ground-support fighter planes from the *USS Essex*, the flagship of the invasion task force.

The brigade hit the beach on April 17, 1961. From the *Cony*, we could clearly see Castro's tanks and troops arrayed on a ridge above the landing beach. Even though they were firing at us, we were not allowed to fire our 5" or 40 mm guns at the Cuban forces or bring in fighter planes to wipe them out. Not surprisingly, the operation soon collapsed in spectacular failure. One hundred eighteen members of the brigade were killed, and over 1,200 were captured. At great danger to themselves, armed *Cony* sailors, using our motor whaleboats, managed to rescue the handful of men that were lucky enough to escape.

USS Cony at sea

To this day, many *Cony* officers and men adamantly insist that Kennedy ordered the American destroyers to withdraw before they had a chance to succeed. Not allowing us to fire on or bomb the enemy was a most egregious mistake. Making matters worse, *Cony* crewmembers were sworn to secrecy about the Bay of Pigs. This secret was not declassified until 40 years later. The

American flag was truly smudged that day. More important, the inevitability of the Cuban Missile Crisis was all but assured.

Kennedy took public responsibility for this fiasco. Nonetheless, he remained determined to rid Cuba of Castro. In November 1961, Kennedy approved Operation Mongoose, a secret plan meant to fuel a rebellion in Cuba. However, Soviet Premier Nikita Khrushchev had a plan of his own. After the Bay of Pigs, he concluded that Kennedy was weak and indecisive. Based on that assumption, in early 1962, Khrushchev secretly began a bold and massive covert operation to smuggle medium-range nuclear missiles into Cuba.

In the summer of 1962, US intelligence acquired evidence of a general Soviet arms build-up in Cuba. On September 4, 1962, Kennedy issued a public warning to the Soviets not to introduce offensive weapons into Cuba. Khrushchev, believing he had Kennedy's number, ignored the warning.

On October 14, a U-2 spy plane over-flight of Cuba provided the first proof of Soviet nuclear missiles that within minutes of their launch could annihilate Los Angeles, Washington, and New York. In total, the Soviets had secretly positioned 42 medium-range nuclear missiles, hundreds of surface-to-air anti-aircraft missiles, and 50,000 Soviet troops and technicians. These weapons and troops were stationed along the northern coast of Cuba as close as 90 miles from our Florida coastline.

Kennedy called together his closest advisers to decide how to resolve this situation, the most dangerous US-Soviet confrontation of the Cold War. The administration hawks argued for an air strike to take out the missiles and destroy the Cuban Air Force, followed by a US invasion of Cuba. The doves favored issuing warnings to Cuba and the Soviet Union. The President decided on a middle course.

On October 22, Kennedy ordered a Naval Quarantine of the island of Cuba, using the term Quarantine as a euphemism to avoid calling this operation a blockade, which according to international law is technically an act of war. Simultaneously, Kennedy raised our national defense readiness level to DEFCON 3. DEFCON is an acronym for Defense Readiness Condition. It prescribes five graduated levels of readiness or states of alert for our Armed Forces. DEFCON 5 is the least severe, and DEFCON 1 is the most severe. That evening, the President delivered a nationally televised speech, describing the critical situation and the actions he had taken. He was speaking not only to the American people but also to the rest of the world, especially the Soviet Union and Khrushchev.

As *Cony's* Communications Officer, I patched Kennedy's speech onto the ship's public address system for all hands to hear. While we, along with the other ships in our task group, steamed at top speed to reach our assigned station along the Quarantine Line.

That same day, Kennedy sent a letter to Khrushchev, demanding that he remove his missiles from Cuba. As in Kennedy's television address, the letter contained the following warning:

> *"It shall be the policy of this nation to regard any nuclear missile launched from Cuba against any nation in the Western Hemisphere as an attack by the Soviet Union on the United States, requiring a full retaliatory response on the Soviet Union."*

This sobering warning caused panic in America. The shelves of grocery stores were emptied to stock American backyard bomb shelters and basements with cans of food and bottles of water.

I wrote the following letter to my fiancée, Susan Parker:

October 23, 1962

Dear Susan,

I guess by this time you're wondering what's up with Cony. *Well, needless to say, we're not pulling into Norfolk on the 25th. We are extended at sea indefinitely. All the ships everywhere are at sea and there's no doubt that this situation is for real.*

It may be a diplomatic ploy, but to us, it's a little different. On the other hand the weather is good, and promotions are good during international skirmishes. (I'm being funny.) It's been grueling out here the last two weeks, and we're anticipating staying at least a couple of more weeks before pulling in someplace. This whole situation is kind of interesting. My being Communications Officer keeps me abreast of everything in the world that's going on. The information about my whereabouts is of course 'For Official Use Only. Handle with Care.'

XOXO

Four days later, on October 26, Soviet freighters, carrying additional missiles and other offensive weapons, appeared to be ignoring Kennedy's demand that they turn around and return home. They steamed on toward the Quarantine Line, an arc connecting two points, one 500 miles northeast of the eastern tip of Cuba and the other 500 miles northeast from the western tip. The distance of 500 miles was chosen, because it was out of range of the Soviet IL-28 bombers based in Cuba.

That day, Kennedy raised the readiness level to DEFCON 2 for the first time in American history. B-52s, our force of nuclear-armed strategic bombers, were put on full alert. A portion of them took off and circled near the northern border of the Soviet Union. One hundred forty-five intercontinental long- and intermediate-range nuclear missiles, positioned as far west as Alaska and as far east as Turkey, stood ready to be launched against the Soviet Union. One hundred sixty-one nuclear-armed interceptor aircraft were dispersed to 16 different airfields to surround Soviet Russia. Finally, a half dozen US ballistic-missile submarines around the world were poised to launch their 16 deadly *Polaris*, medium-range nuclear missiles, at the heart of Russia. Our military state of readiness was only a quick decision away from DEFCON 1, all-out nuclear war with the Soviet Union.

The next day, October 27, was called Black Saturday by those in the Kennedy White House, because two extremely serious events occurred that nearly caused Kennedy to push the DEFCON 1 button. First, with a Soviet surface-to-air missile, the Cubans shot down an American U-2 spy plane. (The pilot, Major Rudolf Anderson, Jr., was the only person killed by enemy fire during the Cuban Missile Crisis.) Technically this was an act of war. Despite intense pressure from his more hawkish advisors, Kennedy took no retaliatory action. Instead, he chose to allow Khrushchev more time to respond to his demand letter and to give back-channel communications the time to produce a breakthrough.

The second serious event occurred later that day: the confrontation between the *Cony* and *B-59*, the Soviet submarine.

The stage was set.

Personal Postscript: In the wee hours of the morning following midnight of *Black Saturday,* Defense Secretary Robert McNamara and Secretary of State Dean Rusk, exhausted from stress and lack of sleep, decided to head home for a few hours of rest to prepare themselves for the critical events of the next day. As they left the White House, McNamara confided to Rusk, "Dean, given the current state of affairs, I'm not sure we'll see tomorrow morning." Rusk sadly agreed. Grimly they shook hands and parted in morbid silence.

USS Cony at sea

Years later, I was lecturing at a think tank in Europe on management of information technology. After my lecture, I flew back to Washington on American Airlines. I was a frequent flyer and a member of the Admirals Club where passengers could relax in comfort while awaiting the departure of their flights. On that occasion, there were only two other people in the club at Heathrow Airport: former Defense Secretary Robert McNamara and his wife Margaret. I introduced myself and explained that I had served on a Navy destroyer on the Quarantine Line during the Cuban Missile Crisis. I also told him that I was a great admirer of the work he had done to advance the science of systems analysis. I explained that I had worked with two of his protégés in that area from his days as Secretary of Defense, Alain Enthoven and Ivan Selin, for whom I worked at American Management Systems.

We thanked each other for our service. Then we began a long discussion of how his work in systems analysis had structured my thinking in developing management software and lecturing on the management of information technology. It was a most stimulating exchange. McNamara was a brilliant thinker, and both he and his wife were extremely pleasant traveling companions. I will never forget our chance meeting in London.

Cuban Missile Crisis - Confrontation

USS Cony – The Quarantine Line
October 1962

I was standing watch on the bridge of the *USS Cony*. Our destroyer was part of the Hunter-Killer Task Group Alpha, comprising a squadron of eight ASW destroyers and the *USS Randolph* (CVS 15), an ASW aircraft carrier. All our ships and aircraft were fully equipped to hunt down Soviet submarines and destroy them using our sizeable array of deadly weapons. Most important, every man in the task force was a professional ASW specialist, trained to a finely-tuned state of readiness and dedicated to the goal of defeating the Soviet submarine threat.

Cony's state of readiness was typical. In May 1962, we had completed a shipyard overhaul equipping us with the latest in ASW weaponry and electronics equipment. Then we had completed a grueling six weeks of Refresher Training at the US Naval Training Station located at Guantanamo Bay. After Refresher Training, which focused heavily on ASW tactics, we had rejoined Task Group Alpha for several months of ASW exercises conducted in the western Atlantic. Our Refresher Training and ASW exercises taught us to launch integrated attacks that combined ASW destroyers and ASW aircraft, fixed-wing, and helicopters from the aircraft carrier and from ashore. We were challenged by our training adversaries, American submarines, whose crews were skilled in employing the tactics of their Soviet counterparts.

Now our task group was operating on the Quarantine Line about 300 miles southwest of Bermuda, where we obtained strategic intelligence from long-range, sub-hunting aircraft and from our top-secret Sound Surveillance System (SOSUS), an array of underwater hydrophones stretching along the eastern coast of North America from Newfoundland to the Caribbean. SOSUS could identify and track Soviet surface ships and submarines from long distances. With these methods of detection, naval intelligence had identified Soviet submarines traveling south toward Cuba in advance of Soviet freighters that were transporting additional nuclear missiles and other arms for Castro's forces. We knew they were coming, and our forces were waiting at optimal locations to intercept them. Earlier in the day, I had written to Susan:

October 27, 1962

Dear Susan,

Well, the old Cony *expects to be 'down' here for quite some time. We haven't seen land for almost three weeks, and we're all wondering what's going to come of it all. In the meantime, we'll stay here and perform our function of carrying out the current Presidential policy.*

Fortunately I speak a little French so I'm an interpreter. So far, I haven't had time to exercise my ability on any French ships, however I'm standing by.

Call it what you may back home, this whole affair is being taken quite seriously here. The ship has gone into battle-watch stations, and we've manned our weapons stations 24 hours a day. It's a grueling period and a long one. We don't expect relief for quite some time.

Paul Goorjian (Gunnery Officer) was extended for 12 months as was Steve (Susan's brother-in-law). *Jim Rowsey had to put off his wedding again. And he's stuck on board and his new command is waiting for him.* (Rowsey, the Operations Officer, was to have taken command of his own ship before the Missile Crisis.)

We are preparing for an extended stay here. Don't ask me what that means. It is my guess that Kennedy will wait out Russia on this one. Keeping us out here and 'mobile.' This has affected everyone. Too bad for a lot of people's plans. I'm happy my car is home and not in a parking lot in Norfolk. I hope we get back before January. But, if not, think of all the good we're doing for World Peace!

I'm really sorry at the brevity of this letter. There's nothing new to report. You know more about the international situation there at home than I do. That's about it. I don't know when you'll receive this, but I'll try to find a mail box.

Bon soir,

Gary

PS. The officers and enlisted men are having a beard-growing contest! I've entered. Wait until you see me. Wow!

On *Black Saturday*, at about five o'clock in the afternoon, *Cony* acquired a solid sonar contact. It was *B-59*, a Soviet *Foxtrot Class*, diesel, battery powered submarine.

Four days earlier, the US Navy had promulgated a *Notice to All Mariners* (NOTAM) to the ships of the world. Simultaneously, a copy of the NOTAM was delivered to the Kremlin by our embassy in Moscow. The NOTAM outlined our protocol for challenging surface ships and submarines crossing the Quarantine Line. Ships were to stop their engines and prepare to be boarded. Submarines were to surface and, maintaining a slow speed, come to an easterly heading.

The NOTAM included two methods for signaling submarines to surface. *Cony* crewmen followed that protocol and dropped five Practice Depth Charges (PDCs) in close proximity to *B-59*. In addition, using our underwater radio transmitter (*Gertrude*), our sonar men transmitted the International code *IDKCA*, which also meant *come to the surface.*

Both the Soviet and American navies were accustomed to using PDCs to signal submarines to surface. On this occasion, our PDCs panicked the *B-59's* already stress-ridden Commanding Officer, Captain Vitali Savitsky. Confused and fearing he was under attack, he ordered his crew to arm the nuclear torpedo. Witnesses aboard *B-59* reported that Savitsky madly screamed,

"Maybe the war has already started up there, while we're down here doing summersaults. We're going to blast them now! We'll die, but we will sink them all. We will not disgrace our Navy."

Savitsky was correct about the damage the *B-59* would have caused. He was about to launch at *Cony* a 15 kiloton nuclear weapon, the same size and destructive power of the A-bombs dropped on Hiroshima and Nagasaki to end World War II.

Stories among *B-59* witnesses differ as to what happened next. Some say Savitsky cooled down and had a change of heart. Others say his acting second-in-command, Captain Vasili Arkhipov, Chief-of-Staff of *B-59*'s submarine brigade talked him out of it. Still others say that the other officers pressured him to change his mind.

Today's Russian version of the story is that Arkhipov used his rank and position to *order* Savitsky not to launch the torpedo. In reality, Arkhipov and Savitsky were equal in rank. Furthermore, because Savitsky was the sub's Commanding Officer, Arkhipov was automatically the acting second-in-command, the Executive Officer in our Navy's parlance. Whatever the reason, Savitsky did not launch his torpedo.

After being detected by *Cony*, Savitsky and his exhausted crew bravely endured four more hours of relentless ASW hounding. With a maximum underwater speed of just nine knots, the *B-59* was caught in our trap, and we weren't about to let her escape. We pounded the submarine with ultra-high amplitude sound waves from the huge sonar dome under our bow. With sound waves crashing against their hull, *B-59* crewmen couldn't hear themselves think.

Toward the end of those four hours, the *B-59*'s batteries were nearly depleted, and her air-conditioning was inoperable, causing temperatures to soar to 140–160 degrees Fahrenheit. Noxious battery-acid fumes escaped from nearly depleted batteries. Her crewmen were dropping like flies. Finally, at nine o'clock that night, *B-59* surfaced. We had won the battle of wills.

Dutifully following dictates of our protocol, *B-59* assumed an easterly heading at a slow speed and turned on her diesels to recharge her batteries. Main deck hatches popped open to allow the fresh night air to flow inside and cool the submarine. The sub's crewmen streamed out of the open hatches, stripping off their sweat-soaked uniforms. They were highly animated and cheerful, apparently delighted to be free of their entrapment. On *Cony*, we observed their expressions of joy and relief as we followed alongside *B-59* from a position about 200 feet off the submarine's starboard beam.

As soon as *B-59* had broached the surface, we bathed the submarine in blue-white light from our huge 24-inch search lights. My first reaction to seeing the submarine on the surface was *Wow! She's huge!* The *Foxtrot Class* submarine was 295 feet long. With a 19-foot draft, she displaced 2,500 tons of seawater, approximately equal to *Cony's* displacement. And *Cony*, with a length of 376 feet, was only about 80 feet longer than *B-59*. The *B-59* had a crew of 80 officers and men; our crew numbered 330.

Soon after *B-59* was on the surface, my lead signalman and I used our flashing light to interrogate the submarine, employing the Cyrillic transliteration table, the International Signals Book, and Morse code. First, I told the submarine to identify itself. Savitsky refused to give me the name of his boat. When challenged, he replied, using his flashing-light operator, that the submarine was *KORABL X SSR* meaning *Soviet Ship X.* When I asked what his status was, he reported perfunctorily, "On the surface, operating normally."

Extending the customary maritime courtesy, I then asked, "Do you require any assistance?"

Savitsky answered with a curt, *"Nyet."*

For the next hour, Savitsky and I simply stared at each other, and the situation settled into an uneasy standoff. I had never seen a Soviet naval officer up close. With his droopy, squatty, and dour face, he looked like an over-the-hill prize-fighter and fit the part of the villain perfectly.

(Later when interviewed for a PBS documentary, I commented that Savitsky looked like he'd come straight from central casting. Noting my comment, Bedlam, the producers of the documentary, *The Man Who Saved the World*, used my description when hiring the actor who played Savitsky in the film.)

Suddenly, out of the pitch-black night sky, an overzealous Navy pilot roared over the scene and disrupted our relative serenity. When his shore-based P2V *Neptune*, a gigantic twin-engine ASW patrol airplane, was directly above the submarine, he dropped several incendiary devices which sounded like a string of large firecrackers exploding. *Bam! Bam! Bam!* While the light flashes were absolutely blinding, they activated his photoelectric camera lenses to photograph the submarine.

Believing he was under attack, Savitsky cleared his conning tower and wheeled his boat around, bringing his forward torpedo tubes to bear on *Cony*.

Cony's Commanding Officer, Captain Morgan, immediately directed me to signal Savitsky and apologize for the provocative nature of the *P2V's* unannounced arrival. Then, using our ship-to-ship radio, the Captain transmitted a scolding rebuke of the Task Group Commander's staff for allowing such an act to occur.

Mercifully, after observing no further provocative actions, Savitsky returned to his conning tower and acknowledged my apology. Closing his torpedo-tube doors, he wheeled to port and returned to his easterly heading. Although I'd had no idea that we were facing a nuclear torpedo, I was greatly relieved not to be staring down the barrel of *B-59's* torpedo tubes.

In the language of a sailor, Captain Morgan, not known for his patience or tact, gave me my standing orders for the duration of the encounter: "Keep that Russian bastard happy."

I spent the ensuing several hours doing just that. First, I nodded my thanks for Savitsky's patience. The Russian even nodded back. Our relationship, such as it was, appeared to be slightly more cordial at that point. Then Savitsky surprised me. His signal was in plain English this time. He had decided that his crew could use some fresh bread and cigarettes after all, if *Cony* could spare them.

Personal Postscript: Later, I learned that B-59's crew included a team of Soviet intelligence specialists trained to intercept and translate our radio transmissions. Their command of English, as well as their knowledge of American ASW maneuvers and tactics, was exceptional. And they were usually very devious. Pretending to be American ships, they would transmit false radio messages to ASW destroyers to draw them away from their submerged locations.

I immediately arranged for a large parcel of freshly baked bread and American cigarettes to be transferred to the submarine by high-line. This involved the use of a special shotgun to propel a floatable projectile attached to a light line over to the receiving ship. In contrast, the Russian high-line procedure called for the use of a hand-thrown, weighted *monkey fist* attached to a light line. No shotgun.

When we'd closed to within 80 feet, our boatswain mate discharged his shotgun. At the sound of the blast, Savitsky, once again, ducked and cleared his conning tower. Apparently, he soon realized that our intentions were benign. He re-manned his conning tower, retrieved the parcel, and came to a northeasterly heading this time. As he slowly chugged toward Sayda Bay, his home base in northwest Russia, he continued to recharge his batteries. *Cony* set a parallel course and followed along, just off *B-59's* starboard beam. Again Savitsky and I exchanged cordial nods and even a small smile or two.

Cony steamed along like this for several more hours, until well after midnight, when Captain Morgan ordered me to call it a night. After a respectful salute to Captain Savitsky, I retired to my stateroom for a much-deserved night of sleep. The next morning, Bob Mitich, a *Cony* crewmember, used his 8-millimeter movie camera to film *B-59* being escorted away by the *USS Waller,* another destroyer from our squadron. I was sad to see the submarine leave. After all, *B-59* was *our* catch.

USS Cony surfaces Soviet Submarine B-59 (October 27, 1962)

Soviet sub B-59 being escorted north by *USS Waller*

The next day, we received word that *B-59* had submerged, taken evasive action, and managed to lose her escort. I found myself somewhat conflicted by the news. I knew Savitsky was the enemy. In these Cold War confrontations, he was sworn and determined to sink us, if necessary, and we were just as determined to sink him. We both had the skills and weapons to do just that. Still I couldn't help feeling ambivalent as I recalled this gruff character staring at me from such a short distance away.

All *Cony* crew members were sworn to secrecy about the entire *B-59* incident. At the time, we didn't know why this was necessary, but when it came to top secrets we took our vows of silence without question, which is why my October 29 correspondence with Susan is silent on the subject:

> *Well, we've been here for quite some time. I'm not sure how much longer we'll stay. It looks like kind of a semi-permanent thing right now. But who knows? Today we replenished at sea, taking on all sorts of fresh stores. We were getting tired of sea biscuits and powdered eggs, so I guess they intend to keep us here for a while. We're sort of on patrol between Cape Canaveral and Puerto Rico, chasing Russians away from Cuba.*
>
> *Our mission has been more than successful thus far, which has proven most interesting to all hands. We're good at our work, and we've proved it this time. I hardly have time to think about what's going on —or even what month it is. We're standing watches regularly 8 off and 4 on, around the clock, plus every time we have sonar contact, we go on a GQ watch until we're all set, then switch to Port and Starboard (4 on and 4 off) watches. What this all boils down to is that most of the officers are standing about 16 hours of watch out of every 24-hour period. This doesn't give you a lot of time to sew, be dainty, or to write mommy. The time really flies however. Oh, and it helps with the beard growing contest. We don't have time to shave anyway.*
>
> *Please continue to write all those letters like I've been receiving and I'll call you from Kingston, or St. Thomas, or Culebra, or Havana, or somewhere come Christmas time.*

The Cuban Missile Crisis – Swatting Mosquitos

USS Cony – Guantanamo Bay, Cuba to Key West, Florida
November 1962

The nominal end of the Cuban Missile Crisis in late October 1962 did not end the presence of the *USS Cony* in Cuba. Two destroyers from Destroyer Squadron 28, the *USS Cony* and the *USS Beale*, were tasked with ensuring that the nuclear missiles had in fact been removed from Cuba. We accomplished this task by patrolling the north coast of Cuba while listening for missile-control radar signals using our specially designed radio receivers.

As *Cony's* Electronics Material Officer, I was responsible for ensuring that the equipment was finely tuned and kept in perfect working order by the Electronics Technicians reporting to me. We listened carefully along every mile of the coastline, making sure we stayed in International waters. Because we steamed slowly at ten knots, it took three days to go from Guantanamo Bay on the southwestern tip of Cuba to Key West on the southern tip of Florida. We repeated this patrol many times before we were certain that there were no suspicious signals emanating from Cuba. We coordinated our listening duties with the *Beale* by ensuring that one of us was on patrol at all times while the other waited in port, either Key West or Gitmo. This meant that each of us spent three days in one of these two ports while the other completed a listening patrol.

When extremely slow, three-day patrols were combined with three-day stays in ports that were not particularly interesting to young naval men, boredom was a constant condition, as reflected in the tone of my letter to Susan:

November 7, 1962

Dear Susan,

Needless to say, we're still out here doing all those things we have been doing for ostensibly the last 4 weeks. We left port on October 11 and we're still going. This is the longest continuous period at sea for any of us. Four weeks is a long time indeed. Morale, etc. is still pretty high and people of course spend a great deal of their time speculating as to when this will all end.

We've done a great deal of steaming since we left port, well over 13,000 miles   which of course in a straight line would put us quite a ways from Norfolk. Unfortunately we've been in one place for the most part. But I'm coming along really well on my beard growing. You'd love it, I'm sure. I've never grown a beard before. I think I like it. I may keep it.

I haven't written in the last week   or maybe less   because the mail wasn't going out anyway. We've only received mail once since we left the Norfolk area, and I'm really starved for any kind of news. We have five tons of mail waiting for us in Norfolk,. Lord knows when we'll be back. (One of my collateral duties was that of the ship's postal officer.)

The trip has been interesting to date and the only thing missing is sight of land and mail. I've spent a great deal of time on watch of course and hope to better my chances of qualifying. The captain will qualify two more before me as I said and in as much as Paul was extended Lord knows when that will be. Rowsey's marriage is scheduled for 10 days from now, and he is generally speaking   antsy.

I'll probably have a chance to send presents from Haiti this year. I'm hoping that this thing stretches out long enough to hit some ports down here. We (right now) have no idea how long we'll be here. We hope not too much longer, but you can never tell. From what I gather, from the sparse news we get, things aren't that much better. Of course, we're here and will be regardless of the news.

I personally am an advocate of invading and cutting out the cancerous growth. I can't see why we don't impose the Monroe Doctrine and stamp the hell out of them while we're still stronger. There is no apparent reason for my attitude – just a passing fancy perhaps. I guess I'd better close before I start sounding nutty!

Your favorite nut,

Gary

Not only were the two crews bored, they were also irritated by the fact that they had already been away from their homeports for a number of weeks during the Missile Crisis. In addition, their fellow destroyer-squadron crews had arrived back home in Norfolk some weeks ahead of them. Frequently, we officers had to deal with crewmembers who were both bored and angry. Although none of us admitted it, we officers empathized with our men in this regard. However, we had another far more serious problem: Our patrolling operations were being threatened by Cuban torpedo boats.

Few people realized that Castro had not wanted the Soviet missiles in the first place. Khrushchev had pressured him to accept them. What Castro actually wanted from the Soviets had already been delivered to the Cubans. This Soviet gift consisted of dozens of nuclear-tipped tactical weapons including rockets and bombs that could be dropped by Castro's medium-range bombers, the Soviet *Ilyushin* (Il-28). In total nuclear power, these tactical weapons were the equivalent of 100 Hiroshima nuclear bombs. More important, unlike what they had done with the nuclear missiles, the Soviets had given the appropriate codes to Castro to use these tactical weapons at his discretion.

After an agreement to remove the missiles was signed, Castro was infuriated with the Soviets for two reasons. First, excluding Castro from the talks, Khrushchev had negotiated, directly with Kennedy, to withdraw the Soviet nuclear missiles from Cuba. Second, the Soviets had had misgivings about having given unrestricted control of the tactical nuclear weapons to Castro. So these weapons were crated and sent back to the Soviet Union with the missiles. Historians believe that, at that point, Castro was angrier with Khrushchev than Kennedy. Nonetheless, Castro displayed his anger by provoking the *Cony* and the *Beale* during our patrolling operation.

The provocation came in the form of threatened attacks by Cuban Mosquito boats, which were equivalent to American PT boats, officially called Motor Torpedo Boats. During World War II, PT boats had been nicknamed Mosquito boats, when Walt Disney responded to a request from *PT-15*'s Commanding Officer. Disney created an image depicting a mosquito wearing a sailor's hat and carrying a torpedo. This image was painted on the cockpit of *PT-15*. The idea was that, like the mosquito, PT boats were small in size and had the ability to *sting* the enemy. Actually PT boats were not that small. There were many different models manufactured during the war, but the average boat was 70 feet long with a 25-foot beam. They were armed with a wide range of weaponry, including two to four torpedoes, depth charges, mines, and guns ranging in size from 50 caliber machine guns to 40 millimeter canons.

The Cuban Mosquito boats would lurk in coves along the coast, and when we passed by, they would dart toward us, presumably to provoke us to fire at them. When we experienced our first mock attacks by Mosquitos, we went to General Quarters and manned our weapons, foiling their efforts by never firing. Usually the Mosquitos would break off their attacks when they were about a thousand yards from us. We became so accustomed to this behavior that we were somewhat disappointed when the Mosquito boats gave up and no longer launched these mock attacks. After all, the Mosquitos broke the monotony of our patrol. I doubt that they knew what a value we placed on their tactics.

Goodbye to the Ghia

USS Cony – Norfolk, Virginia
Late Fall 1962

We remained at our station until the resolution of the Cuban crisis. When we were released, we headed home and arrived in Norfolk on November 10, 1962. Since the *Cony* had been away from Norfolk for more than 11 weeks, I was glad that I had sent the Ghia home with Melvin and that my father had driven it back to Norfolk for my arrival.

During the latter part of November 1962, I applied for and was conditionally accepted as a student at the Naval Destroyer School in Newport, Rhode Island. Established in late 1961, the school had graduated its first class in July 1962. Students were chosen from across the Fleet and were officers with at least 18 months of previous experience on destroyers. The six-month curriculum centered upon engineering, operations, weapons, and executive leadership. On graduation, the students were fully qualified to serve as department heads on destroyers. Graduates could request assignments as Gunnery Officer, Operations Officer, or Engineering Officer. I chose Engineering, because it was the subject I needed to know more about if I chose to be a career naval officer, which at the time was my intent.

Since I had less than 18 months of service on a destroyer, I had to wait nearly ten months before I could attend the school. I would be a member of the fourth class, scheduled to begin in September 1963 and last for six months. When I realized I was going to spend the coming winter in Newport, I remembered my last winter in Ann Arbor. The Karmann-Ghia was not designed for winter driving. It handled terribly in the snow, and its heater produced about as much heat as a lighted match.

I decided to purchase a more suitable car. For help, I turned to an expert on automobiles, my father. He was honored to accept the assignment of finding a replacement. After all, as he reminded me, he had found and purchased my Ghia. I didn't mention the irony that the Ghia had been his choice, and we were now replacing it because of its unsuitability to the type of wintry weather I had experienced during my senior year in Ann Arbor.

I told my father that there was no rush, still he found my new car almost immediately. When he called with the news, I asked him what kind of car it was.

"It's a beautiful car," he answered, and he was right. It was a 1959 Chevrolet Impala convertible. Its body was black with white trim, and the convertible top was white. Rich, deep red leather covered the seats and dashboard.

I thought but didn't say, "Why would I want a convertible in snowy weather?" Instead I asked, "How much did it cost, Dad?"

"Don't worry about that," he said. "I'll sell the Ghia for you when you come to get the new car. In the meantime, why don't you just send me what you've been paying for the Ghia?" That was $20 per month. Knowing my father, I was sure he would not increase it for the Impala. "You better come and get it before it really starts to snow," he advised.

I agreed to try to get there as soon as I could. I recalled the day Melvin was discharged and drove my Ghia to Owosso for me. Then it dawned on me: *Tony!* Tony Oswald was being discharged at the end of the following week. I convinced him that I would provide him free transportation home if he shared the driving. He immediately accepted my offer. The timing was perfect.

As soon as my leave was approved, we were ready to go and decided to drive straight through without stopping. It had taken me 24 hours to drive from Owosso, Michigan to Newport, Rhode Island after I was commissioned. It was a fairly straight shot when you traveled through Canada. This time I estimated the driving time applying a scientific method: I used a ruler and a map of the United States. The distance from Owosso to Newport was five inches. The distance from Norfolk to Owosso was three-and-a-half inches. I divided Norfolk-Owosso distance by the Owosso-Newport distance. The answer was .7. Multiplying 24 hours by .7, I came up with 16.8 hours. Bingo! With two drivers and fewer hours, assuming the weather was good, we'd easily be able to drive it, stopping only for gas and food. Because the Ghia averaged 36 miles per gallon, we wouldn't need to stop very often.

We got a good night's sleep and left right after Tony signed his discharge papers. Both of us anticipated an adventure. What could go wrong? We enjoyed each other's company. We had plotted our route along the best roads we could find on the map. (There were few interstate highways back in those days.) And with an early morning departure, we would be doing the majority of the driving in daylight.

Tony was driving when we crossed into Ohio at sunset. "Looks like we're gonna hit some rain up ahead," he said, perhaps a little too calmly.

"And it's getting dark and we're driving north," I pointed out.

For a long while, we were silent and tense watching the weather ahead. Then sleet began to fall.

The next five hours of driving over sleet-covered roads were sheer hell. I offered to drive, but Tony said he would rather keep the wheel.

"Okay," I said. "Let me know if you get tired. Meantime, I'll tell you some sea stories to keep you awake."

"Better not," he said. "Not on my last day in the Navy."

I had to give Tony credit. Even with terrible road conditions, his driving was steady and smooth. He had a real sense for the Ghia, and I felt calm and relaxed despite the weather.

It took us nearly seven hours to make our way through Ohio. By the time we had reached the Michigan state line, the rain, sleet, and ice had turned to plain old snow. We both uttered sighs of relief, because we were both experienced snow drivers.

"Tony, why don't we pull over at the next truck stop? We both could use some good chow and black coffee. I'll take her the rest of the way. Okay?"

"Aye, aye! Sir!" he answered.

Four hours later, we pulled up at Tony's parents' home just outside of Corunna. He grabbed his sea bag from the back seat, and I grabbed his hand and thanked him. We agreed to talk by phone the next day after a long night's sleep.

"I want to see that new car," he said as he stepped out of the Ghia.

"So do I. So do I," I thought.

It was nearly two in the morning and I was about six hours later than expected. As I parked the Ghia in my parents' driveway, I could see that they had waited up for me.

"Lord! You're home safe," said my mother.

My father shook my hand. He was so overcome with relief that he couldn't speak. I hugged him and said, "That's all right, Dad."

The next day, Dad and I drove through four inches of snow on the unplowed roads leading to my grandfather's farm. When we arrived, he was shoveling the snow away from the horse-barn door.

Dad said, "Looks like we've got some shoveling to do, Son." And we began clearing snow.

When the barn doors finally opened, and I saw my new car, it was love at first sight. What a beautiful piece of machinery! I turned to my father and said, "You did good, Dad."

He nodded, "I know I did, Son," which told me exactly where I had gotten my exceptional modesty.

The Cuban Missile Crisis – Aftermath

B-59 – Sayda Bay USSR
Winter 1963

After my detachment from *Cony,* along with my shipmates, I was awarded two expeditionary medals for my service during the Cuban Missile Crisis. However the recognition that brings me the greatest pride is the *Letter of Commendation* that cited my actions during our stay on the Quarantine Line.

For years, this letter rested undisturbed in a box in our attic. I don't know why I'd never shown it to anyone, not even my wife or children. However, in the summer of 2012, I contributed significantly to Bedlam Productions' documentary entitled *The Man Who Saved the World.* Bedlam asked me for copies of documents like the letter below. At that point, I read the letter for the first time in nearly 50 years.

Citation:

For outstanding performance of duty while serving on board USS Cony *from 23 October 1962 to 7 November 1962. As junior officer-of-the-deck, you consistently exhibited outstanding qualities beyond that required of your rank or experience. During anti-submarine surveillance operations at sea in direct implementation of the Cuban Quarantine, your outstanding performance contributed significantly to the success of the operation. Your conduct, leadership, application of professional skill, and devotion to duty were in keeping with the highest traditions of the United States Naval Service.*

Not a bad letter, especially considering that exactly one month before *Black Saturday*, I had celebrated my 22nd birthday.

You'll note that nothing was said in this letter about the specifics of what I, or we, had done on *Black Saturday*. My lips remained sealed for 40 years.

At the time of the breakup of the Soviet Union in 1991, documents containing the truth were acquired by Peter Huchthausen, author of *October Fury*. He was serving as a naval attaché in the American Embassy in Moscow. Since he was a career naval intelligence officer, he knew whom to contact and where to look for documents related to the mission of the brigade.

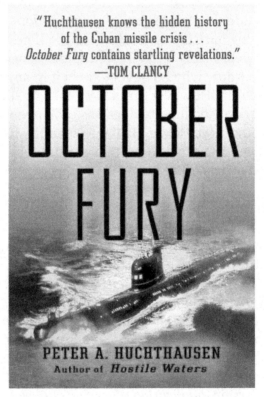

Peter Huchthausen's book, *October Fury*

Huchthausen learned from his Soviet contacts just how close *Cony* came to being sunk by a Soviet nuclear torpedo. In 2000, nearly 40 years after Black Saturday, he contacted me through mutual acquaintances. His name sounded familiar. He informed me that he had served on the *USS Blandy* but he was detached shortly before I reported aboard. When he asked me to tell the *Cony* story, he also assured me that it was permissible to break my vow of silence, because the details of the incident were in the public domain.

October Fury was published in 2002 to celebrate the 40th anniversary of the Cuban Missile Crisis. When I read the book, I learned for the first time that not only was Savitsky a madman but that *B-59* was armed with a nuclear torpedo. I also learned that *Blandy,* like *Cony,* was one of three destroyers that surfaced Soviet submarines on or about October 27, 1962.

I believe I am the only person in the Navy who served aboard two of the three destroyers that surfaced Soviet submarines during the Cuban Missile Crisis. Even more amazing was that during my time on *Blandy*, I never learned their secret, and they never learned mine. This demonstrates just how sacred the vow of silence was to Navy men from that era.

Why was the *Cony* story kept secret? I believe it was one of the conditions that Khrushchev insisted upon with Kennedy. Khrushchev was a very proud man. Having it known that his top submarine commanders had failed would not be something he could countenance.

So what really happened to Savitsky and the other Russians? The four-submarine brigade had been sent to Cuba to establish a forward submarine base in Mariel Bay. After failing miserably to complete this mission, the brigade's officers and men were in serious trouble when they returned to their home base. Their greatest failure was that while the four commanding officers' orders had specifically directed them to take extreme measures to avoid detection, three of the four submarines were surfaced by American destroyers and sent back to Russia defeated.

Needless to say, the brigade did not receive a warm homecoming. A high-ranking Soviet naval officer stated it would have been better for all concerned if they'd gone down with their submarines. Upon their arrival, the four crews were confined to their submarines for a number of weeks while investigations were conducted to establish the facts.

Of all the officers involved in the *B-59* incident, Arkhipov fared the best, going on to command several submarines and submarine squadrons. He was promoted to Rear Admiral in 1975 and served as Superintendent of the Soviet Naval Academy. Yet despite all his successes, Arkhipov never made Fleet Commander. In 1981 he was promoted to Vice Admiral and retired in the mid-80s. Unfortunately, soon after, he died of cancer resulting from his exposure to nuclear radiation during the *K-19* disaster.

During the first half of 2012, I spent many hours working with Bedlam Productions to develop our side of their documentary, *The Man Who Saved the World,* which was shown on PBS stations across America that October to celebrate the 50th anniversary of the Cuban Missile Crisis. The documentary includes excerpts from long interviews with Andy Bradick, *Cony*'s ASW officer at the time, and me. Bedlam filmed our interviews aboard the *USS Barry*, a retired ASW destroyer on exhibit at the Washington Navy Yard in Washington, DC.

In the years following the publication of *October Fury*, I turned down three other documentary filmmakers. I chose Bedlam for two reasons. First, Bedlam had produced the 2010 Best Picture Academy Award winner, *The King's Speech*, which is one of my favorite movies. Second, and most important, Bedlam was able to locate key players on the Soviet side of the incident. Ironically, this second reason led to extreme discontent among many *Cony* shipmates. They felt the documentary was not a true and balanced depiction of the incident. Too much emphasis was placed on the Russian side of the story, including extensive dramatizations, some of which were based on falsifying activities aboard *B-59* before Savitsky brought the sub to the surface.

Cony crewmembers were genuinely disappointed, because the documentary failed to describe the *Cony's* actions after the surfacing of *B-59*. They felt, as I do, that our actions contributed significantly to defusing the anger that Savitsky had earlier focused on *Cony* and the other members of our task force. I strongly agree that this is an important part of the *Cony* story that wasn't told. Finally, *Cony* crewmembers felt that the Americans were portrayed as the bad guys when the historical facts indicate conclusively that we occupied the moral high ground throughout the Cuban Missile Crisis.

Did Bedlam buy the Russian party line? I suggest you view the documentary currently showing on YouTube and judge for yourself.

The Bedlam documentary first aired in the United Kingdom on October 7, 2012. The next morning, I received a telephone call from Fiona Cushley, producer of a BBC documentary on this subject. Fiona and I had become acquainted when she tried to recruit me before I chose to go with Bedlam. Her first words were, "Gary, the Bedlam documentary doesn't tell the *Cony* story." Her next words were, "Will you now work with BBC?"

Without hesitating, I said, "You can count on me."

I was interviewed extensively by BBC who finally included our story in a two-part documentary called *The Silent War,* which discussed the role of submarines during the Cold War. This 2013 film spans the period from the end of World War II until the collapse of the Soviet Union in the early 1990s. Of course, the Cuban Missile Crisis was a significant chapter of this story. I don't believe the BBC documentary is on YouTube yet. When it does appear, you won't want to miss it.

Our Wedding

Highland Park, Illinois
February 1963

Despite the fact that Susan and I had essentially been separated for the year and a half following my electronics training course at Great Lakes, our love continued to grow. We were married in Highland Park on February 2, 1963. I had no difficulty remembering that date, because it was my Grandfather Mitchell's birthday and it was Ground Hog's Day. Still, I did have trouble finding male friends to be members of the wedding party, because most of my friends were in the Navy, either at sea or undergoing flight training.

Under normal circumstances, I would have asked Chuck Nuechterlein to be my best man, because he had been my closest friend in college, my fraternity brother, and a fellow NROTC student. But he was in the midst of flight training and unavailable. So instead, I asked my younger brother Bob, even though he was still in high school. He proudly accepted.

For ushers, I asked my future brother-in-law Steve Groves, who was married to Susan's sister Kathy. Andy Bradick, my *Cony* shipmate and friend, also agreed. My old fraternity brother, Marty Weiss, accepted as well. And Sonny Bushala, my best friend from Owosso, also agreed to serve.

On the day before the wedding, three events were scheduled. The first was nominally the least significant, but Susan and I talked about it for years afterward. We were to be married in her family's church, Highland Park Presbyterian. The church had recently acquired a new minister that the Parkers had yet to assess. Nonetheless, he was assigned the task of marrying us. Before he would conduct a wedding ceremony, he required a private meeting with the bride and groom. While we all thought this was most unusual, we had no choice. So Susan and I made an appointment.

At 10:00 am on February 1, we went to the minister's office. After introducing ourselves, we sat down in two wooden chairs in front of his desk. During the entire meeting, which only lasted about 20 minutes, the minister never made eye contact with us. Instead, he focused on a pencil which he incessantly rolled back and forth across the surface of his desk. It was very distracting. For the first five minutes or so, he asked benign questions about our backgrounds. Where were we born? How long had we known each other? What did our parents do? Then, with great difficulty, he broached the subject that seemed to be the real purpose of the meeting. It came in the form of a brief lecture on the basics of *the* birds and the bees.

This was not a discussion and not a question and answer session. It was a lecture at the highest level of generality imaginable. Our role was to listen to the minister's presentation while he looked at his desk. He never solicited our input, he never asked a question, and he never came close to sharing anything that the average fifth grader hadn't known for years. When he finished, he stood abruptly, shook our hands, and rapidly scurried from his office, leaving us sitting dumbfounded in our chairs. We didn't know whether to laugh or to feel sorry for the poor fellow. It was obviously an extremely painful duty for him to perform.

We left the church in silence, but in the car driving back to Susan's house, we laughed so hysterically that, for safety's sake, I pulled over to the curb. We tried to regain our composure before we arrived at her house. We also agreed not to mention the incident to anyone, because we were certain that no one would believe our story.

The second event on that day was the wedding rehearsal. We assembled at the Parker house, where some of the non-participants had cocktails before we proceeded to the church. Aunt Margaret assumed the role of dispatcher. After she announced who would travel in which car to the church, we all donned our winter coats and hats and headed out the front door. Susan and I were to ride in the last of four cars in the rehearsal procession.

As we pulled out of the Parker driveway, I looked back to see Andy Bradick standing on the front porch with a confused look on his face. He waved meekly at me as if to say, "Help!"

I told our driver, "Hold it, Carl! We forgot Andy."

Carl screeched to a stop, opened the driver's door, and yelled, "Come on, Andy. You can squeeze in with us."

A broad grin swept across Andy's face as he galloped toward our car. He opened the backdoor and slid in beside Susan and me. "I was in the bathroom," was all he said.

The rehearsal went about as well as expected with the new minister's lack of skill in leading the process. Susan and I tried not to make eye contact, because we were afraid we would start giggling again.

When the rehearsal was finally over, Aunt Margaret took charge. "All right, everyone. Now we're heading to our house for cocktails and the rehearsal dinner. Same car assignments. Let's get a move on!" Then she paused. "Andy, you'd better ride in my car so I can keep an eye on you!" Andy shrugged his shoulders and followed dutifully behind Aunt Margaret to her car.

The next day, there must have been 400 people in the church. The wedding was elegant, and the reception held at the Exmoor Country Club was marvelous. Finally, Susan's father approached us and advised, "You two had better think about leaving soon. It'll take about 40 minutes to get to your hotel."

We were both relieved to receive his advice. We said thank you and goodbye to people as we headed out the door. Susan threw her wedding bouquet into a group of about 20 young women, mostly her sorority sisters, and then we left. Outside it was cold and quiet. We were ready to start the next phase of our lives.

Susan and I spent our wedding night in a new hotel on the west side of Chicago. The Parkers had arranged for a bottle of champagne to be iced in a bucket next to our bed. I hadn't had much experience opening champagne bottles, and when I managed to work the cork loose, it flew straight up and stuck in the new ceiling above our bed.

I was mortified. What would the owners think? This was their new bridal suite! I stood on a chair and swatted the cork to the floor with a huge bath towel.

As we sipped champagne, we began to giggle again. What a couple of days we'd had! I admit it was difficult to be intimate that first night, because we continued to giggle over the minister's instructions about how it should be properly done. Somehow we managed.

I was only granted a few days leave and most of it was spent driving from Chicago to Norfolk in my new Impala convertible in the dead of winter. The trip was a nerve-racking drive to say the least.

Our destination was our modest apartment in Norfolk. Two days after we arrived, *Cony* set sail for a two-week stint of ASW exercises off the Virginia coast, and I had to leave Susan in the care of four other *Cony* wives who also were alone. They were happy to indoctrinate Susan in the ways of Bolling Square apartment living and to introduce her to the Navy Exchange and Commissary, where she would purchase her groceries and other sundries. (The established practice among Navy people is to help new arrivals settle into their new homes. In some cases, the families of newcomers would stay in your home while they searched for their own housing.)

Although this was a hurried way to begin our new lives together, we were young and flexible. On top of it all, we were in love, and that's all that really mattered.

My Bodyguard

USS Cony – Norfolk, Virginia
Spring 1963

The military justice system has three levels of courts-martial: General, Special, and Summary. The Summary Court-Martial is the lowest level, designed to resolve minor offenses using a simple procedure. In this type of trial, a single commissioned officer is both the judge and jury. While limited to lower maximum punishments than General or Special Courts-Martial, the Summary Court-Martial provides fewer rights to the accused. Nonetheless, the presiding officer is empowered to sentence the accused to one or more of the following punishments:

- confinement (the brig) for one month or less
- hard labor without confinement for 45 days or less
- restriction (to the ship) for two months or less
- forfeiture of two-thirds pay for one month or less
- reduction to the lowest enlisted grade

During my naval service, I was appointed Summary Court-Martial Officer on a number of occasions. There was one particular case I have never forgotten. The accused was a Steward's Mate and a Filipino.

Since the end of the Spanish-American War, citizens of the Philippines have been able to earn American citizenship by serving in the US Navy. Generally, they were assigned to serve as Steward's Mates. They attended to the personal needs of the ship's officers. Essentially, the Steward's Mate was a commissioned officer's valet.

In this case, the accused was a rather formidable character, much larger and more muscular than his fellow Filipino Steward's Mates. (Later I learned that he was a Bikolanos, an ethnic group that inhabited the mountainous area of Luzon.) After being involved in a physical confrontation in a Norfolk movie theater, the accused had been arrested by the Shore Patrol, who had returned him to the ship. According to the Shore Patrol, the contest at the theater had been one-sided, because three of the Filipino's opponents required hospitalization following the incident. Judging from the physique of the accused, this news didn't surprise me.

After I heard the Shore Patrol's side, I was certain that the accused was not in deep trouble. It appeared to be a case of self-defense, although he may have overreacted a bit. However, as he sat before me in my stateroom, his demeanor was not that of a fighter. Clearly he was a frightened man. I urged him to relax and relate his side of the story. His response caught me off-guard.

"Please don't send me back to the Philippines."

I assured him that he would not be sent back, and he relaxed enough to confess that he had been a member of an organized crime ring in Luzon. While that got my attention, his next piece of information was the shocker. He told me that he had been an assassin for the organization and had no desire to return to his former occupation. Furthermore, if he were forced to return to Luzon, he would certainly be targeted for assassination himself.

I tried not to let this news bias my findings. Since he had not initiated the confrontation, his sentence was not severe: two weeks' restriction to the ship.

Greatly relieved, he pumped my hand and thanked me over and over again. I told him that he was free to go. Before he departed, he said, "Mr. Slaughter, if you are ever in trouble with anyone, let me know. I'll take care of it for you."

High Lines and Helos

During my eleven years in the Navy, I served two midshipman cruises on the ASW aircraft carrier, *USS Valley Forge,* and active-duty assignments as an officer on two ASW destroyers, *USS Cony* and *USS Blandy.* So a great proportion of my at-sea time was spent as a part of an ASW task force with an aircraft carrier as its flagship. The aircraft carrier made it possible for me to be transferred to and from the aircraft carrier by high line or helicopter. I estimate that I was transferred back and forth at least two dozen times.

The basic reason for these transfers was for me to conduct various kinds of inspections of the aircraft carrier or another destroyer in the screen. During my first five years as a naval officer, I became an *expert* on a wide range of topics: electronics, communications, cryptosecurity, and engineering, especially boilers. I am particularly proud of a document I have kept all these years that certifies me as a qualified high-pressure boiler inspector. Not too many people can claim this distinction.

To inspect another destroyer, two pairs of transfers were required. First, I was transferred from my destroyer to the carrier, and then from the carrier to another destroyer. After the inspection was completed, I was transferred back to my destroyer via the carrier.

Most of my many transfers were accomplished by high line, a pair of rope cables on which a trolley moves back and forth between two ships. A metal caged chair hangs from the trolley. The passenger sits in the chair, and the cage is closed to prevent the passenger from falling out. Because the two ships are moving, admittedly at a slow speed, both ships must maintain a steady course to keep the high-line cables taut. If the ships move too close to each other, the rope will slacken, causing the cage to dip into the water between the ships. This happened to me on one high-line trip when the sea was very rough, so I can attest to the fact that it's no fun to go under water sitting in a closed cage. Other than that one occasion, my high-lining experiences were first-rate. To view a high-lining operation in action, I suggest one of the *Ship High Line* videos on *YouTube.com*.

Lt. Slaughter being high lined at sea

On two occasions, I left and returned to the carrier by airplane, specifically the mail plane, as it was called. Technically, the mail plane was a Grumman C-1A *Trader*, the COD (Carrier Onboard Delivery) variant of the S-2F *Tracker*, which had seats for two people, the pilot and one passenger. When I was required to go ashore for one reason or another, I was that passenger. Once I went ashore to attend a class offered only when I was at sea. I must admit that taking off and landing on the aircraft carrier was a thrilling experience.

Each day, the mail plane flew to shore to deposit and pick up mail for distribution to the ships in the task force. The pilot also returned movies that had been viewed and picked up the latest films to distribute throughout the task force as well. Once viewed, the movies would be returned to the carrier for distribution to ships that hadn't seen them yet. We always had two or more movies aboard, which enabled us to show one to officers in the Wardroom while the crew watched another on the second deck amidships. The mail and movies were also transferred by high line.

A few times, I was transferred by helicopter. My worst helicopter experience, again attributed to rough seas, happened when I was taken by helicopter from the aircraft carrier back to the *Cony*. The helicopter flew to a position above the fantail, a section of the main deck at the rear of the ship. I was riding in the helicopter's cargo compartment, where a sailor had slipped a hoop of canvas-covered rope over my head. The hoop was connected to a length of cable wound around a winch, which would lower me to the deck below. After I had raised my arms and brought them down over the hoop, the sailor led me to the open door and instructed me to step off. Then, when I was hanging outside, the sailor began to lower me toward the fantail.

However, there was a major problem: the sea was so rough that the fantail was bouncing all over the place. Seawater even covered it now and then. To make matters worse, dangling at the end of the line from the helicopter, I began to swing from one side of the ship to the other. Though two *Cony* sailors had been dispatched to assist in my landing, I was swinging radically and far too fast for them to catch me.

For me this was not only frightening but also painful. I slammed into the depth-charge rack, the bulkhead at the end of the second-deck superstructure, and the lifeline posts surrounding the fantail. Finally, I raised my arms and dropped to the deck from a height of about 12 feet. Although it was a painful landing, I was relieved to be standing on the solid, albeit tipsy, deck. That was the last time I was transferred by helicopter. High lining was a piece of cake compared to dangling from the end of a tether from a helo.

Loss of Appetite

USS Cony – Punta Delgada, Azores
Summer 1963

During the late summer of 1963, *USS Cony* was assigned to assist in the Operational Readiness Inspections (ORIs) of two nuclear ballistic-missile submarines (SSBNs). The most significant aspect of the ORIs involved the actual firing of the submarines' ballistic missiles, from a position near the Azores Islands, down range to a monitoring station east of the Caribbean Islands. We carried several observers and the appropriate telemetry equipment required to measure transmissions from the submarine and missiles to assess the effectiveness of the launches.

Of course, we had an unwanted visitor in the form of a Soviet trawler that constantly shadowed our ORI activity. It wasn't really a fishing vessel. By the number of antennae draping its masts and riggings, we knew the Soviets were fishing for the same information our telemetry equipment was capturing. The presence of Soviet trawlers snooping on our operations was so common that no one paid any attention to it.

To us *Cony* crewmembers, these kinds of assignments typically involved a lot of sitting around and waiting between significant events. But our perceptions were from the standpoint of the bus driver and not from the view of the important passengers and their equipment. The real excitement occurred on one occasion when a missile was launched and, instead of heading down range, it turned around and dove down toward the submarine. Moments before it struck the submarine, the missile's first-stage fuel supply exploded, giving us all the scare of our lives.

To compensate for the unavoidable tedium of playing our role in the inspections, the ORIs were scheduled nearly two weeks apart, allowing the *Cony* to spend ten days in Punta Delgada, the largest city in the Azores. Ray Schmaltz, our beloved First Lieutenant, who also served as the *Cony's* Welfare and Recreation

Officer, had the responsibility of researching and reporting on new ports of call. He presented his initial report on Punta Delgada to his fellow officers in the *Cony* Wardroom. If we approved of his presentation, as we usually did, he would deliver his talk to every division on the ship prior to our arrival. His Punta Delgada highlights included:

Both Portugal and Spain are ruled by the Fascist dictators, Salazar and Franco. During World War II, they were both neutral countries, but Portugal was slightly friendlier toward America than Spain. Because of their Communist leanings, both are ripe targets for the Soviet Union. This last part is Top Secret, Gentlemen.

Both Portugal and the Azores are very poor places. I'm told that Portugal sends its poorest people to the Azores. When you see the residents of Punta Delgada, you will be struck by their appearance. For one thing, they are very short compared to Americans. And they only wear black. Long black dresses and black scarves for women. Black suits, white dress shirts, black ties, black shoes, and black hats for the men.

Punta Delgada is the largest city in the Azores, nine volcanic islands, which are possessions of Portugal. These are situated about 550 miles from Portugal's coast.

There is very little industry here and only the most meager form of farming. While the soil looks like humus, it's volcanic soil, which lacks minerals to make it fertile.

However, there is one commodity that tops the exported-products list. You'll never guess what it is: Pineapple Brandy – from pineapples grown in greenhouses on the mountaintops of these nine islands.

Because of the warmth carried here by the Gulf Stream, the climate is very mild. Near 70 in the winter, and when we arrive it will likely be in the 90s.

Finally, this is one key piece of historical information that everyone must be aware of: Cony is the first American man-of-war to visit Punta Delgada since the First World War.

The seawall-enclosed harbor was a base for American colliers, coal ships, during that time. American combat ships with coal-fired boilers stopped there to have colliers replenish their coal supply before they continued on to Europe.

As Ray shared this last piece of information, I remembered the Eyes-Only Special Intelligence Requirement Memorandum (SIRM) that I'd decoded and stored in the Top Secret safe in my stateroom. Despite the fact that I was *Cony's* Engineering Officer, because of my special training in Communications Officers School four years earlier, I was also *Cony's* Cryptosecurity Officer. While SIRMs were addressed to me personally by the Office of Naval Intelligence (ONI), the intelligence requirements were usually originated by the CIA. *Eyes-Only* meant that only I, as Cryptosecurity Officer, could decode the message and then share it with the Captain. The message was to be read by only the two of us and then destroyed.

As the meeting broke up, I whispered to the Captain, "Sir, we've received a SIRM that I need to discuss with you. Do you have a few minutes?"

After I retrieved the SIRM, the Captain and I met in his stateroom. The SIRM instructed us to photograph the Punta Delgada harbor and all associated heavy equipment and facilities. Photos were to be taken at various angles from the seawall and from the shore. Upon our arrival back in Norfolk, I was to hand-carry the film negatives immediately to the headquarters of the Commander-in-Chief of the Atlantic Fleet (CINCLANTFLT) and turn them over to the top-ranking ONI officer whose code name I recognized in the message.

"The Soviets obviously have a special interest in the island," said the Captain. "As Ray mentioned, we'll be the first US war ship to visit Punta Delgada since World War I. If we stick to our present plan, we should be back in Norfolk in about two weeks. After we tie up in Punta Delgada, you'd better get those photos while this sunny weather holds."

Early the next morning, we pulled into Punta Delgada. To impersonate a tourist, I donned my brightly colored, madras sports coat and tan slacks. After placing my sporty straw hat on my head at a jaunty angle, I hung my camera around my neck and headed for the quarterdeck. We were moored adjacent to the main harbor, so I didn't have far to walk.

The harbor was shaped like a gigantic horseshoe with the shoreline on one side and the solid piled-stone seawall on the other. Ships entered and departed from the harbor through a wide opening at the leeward end of the horseshoe. I walked up and down the horseshoe for about an hour, shooting two full rolls of film. I saw no signs of anyone suspicious, let alone anyone resembling a Russian.

As I stored my civvies back in my locker, I heard a light tap at the door. "Come," I responded in the Navy manner.

Ray Schmaltz entered. "Morning, Sir. I bring you tidings of great joy. Our wonderful Executive Officer has selected you and your beloved Chief Engineman to serve in the capacity of Shore Patrol Officer and Assistant at tomorrow's Gunnery Department softball game and hotdog fest. The party will be held at a makeshift ballpark at the top of the hill overlooking the city. Yours truly will serve as bus driver. We leave from the pier at 0930 tomorrow morning and should arrive at the park in about 15 minutes.

"Uniforms for Shore Patrol and bus driver will be tropical dress whites, in shorts, if you please. It's going to be hot. Your Gunnery Department guests will be in dungarees so they can slide around in the dust on the ballfield. The bus will be loaded with bats, balls, and gloves for the game.

"The menu includes a keg of local beer that I have personally sampled and heartily recommend soft drinks for the nonbelievers, hotdogs and rolls, pork and beans, and potato chips, served on elegant paper plates with plastic silverware and paper napkins.

"Oh, I almost forgot: mustard, ketchup, pickles, and diced onions for the garnish." Ray handed me two stacks of Shore Patrol accessories and clicked his heels.

"Gee, Ray. I can't tell you how honored I am. I'm all choked up. And if you don't get out of here, someone else will be choked up as well."

Ray gave me a broad grin and a snappy salute. I could hear him chuckling as he made his way down the passageway. After his departure, I grinned too. I had served on Shore Patrol duty before and rather enjoyed it.

The next morning, I donned my tropical whites, my Shore Patrol armband and badge, and my obligatory sidearm, a Colt .45 automatic, with holster mounted on a white web belt. My assistant would wear the same uniform but would be armed with a highly polished night stick stowed neatly in a sheath attached to his white web belt.

As we boarded the bus, spirits were high. Some ball-playing enthusiasts began singing, "Take me out to the ball game . . ." in loud voices. Punta Delgada residents stared at us. But none of us seemed to care. We all were looking forward to the fun, and nothing was going to spoil it for us.

After arriving, we gathered several picnic tables and positioned them just off the first-base line. Soon the fire was blazing, and the volunteer cooks began roasting hotdogs which they offered with all the trimmings and tall glasses of frothy ice-cold beer. Even though my mouth watered, being on duty, I restrained myself. The gunnery guys were really enjoying themselves, those on the ballfield as well as their cheering squad on the sidelines.

As the sun rose higher, the temperature soared as did the level of beer and food consumption. Some of the huskier fellows downed three beers and an equal number of hotdogs before the second inning came to a close. The trash barrels next to the picnic tables began to fill with partially eaten hotdogs and paper plates soaked through with pork and bean juice and spilled beer, discarded with the other leftovers and a half dozen charred hotdogs from the grill.

I was enjoying my first hotdog when one of the cooks came up beside me and pulled my sleeve. As I turned his way to hear him over the noise of the crowd, he pointed his thumb over his shoulder in the direction of the trash barrels.

When I saw what he was pointing to, I was stunned. Four children were retrieving discarded food from the barrels and stuffing the scraps into their mouths. The children were extremely thin, very dirty, and all dressed in tattered clothing. None wore shoes of any kind. It shocked me to see the kids pick up the soaked paper plates and suck them dry of pork, bean, and beer juice. At least 30 more children just as thin and dirty were running up the hill toward their friends to join the feast.

The crowd of sailors standing along the first-base line turned and walked slowly and incredulously toward the children surrounding the barrels. By the time the running children arrived, all the sailors had circled around the barrels to watch this heart-wrenching scene. Any sailor with food left on his plate handed it to a child, who nodded appreciatively before ravenously choking down the gift.

Our cooks didn't wait for permission to support the cause. They loaded the grill with the remaining hotdogs and opened bag after bag of rolls. The sailors joined in, opening bottles of soft drinks and distributing them to the kids. Then, the cooks reached under the picnic table, brought out our surprise dessert, a huge box of peanut-butter cookies, and gave these to the children as well.

All the while, the flow of children up the hill never stopped. In all, about 80 children enjoyed our picnic. When the supply of food was exhausted, each child shook the hand of the nearest sailor, waved goodbye, and wandered back down the hill.

We were speechless. None of us had ever seen anything like that. Without saying a word, the sailors gathered up the ball equipment and cooking gear and stored it in the back of the bus. Then, one by one, we boarded the bus and headed back to the ship. No one said a word. Not as we unloaded the bus. Not as we walked up the gangplank. Not as we retreated to our compartments. As a matter of fact, to my knowledge, none of us has ever spoken about this incident since it happened in 1963. It was too painful to remember.

Plane-Guard Duty

USS Cony – ASW Screen in the Atlantic
Summer 1963

Frequently, Desron 28 provided ASW screening services to attack aircraft carriers like the *USS Roosevelt* (CVA 42). On one occasion, as *Cony's* OOD, I witnessed a remarkable event, involving the *Roosevelt,* which is as vivid in my memory today as it was the day it occurred.

Carriers conducting flight operations required one of the destroyers from the screen to perform plane-guard duty. On that day, as the designated plane guard, I maneuvered *Cony* away from the screen and into position on the carrier's starboard quarter, about 600 yards aft of the carrier, which enabled me to clearly see aircraft taking off and landing on the carrier. This was not a fixed position, because the carrier often changed courses to ensure that it was steaming directly into the wind to provide maximum lift for aircraft being launched.

When a carrier was about to change course, the new course was communicated to the screen and the plane guard by signal flags. The series of appropriate signal flags were attached to a halyard and hauled up to fit snugly under the signal yard-arm. All destroyers in the formation would mimic the carrier's series of flags and haul them up to their signal yardarms. After the carrier signal gang verified that everyone in the formation was displaying the correct series of flags, the lead signalman would inform the carrier OOD, who would execute the order using the command, "Standby. Execute."

The moment the order was received, the carrier signal gang quickly hauled down the signal flags, which was acknowledged by all the ships in the formation by immediately hauling down their signal flags as well. Simultaneously, all ships came to the new course by turning in the direction called for in the signal itself. For example, the signal might order the formation to "Turn starboard and come to course 090." The order cannot simply be delivered to the formation by radio, because in combat situations, radio silence is ordered to prevent the enemy from knowing your intentions.

While the function of the plane guard was to rescue a pilot from the water who, for any reason, parachuted from his aircraft, this rarely happened. When it did, the cause was usually attributed to a mechanical failure that prevented the pilot from landing safely on the carrier. In preparation for rescuing an aircraft crew member from the sea, the plane-guard crew swung out its lifeboat's davits and had a crew standing by to launch the boat and rescue the downed man as quickly as possible. In addition, helicopters from the carrier were prepared to assist if necessary.

The case I witnessed resulted from a collision of two aircraft almost directly over the *Roosevelt*, from which they had just been launched. The first aircraft was an F-4 *Phantom*, with a crew of two men, the pilot in the front seat and a radar-intercept officer in the back. The second aircraft was an F-8 *Crusader* with only a pilot. The F-4 *Phantom* took off and headed almost straight up from the carrier. A minute or so later, the F-8 *Crusader* was launched. It also rose straight up and collided with the underside of the *Phantom*. Both airplanes broke apart and burst into flames. Fortunately, three parachutes opened, and the pilots floated down to land in the sea about 500 yards from us.

By this time, our lifeboat was in the water, heading at top speed toward the spot where the parachutes would likely land. The *Roosevelt* also launched a helicopter, which arrived at the scene at about the same time as our lifeboat. The rescue was a joint operation. The helicopter dropped lines. Our lifeboat crew helped the downed men into the rescue loops on the ends of the lines. Finally, the helicopter lifted the men from the sea and into the helicopter. By the time our lifeboat returned to the *Cony*, the three rescued men were back, safely aboard the carrier.

Over the years, the capability of helicopters has advanced, so they have replaced the need for plane-guard ships. A helo's greatest advantage is its speed, especially in cases in which the downed man is a great distance from the carrier.

I will never forget the frightening images of those two aircraft crashing together, their flaming pieces hurtling toward the sea. Most important, I will always remember the relief I felt when the three billowing white parachutes appeared in the sky. I later learned that the three rescued men were completely unscathed and were eager to be airborne again. Evidently, we witnesses were more traumatized than the aviators.

The Bancroft House

Destroyer School – Newport, Rhode Island
Fall 1963

After I was detached from the *USS Cony*, I was ordered to the Naval Destroyer School in Newport. There I would spend six months of intense schooling to qualify me to serve on another destroyer as department head. I truly hoped my second destroyer would be located in a southern port. I thought I deserved it.

When I was first commissioned in June 1961, I had been ordered to the *USS Power* (DD839), which was homeported in Mayport, Florida near Jacksonville. Having had my fill of Michigan winters, I had been ecstatic about serving on a ship stationed in a warm-water port. I was to report to the *Power* after completing six months of training in naval communications and electronics. About halfway through the electronics phase, my orders had been changed, directing me to report to the *Cony* out of Norfolk, which is not exactly on the Arctic Circle, but it's not Florida. Needless to say I was extremely disappointed. Still I held out hope. Now, after destroyer school, I might still have another shot at the balmy breezes of Mayport or even San Diego!

Susan and I had begun our married life with several other young *Cony* naval officers and their wives living in small furnished apartments in Bolling Square, a huge complex of a dozen or more plain brick buildings, each jam-packed with six or eight one-bedroom apartments. Bolling Square was across Granby Street from what is now Old Dominion University. For a one bedroom, sparsely furnished apartment, we paid $90 a month, which was about all we junior officers could afford.

I was now eager to move my new bride from these dingy quarters to something much classier in beautiful Newport. As I look back, I was a bit unrealistic, because Newport, with all its mansions, was considerably pricier than Norfolk. But I didn't think about that as we drove north in our classy black Chevrolet Impala convertible. Visions of sugar plums danced in our heads.

When we arrived in Newport, we checked into the motel near the base where I had stayed when I drove my Karmann Ghia straight through from Michigan. We rose early the next morning, had a solid breakfast, and perused the paper for furnished rental apartments. We limited our search to candidates in the Norfolk price range.

We spent a full day and a half looking at the furnished rentals we could afford, but we rejected each and every one of them for a myriad of reasons. After the second morning of searching, dead tired and emotionally spent, we decided to suspend our search for the afternoon. Instead, we drove around Newport, and I pointed out the attractive sights that I'd described at great length since we learned we were moving there.

I drove east out of Newport proper and crossed a spit of land that took us to Middletown, playing tour guide along the way. "This is Easton Pond on the left and Easton Bay on the right. Some call this beach along the bay *First Beach*. We've just passed into Middletown where our destination is located. Notice the name of this road?"

"Purgatory Road," said Susan. "That's certainly an odd name."

"Wait until you see what's next. Check out this intersection."

"My gosh! We're at the corner of Purgatory and Paradise Roads. Halfway between heaven and hell. How bizarre!"

I parked the car in a space near the beach. The white sand was, at its narrowest, about a hundred feet wide, although it was much wider in some spots. Even in midafternoon on that Friday in late August, there wasn't a soul to be seen in either direction.

"The locals call this Third Beach, but I prefer to call it by its official name, Sachuest Beach. And, why not? That body of water out there is Sachuest Bay. Besides, it sounds more descriptive to me. This is one of my favorite spots for sitting alone and watching the waves roll in. It's very peaceful."

Susan agreed. "We can use some peace after two days of rejecting one rental property after another."

"Not to change the subject, but after the Newport Jazz Festival in 1961, this is where I found the capo I use with my guitar."

"Speaking of the Jazz Festival wasn't the movie *High Society* with Bing Crosby and Grace Kelly set here in Newport? Oops! Sorry. Where did you find your capo?"

"Buried under the sand over there." I pointed toward the edge of the water. "It was probably lost by Louis Armstrong's group when they were making *High Society*."

Susan laughed and slapped my arm.

We hadn't eaten in hours, and I was getting hungry. "What say we head back into town and have an early dinner followed by an early bed time? We can hit it hard again tomorrow if we rebuild our enthusiasm. Maybe we'll have better luck."

Susan agreed and we hopped in the car. As we drove along Purgatory Road, we noticed a street that veered off to the left, Tuckerman Lane. We followed it as it ran along and discovered that Tuckerman Lane was a scenic route lined with gigantic, majestic old mansions. On our right, we saw a huge sign for *St. George's Boys School.*

"Wow! Look at that house. It's beautiful, with the siding and roof covered with weathered shake shingles. And the lot must be four or five acres.

"The house looks to be three or four stories high," said Susan. "Maybe five if you count the attic. And it has a great view of Sachuest Bay and those huge rocks in the water a few feet from the shore. I don't see any cars, and there's no garage. Why don't we pull in the drive and take a walk around back?"

"Okay. We can say we're looking for our cat." I was being only half sarcastic.

I had just turned into the driveway when Susan said, "Wait! Look at what that sign says."

"What sign?"

"The one nailed to the mailbox. A branch is covering part of it."

I leaned over to get a better view. "Does that say what I think it says?"

We got out of the car to read the sign up close. Susan lifted the branch to reveal:

BANCROFT HOUSE
FURNISHED APARTMENTS
FOR RENT
INQUIRE WITHIN

We drove up the driveway, parked, walked up the stairs, and rang the doorbell. We heard footsteps inside, and then the door opened.

A thin middle-aged lady with black hair streaked with white greeted us. She smiled warmly. "I'm Hazel Moore. My husband and I own Bancroft House."

"Pleased to meet you, Mrs. Moore," I said. "We're Gary and Susan Slaughter."

She smiled and asked, "Are you Navy folks?"

"Yes, Ma'am. We've arrived in Newport on Tuesday, and we've spent the last two days searching for a reasonably priced, furnished apartment. By chance, we turned onto Tuckerman and saw your sign."

"Well, your search is over," said Mrs. Moore. "I have just the apartment for you, a lovely furnished two bedroom on the top floor. You even have a fire place if you want to carry wood way up there. If you join our family of tenants, you'll be our – wait a minute. I lose count. The Kings, Fred, Brian, Nancy – I must be forgetting someone.

Anyway, in 1950 this house was divided into eleven apartments. My husband kept one for his office, and we live in the other one here across from the stairwell, which leads to two apartments on the top floor. One apartment is open, and Brian and Mary Catherine Kelly live in the other. He's a Navy lawyer, and Mary Catherine is a sweetheart. Your front doors will be right across from one another. You'll get to know and like them quickly.

"On the floor below that, there are three apartments. Nancy Clark has one. She's a quiet person, a Lieutenant Commander in the Supply Corps."

The Kings have the second apartment, the one at the top of the stairs. Rufus King, a retired Captain, has been teaching Spanish at colleges and prep schools around here for years. Graduated Annapolis in the early 1900s. His wife Helen is lovely. And Fred and Bonnie Zimmerman have the third apartment on that floor. They're new. He's going to some kind of school here.

"Finally we have two ground floor apartments in the back that are occupied by older friends of ours, who will be here until they pass. The point is if you join us, you'll be the fifth naval family in the building."

"That's amazing," I said. "So many Navy people."

"In case you're wondering why, my husband served in the Navy during World War II," said Mrs. Moore. "Come to think of it, I guess he's the sixth Navy person in the house. How 'bout that? Now before you make up your mind, you have to inspect the apartment and the view from there. It's absolutely glorious. You'll also want to tour the grounds. We have four acres, including a beautiful sunken garden. Not many of those around here anymore. Too hard to maintain. And you'll want to walk down and see Sleeping Elephant Rock just off our shoreline."

"That sounds like a good plan, Mrs. Moore. Perhaps we should spend a bit of time talking about the rental fee before we waste your time giving us a tour," I suggested. "I'm only earning the pay of a Lieutenant (jg). My wife will be a substitute teacher for eighth-graders in the Portland school system, and as you probably know, substitutes aren't paid as much as full-time teachers. So I –"

"You're absolutely right, Lieutenant Slaughter," said Mrs. Moore. "I must be getting forgetful. The rent is usually one of the first things I mention. Every naval person in this house pays $100 per month. I know that may strike you as low compared to other apartments you could find here in Newport. Still, that's what we charge. As a result, we get and retain a high class of mostly naval folks here. You might say we're one big Navy family. How's that sound?

I looked at Susan, who was grinning from ear to ear. Her grin was contagious. All I could think was, thank God she saw that sign on the mailbox.

"Shall we start the tour then?" asked Mrs. Moore.

When we agreed, she said, "Before we go upstairs, I should tell you something about the history of this marvelous old house that was built in 1895 by John Chandler Bancroft. It is described by people in many ways. Some say it is a grand summer cottage. Others call it a shingle/arts and crafts/cottage style. In any case, it's quite unique, even among the other beautiful old homes in Newport. The interior reflects John Bancroft's interest in oriental art, and we have several panels of Japanese prints. You'll notice the elaborate wooden staircase, paneled walls, and artistically designed wooden ceilings. Outside you'll see this theme carried out by a sunken Chinese garden."

Mrs. Moore paused to check on us. "Am I overloading you with details, my dears?"

"No, no, please don't stop," said Susan. "It's fascinating! We want to learn as much as we can, so we can inform our visitors about our new home."

That feedback was obviously what Mrs. Moore wanted to hear. "Let me show you your apartment now."

Even though we climbed two flights of stairs to reach our floor, the stairs seemed to slope in a way that made them easy to climb. When we stepped into the apartment, we were delighted with what we saw. The apartment was spacious, with a living room that easily accommodated large, red-leather-covered chairs and couches plus a sizeable coffee table.

The dining area held an enormous table that would seat six or eight people. The kitchen was completely equipped with modern appliances and a small table and chairs for breakfast. The laundry room had, what appeared to be, a new washer and dryer. In addition, there were two spacious bedrooms and two complete baths.

This was a perfect apartment for hosting house guests. The walls and ceilings were tastefully finished with light-colored wood paneling, and t closets were huge and equipped with wooden hangers. Perhaps the most dramatic features were the beautiful stone fireplace and large windows that looked out to sea and down on the back gardens and the shoreline that featured the huge Sleeping Elephant Rock, which lay in the roiling waters a few feet off shore.

A check of the mattress in the master bedroom showed it to be firm, the way we liked it. We peeked into both bathrooms and could hardly believe our eyes. The fixtures were solid silver, and the bathtubs were equipped with showers as well.

We looked at each other with a mixture of disbelief and pure joy. We were going to pay only $100 a month for this luxurious apartment. What a gift! "When can we move in?" we asked.

"There's no time like the present. We're delighted you've decided to join our little gathering of Navy folk. Once you've emptied your motel room and unloaded your car, we'll organize a little cocktail party for you to meet your new friends and neighbors. Will six o'clock work for you?"

As we left the Bancroft House to fetch our things from the motel, I told Susan, "I'm really going to miss those plastic covers over all of our Bolling Square furniture."

We both laughed until we cried. How lucky we were to have found the Bancroft House.

"You may have to resign from the Navy, so we can live here forever," Susan said.

I knew she was half serious. "I've already thought of that. Let's wait until we experience a Newport winter before we make that decision."

"Oh, right. I forgot about your desire for balmy breezes and coconut trees."

Although our apartment at the Bancroft House was beautifully furnished, we knew the furniture wasn't exactly right for us. More important, it belonged to someone else. One of Susan's fellow teachers suggested that we visit a craftsman named James Buchanan, who owned a modest showroom-workshop in a barn near Dorchester, Rhode Island. He frequented auction sales in his area to acquire sturdy pine and maple farm furniture and was renowned for his ability to transform it by adeptly stripping off the paint, sanding the surface, and professionally refinishing the pieces with stain, varnish, and lacquer. He knew exactly how to work with these woods to produce admirable results.

When Susan and I visited his showroom, we immediately fell in love with the restored furniture. Even more impressive was its unbelievably affordable price. We chose several pieces, which Mr. Buchanan agreed to hold until we checked with Mrs. Moore for her approval to replace the current furniture.

Mrs. Moore readily agreed, and the first truckload of furniture arrived the next day: a handsome dining-room table with six matching chairs, two large book shelves, a double bed frame, and, looking to the future, a beautifully carved cradle that our firstborn would find comfortable and cozy. Mr. Buchanan and I moved Mrs. Moore's furniture into a storeroom on the top floor of the mansion. When we finished, I wrote a check and shook hands with the craftsman. We also gave him a list of additional pieces we wanted if he could find them at future auctions. After he left, we sat down on the couch to admire the new look of our lovely apartment. It had taken on new warmth. We knew we would enjoy our new furniture for the rest of our lives.

Captain Rufus King

Destroyer School – Newport, Rhode Island
Fall 1963

Among the most interesting individuals I met during the course of my naval career was Captain Rufus King. He and his wife Helen lived in the apartment at the top of the stairs on the second floor of the Bancroft House. When we met, Captain King was in his late seventies, but he was mentally as sharp as a tack. The stories he told us about his lifetime of experiences were absolutely fascinating.

Captain King was a member of a prominent family. His great, great grandfather, the first Rufus King, had represented the young state of Massachusetts and contributed significantly in the drafting of the United States Constitution, which he signed at the Constitutional Convention in Philadelphia on September 17, 1787. Captain King's grandfather was General Rufus King, a Civil War General. And his father, General Charles King, was not only a soldier but also a distinguished writer who was a close friend of Edgar Rice Burroughs, the creator of *Tarzan*.

Captain King had graduated from the US Naval Academy in 1909 and had served with distinction as a naval officer for 30 years, at which time it was mandatory that he retire. A few months later, Pearl Harbor was attacked, and he requested to be reactivated. He was promoted to Captain and returned to active duty. When the war ended, King asked to continue on active duty, but his request was denied, because he was told that he suffered from heart disease.

Reluctantly Captain King agreed to retire from the Navy for a second time. Nevertheless, he was determined to prove to his naval superiors that his heart was perfectly fine. So with his son, he traveled to New Hampshire and the two of them climbed to the summit of Mount Washington, at 6,288 feet, the highest peak in the Northeastern United States.

During his naval career, Captain King received extensive training in foreign languages. He had been blessed with a natural proclivity for absorbing languages quickly. Although he received much of his language training during his first 30-year stint, he also received training from the newly established Defense Language Institute during World War II.

When Captain King faced the fact that his naval career had come to an end, an idea struck him: Why not take advantage of his foreign language skills? He had stayed in touch with a classmate from St. George's Boys School in Newport, Rhode Island. His friend Sam also had an extraordinary ability with languages. He was now the Chair of the Romantic Languages Department at Brown University in Providence. As it turned out, he was in need of a top-notch Spanish teacher who, if required, could cover Italian and French as well. Captain King fit the bill perfectly. At the age of 59, Captain Rufus King became Professor Rufus King, teaching Spanish to college students at the prestigious Brown University.

However, as Professor King had experienced in the Navy, all good things come to an end when one crosses certain milestones, such as reaching Brown's mandatory retirement age of 65. Did that stop him? No. He joined the faculty of Providence College, which at the time had a mandatory retirement age of 70.

When Professor King hit 70, he knew his teaching days were over, but before hanging up his book bag, he decided to check in again with his old classmate Sam who was now back at St. George's serving as the Chairman of the Foreign Language Department. Once again, Captain King became Professor King.

When Captain King and I first met in 1963, he was 76 years of age and still going strong, because there was no mandatory retirement age at St. George's. If you did a good job, you could stay forever. He proudly told me that he intended to do just that.

After I completed Destroyer School in March 1964, I was ordered to report to the *USS Blandy* to assume the position of Engineering Officer. The good news was that *Blandy* was homeported in Newport, Rhode Island. Susan and I kept our apartment in the Bancroft House and maintained our friendship with the Kings. As I have said, all good things eventually come to an end. In October 1965, *Blandy's* homeport was changed to Norfolk.

Over the years, we stayed in touch with our old neighbor, Captain King, exchanging Christmas cards and occasional telephone calls. In August of 1967, I resigned my commission and gave up my naval career for a business career in the emerging field of information technology. In 1979, my first book on this subject was published, and my career soared. I proudly sent a copy of the book to Captain King.

When he received it, he called me. I assumed it was to congratulate me on my new book. But that was only partially true. His real purpose was to ask for my help. He'd written a book describing his revolutionary method of teaching Spanish to high school and college students and wanted to know if I would help him find someone to publish this breakthrough book. The manuscript had been written by hand using several colored pencils to illustrate the models he had invented to make learning Spanish much easier. He only had one copy of the manuscript and said that, if I agreed to help him, he would risk sending it to me.

I had been schooled in French, and, when I received the manuscript, I saw immediately that Captain King indeed had created a revolutionary approach to teach Spanish. I called him the night the book arrived in the mail and told him how impressed I was with his method. He was clearly encouraged by my words. For the next three months, I ran his manuscript past dozens of people in education, in publishing, and in the diplomatic service. Since we had settled in Washington, D.C., embassies were convenient targets. After spending hours and hours on this project, I finally gave up and had to phone Captain King, then the ripe old age of 92, and inform him that I had done all I could to get his book published, but I had failed. He thanked me profusely for my effort and requested that I return his manuscript by special delivery. The next day, with a feeling of failure and loss, I mailed the manuscript back to Captain King.

We never communicated again, but about a year later I heard from the owner of Bancroft House that both Captain King and his wife had passed away within a few days of each other. There was no formal memorial service. I felt a profound loss that to this day, I cannot seem to shake.

Shock

Destroyer School – Newport, Rhode Island
November 1963

In September, after my departure from *Cony*, I joined a class of about 30 other officers in the vaunted Naval Destroyer School in Newport. Forty hours of classroom instruction per week plus homework and studying for exams left me little time for anything except work. Fortunately, my grades were high, and I'd made good friends with a number of fellow officers. In short, I was very pleased to be in Newport, and Susan was too. After two months, we had settled into a routine. Susan was teaching eighth-grade English and was guaranteed to be there for the remainder of the school year, which helped our family budget and gave her something interesting and rewarding to do while I labored away as a Destroyer School student.

One sunny and unseasonably warm day in November, all instructors and students from schools, men from ships who could be spared, and those working in various facilities on the base were assembled in the OCS Great Hall to hear an address by Paul B. Fay, Jr., the Secretary of the Navy. About four hundred of us were in attendance. The majority were instructors and students from:

- Naval War College
- Communications Officers School
- Naval Destroyer School
- Officers Candidate School
- Dental Officer Naval Orientation Program

Later I learned that Paul Fay had enlisted in the Navy after the bombing of Pearl Harbor in December 1941. At Officers Candidate School, he had been assigned to PT boat training with John F. Kennedy as his instructor. Both men were stationed at the same base in the South Pacific but not on the same boat. As it happened, a Japanese plane dropped a torpedo on Fay's boat. While the torpedo did not explode, it did pierce the hull below the water line. Fay got the boat back to base, where it sank. Later, he received a Bronze Star for his role in the incident.

After the war, Fay and Kennedy became close friends. Fay worked on Kennedy's campaigns for the US House of Representatives, for the US Senate, and for US President. During Kennedy's presidency, Fay served as Under Secretary of the Navy. Then, by November 1963, when he spoke to us in Newport, he was Secretary of the Navy.

Shortly after Secretary Fay began his address, a Lieutenant, wearing the epaulet of an Admiral's Aide on his shoulder, stepped onto the stage, proceeded quickly to the podium, and whispered something to the Secretary. After excusing the aide with a nod, the Secretary removed his glasses and pinched the bridge of his nose with his thumb and forefinger.

After a few seconds, which he apparently needed to regain his composure, he addressed us in a somber voice. "Ladies and gentlemen, I have some terribly bad news. It has been confirmed that John Fitzgerald Kennedy, the 35th President of the United States, was assassinated at 12:30 pm, Central Standard Time today, November 22, 1963, in Dealey Plaza in Dallas, Texas. I have no further information to share with you at this time, except that our President is dead."

After we heard the word *assassinated*, a monumental *GASP* erupted from the audience. Then there was utter silence.

"I am now terminating this program," said Fay. "Officers, please organize an orderly withdrawal from the building. I suggest you return to your classrooms, ships, or base organizations to await further instructions. In closing, I have only this to say, God Bless President Kennedy and may he rest in peace. Amen." With those words, the Secretary turned and walked off the stage. It was so quiet in the Great Hall that you could have heard a pin drop.

When we arrived back at our school, we were dismissed for the remainder of the day and, of course, the weekend. We would recommence classes at the regular time on the following Monday morning. As we left school, we married officers ran toward the parking lot and headed for home. Fred Zimmerman, who attended Destroyer School with me, was also a resident of the Bancroft House. When Susan had landed the substitute-teaching job, Fred suggested that we commute to school together in his car, and I gladly accepted his generous offer.

We headed home together. Coincidentally, Susan pulled into the parking lot just as Fred and I arrived home.

Over the weekend, like most Americans, we stayed glued to the television, watching the bizarre story unfold. I don't know about other people, but I felt dead inside.

Paul Fay resigned his position as Secretary of the Navy effective November 28, 1963, following Kennedy's assassination on November 22. However, he remained Undersecretary of the Navy until 1965. In 1966, he wrote a best-seller about Kennedy, *The Pleasure of His Company.*

Mystery Transmitters

Destroyer School – Newport, Rhode Island
Winter 1964

As part of the Destroyer School curriculum, we were required to write a professional research and evaluation paper concerning something of interest to us that might be of value to the Navy. I chose to describe our experience on *Cony* with a pair of huge transmitters that we never used. Extensive research revealed that these transmitters cost the Navy $90,000 each. $180,000 had been invested in useless equipment.

In January 1962, the *Cony* had entered Portsmouth Naval Shipyard for a complete overhaul. A major part of the work done related to a complete upgrade of communications and cryptography equipment. Put simply, we converted fully to Single Side Band (SSB) radio equipment and online cryptography equipment. As the ship's Electronics Material Officer (EMO), my Electronics Technicians (ETs) were charged with the responsibility of maintaining this extensive array of new and radically different electronic equipment. Drick Simpkins, the Communications Officer, was also challenged, because his people were required to learn to operate this new equipment. For both our groups, this was the electronics equivalent of learning to drive an automobile after having driven only a team of horses all your life.

Prior to the overhaul, *Cony* was equipped with two other low frequency radio transmitters, the AN/WRT1 and the AN/WRT2. These behemoths were six feet tall with a footprint measuring two feet by two feet. They were so large they would not fit in the Radio Room on the second deck, where all other communications and cryptography equipment was located. Instead, these transmitters were installed in a compartment on the main deck amidships. In August 1962, Drick took over the position of Combat Information Center (CIC) Officer, and I relieved him as Communications Officer. In recent conversations with Drick, neither of us could remember exactly why we had these transmitters, especially after the installation of the SSB equipment. In fact, we could not recall a time before having the SSB equipment that we had used them. Drick speculated that perhaps they were supposed to have been removed during the shipyard overhaul. That made sense to me. In September 1963, I left the *Cony* to attend Destroyer School in Newport. During my 12-month tenure as Communications Officer we had never used these transmitters.

In Honor of the Loyal Crew of the

U.S.S. CONY (DD/DDE-508)

Commissioned as DD – 30 October 1942
Recommissioned as DDE – 17 November 1949

World War II
11 Battle Stars
8 Combat Deaths

Korea
2 Battle Stars

Vietnam – Cuban Blockade

Presented by the
U.S.S. CONY Association

Historical highlights of the *USS Cony*

In my paper, I challenged someone in authority to investigate this situation and inform the *Cony* and any other ships with this equipment of the reason for having these transmitters and the way they could possibly be used. For my efforts, I received a Letter of Commendation signed by Captain R.R. Carter, the Commanding Officer of the Destroyer School. In part, his letter read:

> *Your professional paper has been evaluated independently by two officers of the staff. Their reports have been reviewed with a final determination that your paper merits a rating of* Outstanding.
>
> *You are to be commended for your initiative, imagination, and literary effort in producing a truly fine professional paper. A copy of this letter will be attached to your next report of fitness.*

Naturally I was pleased to receive an *Outstanding* rating. However, no one to my knowledge ever informed the *Cony* of how this equipment was to be used. So much for the effectiveness of whistle-blowers.

On July 2, 1969, the Cony was decommissioned, and on March 20, 1970, she was sunk as a target off the coast of Virginia. We can only assume that the old AN/WRT1 and AN/WRT2 nobly went down with the ship.

Old Navy Habit

USS Blandy at Sea
Spring 1964

When I was Chief Engineer on *Blandy,* and we were underway,
my principal point of contact with my department was Main
Control. Like most destroyers, *Blandy* had four engineering
compartments. The forward-most compartment was Fireroom
#1 or the Forward Fireroom in which two 1200 psi boilers with
associated feed-water pumps were located.

Just aft of this fireroom was Engine Room #1 or Main
Control. This Engine Room contained the following major
equipment:

- a control board with meters measuring all the critical
  readings (water and steam pressures, RPMs, etc.)
  throughout the entire engineering plant
- engine order telegraph to acknowledge speed changes
  signaled from the bridge
- throttle wheel to change RPMs of the #1 Engine
- a main turbine through which steam passed, causing
  the turbine to turn like the drive shaft in an automobile
- a reduction gear serving the same function that a trans-
  mission does in an automobile, to reduce the RPM of the
  turbine to that number of turns required to revolve the
  main shaft
- a main electrical generator to power electrical motors
  and lighting throughout the ship
- an evaporator, which recaptures low pressure steam
  from the turbines and condenses it back into feed water
  for use in the boilers

In Main Control, the top watch, usually a Chief or First Class Engineman was in charge of the ship's engineering plant when we were underway.

Aft of Main Control was Fireroom #2 or the After Fireroom, containing the same equipment as Fireroom #1. Finally, Engine Room #2 or the After Engine Room contained the same equipment as Main Control with the exception of the Control Board.

The Engine Order Telegraph was located in the wheelhouse just aft of the bridge where the Officer of the Deck stood his watch. There he was close enough to transmit verbal orders to the Helmsman, who steered the ship, and to the Lee Helmsman, who operated the Engine Order Telegraph to send speed orders to the Engine Rooms. There were two handles on the Engine Order Telegraph, one on the right and another on the left. The right handle transmitted speed orders for the starboard engine and the left handle transmitted orders for the port engine. Each handle could be used to send the following speed orders:

12 o'clock position - *Stop*

Ahead Speeds
1 o'clock position - *Ahead 1/3*
2 o'clock position - *Ahead 2/3*
3 o'clock position - *Ahead Standard*
4 o'clock position - *Ahead Full*
5 o'clock position - *Ahead Flank*

Back Speeds
11 o'clock - *Back 1/3*
10 o'clock - *Back 2/3*
 9 o'clock - *Back Full*

The handles could be operated together to order the same speed on both engines. In this case, an order from the OOD might be *All Ahead Standard.* Or in turning situations, the OOD could order one engine to go *Ahead* and the other to go *Back.* For example, if the OOD wanted to turn sharply to port, he could order *Starboard Ahead Standard. Port Back 1/3.*

The order from the OOD via the Lee Helmsman was sent to Main Control, where a second, simpler Engine Order Telegraph was located. When Main Control received the signal to change speed for the starboard engine or Engine #1, it acknowledged the signal by placing its Engine Order Telegraph in the same position(s) as that of the bridge Engine Order Telegraph. Engine Room #2 did the same for the port engine or Engine #2.

As Engineering Officer, I prepared a set of Standing Orders inventorying the conditions or situations having to do with the operation of the Engineering Plant that required Main Control to notify me by telephone. It was my responsibility to keep Main Control aware of my location at all times so they could reach me if necessary. When we were underway, if I were absent from the ship for any reason, a Duty Engineering Officer would be appointed, and Main Control would communicate with that officer as they normally did with me.

A telephone was installed on the cabinet next to the head of my bed. When I went to bed at night, I made it a habit to sleep on my left side so I could grip the telephone receiver with my right hand. When the phone rang, I immediately put the receiver to my right ear and listened to Main Control's report. For years after I was out of the Navy, I continued to sleep on my left side and grip the bedpost with my right hand. An old habit is hard to break!

Narragansett Prizes

USS Blandy – At Sea in Northern Atlantic
Summer 1964

One clear, moonless night, we were steaming solo off the coast of Narragansett Island, not far from Newport. In that part of the Atlantic, it was not unusual to encounter a fleet of fishing boats. Unless it was inclement weather, you could identify them from afar, because they were so brightly lighted, resulting from the combination of running lights and work lights. Maritime law requires running lights on all vessels after dark so other vessels can observe and judge their speed and bow angle relative to theirs. Work lights simply enable fishermen to do their jobs: catch seafood, sort it by size, stow the keepers, toss the non-keepers overboard, and rebait traps or hooks.

In this case, the fleet of fishing boats comprised only one vessel, and it was not actively fishing. Its lights were dimmed to only those required by law. But the fishing boat was apparently attempting to get our attention by sounding its foghorn and having its crewmen wave and shout madly in our direction. And the vessel was headed our way at what I guessed was their top speed.

I was Officer of the Deck at the time. Frankly, I didn't know what to make of it. I conferred with my watch members, and they were as baffled as I.

"I don't know what their intentions are," I said. "We're only making ten knots, and by my radar plot, they're slowly gaining on us. Whatever their intentions, I hope they're benign. I'd hate to have to open up on them with our three-inch guns. It would wake the whole crew and ruin a perfectly good fishing boat."

Joe Hanson, my Junior Officer of the Deck, asked, "Do you think we should wake the Captain?"

"Let's hold off on that for a minute. I'm not anxious to wake him, especially if this is something trivial. Maybe they want to borrow a cup of sugar or something."

Several members of the watch snickered. Mid-watches were usually not that entertaining.

"Joe, why don't you take the megaphone down to the fantail and simply ask them what they want?"

Joe carefully made his way to the fantail. While the fishing boat was far enough away to prevent me from hearing the conversation between him and the fishermen, I could see them nodding at Joe and his nodding back. He held up a finger and trotted to the quarterdeck, where he picked up the phone and called the bridge.

"It's for you, Mr. Slaughter," the messenger said. "It's Mr. Hanson."

I took the phone. "Slaughter, here. What's up, Joe?"

"You're not going to believe this," he said and hesitated.

"Com'on, Joe. What do they want?" I asked.

"You're not going to believe this, but they want to give us ..." He began to laugh hysterically.

"Joe, get serious!" I ordered. "What are they trying to give us?"

"A pair of lobsters!" he guffawed.

"All this for a couple of blinking lobsters. You gotta be kidding."

"Well, Sir. These are not common lobsters," Joe paused, apparently wondering whether or not I would believe him.

"What's different about them?" I asked.

"They must each weigh at least fifty pounds!"

"Fifty pounds? You're kidding me."

"No, I'm not. By law, they'll have to toss the lobsters back, and they wondered if our crew would like them for dinner tomorrow. One of the fishermen used to be in the Navy. He says it would be a nice treat for our men."

"Holy Smokes! Tell them to tie up alongside. I'm going to wake the Captain on this one."

The Captain came out of his sea cabin rubbing his eyes. I waited a few seconds and then laid the news on him. After he thought a minute, he decided. "Well, this is international waters, and I'm the Captain. Go for it! Give the crew a real treat for dinner tomorrow, but swear your watch section and the cooks to secrecy. And thank those lobstermen with a couple cases of cigarettes. Questions?"

"No, Sir. Mums, the word, Sir."

"You bet it is. Goodnight," he said and stumbled back to his sea cabin.

Mum's the word, readers. Captain's orders!

Sleeping Elephant Rock

Destroyer School – Newport, Rhode Island
Early Fall 1964

As Mrs. Moore, the owner of the Bancroft House, predicted, we became close friends with Brian and Mary Catherine Kelly, who occupied the other apartment on the top floor of the mansion. The four of us shared a fascination with the flow of seawater around Sleeping Elephant Rock, which lay parallel to the rocky shoreline at the base of the mansion's four-acre lot. The Rock was about 60 feet long and 20 feet wide, and it stood about 15 feet above the water. And it did indeed resemble a sleeping elephant.

The most alluring feature of that stretch of the bay was the rush of water between the Rock and the rocky shoreline, which only occurred when the huge waves of the bay were receding from the beach. While these rapids not only fascinated Brian and me, they also attracted schools of small herring that, in turn, attracted the huge striped bass that were the favorite of anglers in the region. Neither Brian nor I was particularly interested in the fish that inhabited the rapids. We were attracted to the rapids themselves and were obsessed with how we might exploit the rush of water for our enjoyment. Should we purchase a canoe? A boat? No, the rapids were too dangerous for solid crafts, which would quickly be dashed into the Rock or the shoreline and be damaged. We finally realized that we needed a craft that was flexible and resilient enough to withstand being bashed against the rocky surfaces on either side of the rapids.

Brian and I found everything we needed at an Army surplus store. We each purchased a one-man, inflatable life raft with a paddle. The rafts were made of heavy rubber, that was brilliant yellow and perfect for showing off.

Because the ebb and flow of the water created the rapids, we calculated that we could position ourselves at the top of the rapids and ride the receding waves downward away from the beach. Then as the waves returned to the beach, it would be easy for us to use them to paddle back to our starting point and repeat our ride over and over again. And that is exactly what we did.

Another issue we grappled with was what to wear. It was fall in Rhode Island and not sunbathing weather by any means, but if we dressed warmly, our clothing would soon be soaked with freezing seawater. Our solution took us to a store that sold underwater diving equipment, where we each bought a rubber diving suit. We also wore goggles, which enabled us to see where we were going more clearly. An old pair of tennis shoes without socks completed our rapids-shooting attire.

When we were all set for a trial run, our wives stood on the shore to watch the show. Dressed in our diving suits, we put our rafts in the water below the Rock and waited for the seawater to turn beachward. We hopped in our rafts and paddled with the water to the top of the Rock. Then we waited until the rush of the returning sea created the rapids we sought, at which point we shoved off and shot down the rapids in *rapid* time. Then we paddled once again to the top of the Rock, waited, and repeated the rapids ride to the bottom. It was a thrilling experience, and we were perfectly equipped.

After about six runs, I felt a bit exhausted, but I didn't want to stop, because the ride was so exhilarating. On our next run, a strange thing happened. Large schools of herring leaped out of the water and into our rafts. At the same time, we saw huge striped bass rolling in the waters around us, obviously feeding on the herring. To top it off, running down the hill toward our Sleeping Elephant was a gang of fisherman with casting rods in their hands. They evidently had spotted the stripers from afar and had driven to our driveway. From there, they ran to our shoreline to cast their bait into the feeding school of stripers.

This was the signal for Brian and me to call a halt to our rapids-riding session. We quickly paddled ashore to avoid being hooked by a fisherman's lure and joined our wives to observe the catching of several huge striped bass by the able anglers who had invaded our privacy.

After we tired of the fishing binge, we returned our rafts and paddles to their storage place under the back deck of the mansion and sought hot showers. As agreed, we reconvened in our apartment, which had windows that looked down on Sleeping Elephant Rock. We shared a bottle of wine as we watched the fisherman lift their last catches from the rapids.

I must admit that I felt that they had invaded our personal playground. On the other hand, a dozen rapid rides were quite enough for our first day. After a bit of wine, we boasted that we would set a new record the next day. And we did. Of course, Mrs. Moore's call to a friendly newspaper reporter and photographer, who came out to observe us, enhanced our performance immensely.

Oddly enough, this was not the last time we would see that reporter and photographer. Months later, after a heavy snowfall, Susan and I joined Brian and Mary Catherine in building a snow elephant in the sunken garden. We spent hours sculpting our subject. The result was so impressive that Mrs. Moore once again called the newspaper and suggested they send their reporter and photographer to record our accomplishment. The next day's front page featured a picture of the four of us and our elephantine work of art.

Our Firstborn

Destroyer School – Newport, Rhode Island
October 1964

Out of the five naval tenants in the Bancroft House, Susan and I were one of those couples who were young, fairly recently wed, and had no children, a demographic description was common to about 90% of my 30 Destroyer School classmates. In fact, I was amazed at the number of discussions that revolved around efforts to ensure that the men didn't go back to sea after Destroyer School without their wives being pregnant. To our credit, almost all of us accomplished our mission. Happily, Brian and Mary Catherine, the couple who lived in the apartment across the hall from us, achieved the same goal. In fact, our firstborns arrived within days of each other the following October.

As a final Destroyer School event, our class cruised to Guantanamo Bay on the school ship, which was, like *Cony*, a *Fletcher Class* destroyer, where I really knew my way around. We 30 classmates were trained to operate the ship by performing the functions that were normally those of enlisted men on a destroyer. This hands-on experience was designed to make us sensitive and knowledgeable about the roles of the men who would make up the departments we would soon be managing. I learned how to light-off a boiler with a flaming kerosene-soaked swab attached to the end of a long metal rod. I also loaded a five-inch gun with both projectiles and powder cases in rapid order. All in all, it was a very effective teaching method, and we enjoyed ourselves too. We watched a recently-released movie every night and spent almost all of our spare time talking about the impending birth of our babies.

When that time came, Susan went through a number of false starts. Three times we went to the Newport Naval Hospital and back home without a baby, and I didn't mind. According to hospital rules, at check-in time, we fathers were required to provide a huge carton of sanitary napkins, which we bought at the Navy Exchange. The entire waiting room was filled with naval officers and enlisted men holding huge boxes with the word *Kotex* clearly marked in large letters. Susan's three attempts subjected me to three embarrassing moments. I guess that was the price for having our baby delivered for an out-of-pocket cost of a mere $8.00.

While Captain George Grove was sometimes cantankerous, he was extremely generous when it came to babies' births. He always granted the father seven days of *basket leave,* which meant that our absence from the ship was not charged against the 30 days of regular leave that Navy men were granted each year.

When it was time for Wendy Elizabeth Slaughter to be born, Susan's mother, Virginia Parker, flew in to assist us by preparing meals, tending to the house, and caring for the mother and baby. My role was not as clearly defined. In fact, when Susan arrived home with the baby, I felt extremely superfluous and decided to go fishing. The trouble was that I had no fishing equipment, nor did I have the faintest idea of what kind of fish I might catch in waters around Newport. I decided to take a scouting trip.

I drove along Ocean Avenue, which follows the shoreline of the peninsula on which Newport is located. At the most southern tip of the peninsula, I saw a lone fisherman sitting on the rocks above the surf. I stopped the car, introduced myself, and told the man about my lack of Newport fishing knowledge. He was very understanding and quite eager to help. He explained that he was fishing for *blacks*, which are technically a type of grouper called tautogs. These dark brown fish with white blotches were a good-size, weighing one to three pounds. They were extremely delicious, having firm white flesh with a delicate flavor. But they were difficult to catch, because they hid in rocky areas along the shore.

The man showed me the rod and reel he used and the kind of bait I would need. He then directed me to a sporting goods store where I could properly outfit myself and buy a supply of bait, which were small crabs. He invited me to return after making my purchases, saying he would enjoy my company.

As I would learn, my new fishing partner was a retired telephone-company employee whose name was Ned Jordan.

After I returned, I proved to Ned that I was not a novice. I had gained considerable experience fishing while growing up in Michigan. It didn't take me long to catch my first black. As the day wore on, Ned and I caught a total of eight huge blacks. We decided to call it a day when the sun began to sink. While I suggested that we divide our catch evenly, Ned demurred saying, "Gary, you take all eight. Neither my wife nor I eat fish. We just don't like the taste. But I love to catch 'em."

Frankly, I had no idea what I would do with eight huge fish. Reluctantly, I agreed to take our entire catch. Ned loaned me a huge gunny sack in which to carry the trove of fish, and we agreed to meet again the next day. I told him I would stop at the sporting goods store and buy the bait for both of us. It was the least I could do.

When I arrived home, I was eager to present the results of my day's fishing. I decided that the best way to display my catch was to dump the contents of the gunny sack into the bathtub. Then I invited Susan and her mother to come and see my prizes.

Instead of being pleased, the two of them were disgusted. Virginia ordered, "Remove those fish from the tub and throw them into the garbage."

"I agree," said Susan.

Taken aback and a bit hurt, I politely refused. I explained that I would clean the fish in the kitchen, and they could stay clear of that process. I added that the fish would make a delicious meal for us and our neighbors. Susan and her mother grudgingly agreed, and I was quite proud of myself. For the first time, I had faced down my mother-in-law.

By the time I finished cleaning the eight fish, I must have had a dozen pounds of fillets. I saved a good portion for us and delivered the remainder to our neighbors, who were delighted with my gift. I didn't mind sharing my catch, because I had a feeling that Ned and I would have more good luck in the days ahead. And I was right. Our luck was so good that finally our neighbors began to tire of fish dinners. Then I made arrangements to share my catch with *Blandy* shipmates to spare the embarrassed neighbors having to say, "Please, no more."

Susan's father Carl was due to arrive on the fourth day of my seven-day basket leave, and I agreed to pick him up at the Providence airport. To the relief of Susan and her mother, Carl's visit would mean the end of my fishing. The day before Carl's arrival, I had to break the news to Ned. Frankly, I thought he was going to cry. He told me that he would really miss my company. Naturally, I felt the same way about him, but I felt obligated to spend my time with Carl.

For the evening when Carl arrived, Susan and I planned a surprise lobster dinner for her parents. Being Midwesterners, neither Susan nor I had eaten lobster before we came to Newport, but we had developed a taste for it while I was in Destroyer School. We had learned that the best time to purchase lobster was in the late afternoon when the boats returned to their berths in downtown Newport. Upon their arrival, the lobstermen would separate their catch into two categories. First were the lobsters sizeable enough to sell to wholesalers, who in turn would sell them, fresh off the boat, to local restaurants. Second were the lobsters large enough to be a legal catch but too small to sell to wholesalers. These smaller specimens were called chicken lobsters. Their average weight was one-and-a-half pounds. The price? Ninety cents! What a bargain.

On the way back from the airport with Carl, I stopped at our favorite lobster boat. I left Carl in the car while I purchased five chicken lobsters. I returned, carrying them in a shopping bag, which I placed in the trunk next to Carl's suitcase.

When we arrived at the Bancroft House, Carl carried his suitcase inside, and I carried the shopping bag. Susan and her mother were in the kitchen, so we joined them there. As Susan was hugging her father, I opened the shopping bag and dumped the five live lobsters on the kitchen floor. Naturally, the lobsters began to scurry about.

Susan and her mother shrieked. "Get those out of here! Do you hear me?" Virginia screamed as she ran toward the guest room. Carl, who wasn't even in on the joke, joined me in a bout of hysterical laughter. Susan just glared at me with her hands on her hips.

After I showed Virginia that the claws of the lobsters were held safely closed by heavy rubber bands, she finally joined in the laughter and saw the humor in my joke. At least, I hoped so. And the lobsters were delicious, especially when the pieces were dipped in melted butter before popping them into your mouth.

Susan smiled at me as her father, holding little Wendy in his arms, rocked back and forth.

Virginia continually admonished him to be careful about how he handled the baby.

Accustomed to her nagging, as usual, he ignored her.

Man Overboard

USS Blandy – Portland, Maine
Late Fall 1964

In the US Navy, the position of Officer of the Deck (OOD) confers a great deal of authority and responsibility. The OOD is the direct representative of the ship's Commanding Officer (CO), with full responsibility for carrying out the operations and mission of the ship.

Qualification for OOD does not depend on an officer's rank, but solely on the officer's ability to command and maneuver the ship. I became a qualified OOD when I was a 22-year-old Ensign. While other officers aboard my ship outranked me, they were not OODs, because they didn't possess the unique ability to *drive* a 418-foot destroyer.

In port, the OOD is called the Command Duty Officer (CDO). In an emergency, a CDO must be qualified and capable of getting the ship underway without the presence of the CO or the Executive Officer (XO). At sea, the standard OOD watch is either two or four hours in duration. In port, the standard CDO watch is 24 hours commencing at 0800 in the morning and ending at 0800 the next day. Because most destroyers had four qualified OODs aboard, watches were stood in four sections. That is, as OOD and CDO, we were off watch for three periods and then on watch for one period.

In general, I enjoyed standing my CDO watches, because they gave me an opportunity to catch up on my paperwork, watch a movie in the Wardroom after dinner with my fellow officers, and get a good night's sleep. My luxury of a good night's sleep ended when a 3rd class petty officer named Balmer reported aboard.

It's not that Balmer was a bad sailor. In fact, he was a highly respected Fire-control Technician (FT), but he had a serious character flaw. Every month or so, he would go ashore on liberty and drink too many beers. As luck would have it, he always did this when I was the CDO. Just as I would fall asleep, the telephone beside my bunk would ring, and the quarterdeck watch officer would be on the line reporting that the Shore Patrol had brought Balmer back to the ship, and I had to sign for him.

This situation was both good news and bad news. The bad news was that I had to get out of bed, dress, and make my way to the quarterdeck to take possession of a drunken Balmer. The good news was that Balmer would soon be restricted to the ship by a Summary Court-Martial, and I would be assured of two months of peaceful CDO watches, free of being Balmerized in the middle of the night.

The oddest of all my midnight interactions with Balmer occurred when the ship was paying a goodwill visit to Portland, Maine. It was late October, and we were enduring a blast of unseasonably frigid weather, even for Maine. Once more, I was awakened by the call from the quarterdeck. Balmer had struck again. This time, however, the outcome was radically different. After arriving at the quarterdeck wearing my foul-weather jacket to ward off the freezing weather, I signed Balmer's paperwork. Then, when the Shore Patrol removed Balmer's handcuffs, instead of drowsily heading for his bunk, he abruptly raced toward the forecastle.

At a leisurely pace, I followed Balmer, more out of curiosity than anything else. I wondered what he could achieve by running to a virtual dead-end like the forecastle. As I rounded the forward gun mount, I saw Balmer standing on the base of the jack staff, a small vertical spar on the bow of the ship, on which a type of flag called a "jack" is flown when a ship is in port. During my time in the Navy, the jack was the blue star-filled field of the American flag.

When Balmer spotted me, he yelled in his predictably slurred voice, "Don't come any closer, Mr. Slaughter. If you do, I'll jump!"

I ignored Balmer's threat and walked toward him. Stopping just short of the jack staff, I ordered, "Balmer, get down off that jack staff! And go to your compartment. Right now!"

"Don't come any closer or I'm really going to jump!"

I looked down at the water below the bow. The frigid wind had whipped up a white frothy target for Balmer if he wanted to take the plunge. "It's too cold out here to play games. Get down – on the double!"

"No, Sir. I'm gonna jump!"

By this time, I was cold and impatient. I turned around and marched back toward the quarterdeck, yelling over my shoulder, "Go ahead and jump, Balmer! I don't give a damn."

A second later, even with the wind howling in my ears, I heard a loud splash, followed by a wild scream. I ran to the lifeline to see Balmer swimming frantically toward the pier right where the pair of Shore-Patrol sailors was waiting to greet him.

This time I ordered the Shore Patrol team to lock Balmer up in their brig, and I went to bed. The next day when Balmer was returned to the ship, he gave me a sheepish look. That was the last time Balmer deprived me of enjoying a full night's sleep.

Blandy's Underside

USS Blandy – Boston Naval Shipyard
Winter 1965

In March 1964 after completing Destroyer School at the top of my class, I reported to *USS Blandy* with high hopes and enthusiasm, as I assumed the position of Engineering Officer. Early in 1965, *Blandy's* regularly scheduled overhaul took place in the Boston Naval Shipyard. Special emphasis was to be given to correct our extremely unreliable 1200 psi boilers, which would become the bane of my existence for the next two years. Following the shipyard's standard practice, the ship spent a portion of its overhaul period in dry dock. This enabled shipyard personnel to inspect its underside of the ship, make necessary repairs, strip any rust, apply a special *red lead* primer seal, and repaint *Blandy's* underwater hull in standard navy gray.

The dry dock was essentially a mammoth steel bathtub filled with sea water. At one end were huge doors through which *Blandy* was pushed by tugs and hauled by steel cables attached to giant cranes. The top rim of the dry dock was even with the ground into which the dry dock had been dug. When *Blandy* was positioned properly, the open-end of the dry dock was closed. Then the water was pumped out over a period of hours, leaving *Blandy* at rest on a cradle of sturdy, wooden supports constructed earlier to keep the ship upright but off the floor of the dry dock. Shipyard personnel then descended into the dry dock using a long staircase attached to the dry-dock wall. Needed equipment was lowered to them by rope or with the assistance of cranes located in appropriate positions along the rim of the dry dock to enable them to perform their work beneath the ship.

I had experienced my first shipyard overhaul on the *USS Cony* some three years earlier in the Portsmouth Naval Shipyard. During that overhaul, my concerns as Electronics Material Officer were largely focused upward toward radio and radar antennas or inward to where our vast array of electronics equipment was installed and operated. However, I entered the Boston Naval Shipyard as Engineering Officer, as well as the ship's Repair Officer, and I was responsible for all aspects of the overhaul activity. During our dry-dock period, I centered my attention downward into the engineering spaces where our fragile boilers begged for creative and competent help. I also concentrated on the hull of the ship normally underwater except when *Blandy* was propped up in the empty dry dock.

To carry out my responsibilities, I teamed with Warrant Officer Reading, the Shipyard's Overhaul Liaison Officer assigned to *Blandy*. Unfortunately, owing to Reading's lack of effectiveness, especially in the critically important area of improving our high-pressure boilers, this relationship proved to be unsatisfactory. Aware of Captain Grove's high priority to improve the reliability of our 1200 psi boilers, I recommended that Reading be relieved and that a more qualified boilerman replace him. Captain Grove concurred, and Reading was relieved of his *Blandy* responsibilities.

I had never been down in a dry dock before. When the shipyard engineers signaled that it was safe for me to descend, I donned my hardhat and carefully followed the long flight of stairs down into the massive bathtub containing my ship. As I walked down those stairs, an unusual sensation overcame me. I was not prepared emotionally for the reality that *Blandy* was downright enormous. I had known that she was 418 feet long, longer than the football fields I'd played on as a student, and that she had a 45 foot beam, longer than the distance from the pitcher's rubber to home plate in the softball games I'd pitched since I was in third grade. But not until I reached the floor of the dry dock and looked upward did I realize just how massive *Blandy* really was.

Normally, as a member of the *Blandy* crew, you would not be aware of the gigantic size of the elements that were installed on the underside of the ship: Two four-blade propellers, each taller than 15 feet. A sonar dome about the size of an Airstream Travel Trailer. Rudders, each the size of a large barn door and each weighing some 45 tons. After being overwhelmed by *Blandy's* sheer size, a second sensation hit me: How small and physically insignificant I was. And to think as the leading OOD on *Blandy*, I was privileged to drive this massive machine, weighing over 4,000 tons when fully loaded, through the water at nearly 35 knots and turning on a dime to snare an elusive submarine that was almost as large as the *Blandy*! What an honor! What a thrill!

USS Blandy at sea (1962)

Actually, for her size, *Blandy* weighed far less that other ships of the fleet with similar dimensions, because *Blandy* had a steel hull, topped by an aluminum superstructure. Had her superstructure been made of steel like other ships in the fleet, her fully loaded weight might well have exceeded 5,000 tons or more. The relative lightness of the aluminum superstructure not only increased *Blandy's* speed but also decreased her fuel consumption. This resulted in increasing *Blandy's* range when fully fueled. That was the good news. The bad news was that, because steel and aluminum are dissimilar metals, they naturally produce galvanic corrosion or dissimilar metal corrosion. This is the corrosive damage that occurs when two dissimilar materials are coupled in proximity to corrosive electrolyte materials between them. In this case, the electrolyte was salt water and, to a limited extent, simple salt sea air located in close proximity to the hull where these two metals were joined. During my tenure as Chief Engineer no type of insulation or non-corrosive barrier employed managed to reduce this damage significantly, which was a constant challenge to those of us who were charged with maintaining *Blandy*.

Combining steel and aluminum to derive the benefits of less weight worked well on the drawing board, but out at sea in the natural elements, it proved to be a disastrous combination. Between its unreliable boilers and troublesome superstructure, *Blandy* served fewer years of active duty than many other destroyers of her era. For all her faults, I was proud to serve on her. As *Blandy's* Chief Engineer, I felt she was mine.

Tricky Dicky

USS Blandy – Boston Naval Shipyard
Winter 1965

While serving as a naval officer, I took pride in my professionalism. I strived to live up to the time-honored standard of an officer and a gentleman. However, I had one supervisor who had the uncanny knack of bringing out the worst in me. During my first year as Chief Engineer on the *USS Blandy*, I reported to the ship's Executive Officer. His nickname, used irreverently by the ship's officers and members of the crew, was Tricky Dicky, TD for short.

I'm not sure how he came by that nickname, because I was certain he wasn't clever enough to be all that Tricky.

Tricky Dicky was especially uninformed in the area of engineering. I can't remember one occasion when he inquired about anything in my area of responsibility. Yes, I was truly blessed, but the other department heads weren't as fortunate. TD seemed to think he knew something about weapons, operations, and supply. Those department heads devoted an enormous amount of time and energy explaining to TD why he was wrong and how things really worked.

Captain George Grove, the Commanding Officer, did not approve of our making fun of his Executive Officer. Whenever he heard us start to tell the latest TD story, he frowned at us, and of course, we stopped immediately. He was a real spoil-sport.

When *Blandy* entered Boston Naval Shipyard for a complete overhaul in the late fall of 1965, much of the work involved improvements to our 1200 psi boilers. So the ship went *cold plant* for most of the four-month shipyard period. With no heat from boilers, it was impossible to sleep aboard the ship, especially during the winter in Boston which meant the enlisted men were moved into shipyard barracks. Many officers were sent to schools and some stayed at the BOQ in the shipyard. Others of us commuted between Boston and Newport, the ship's homeport as well as home to many of us married men. Because the drive took 1 hour 45 minutes one way, when we returned to the ship, we left Newport at about 5:30 am. If not, we were in danger of missing Quarters, held at 8:00 am. If snow was predicted, our departure was even earlier. When I commuted, which was most of the time, I drove my Impala convertible, because it could comfortably accommodate four passengers and the driver. Since the driver had to make the rounds of his passengers' homes, he didn't get as much sleep as the others.

On one occasion, TD was the last passenger I picked up that morning. We were running a bit late. Following our normal procedure, we pulled into his driveway and waited for him to emerge from the kitchen door. We waited and waited. At last, I asked Bill Poteat, who worked for me as Damage Control Assistant (DCA), to go and tap on the kitchen door gently, since TD's family would likely still be asleep.

Bill knocked on the door and waited, still TD didn't come out. Bill knocked again. Still no TD. Bill shrugged his shoulders and looked to me for help. I got out of the car, went to the door, and knocked very hard this time. I could hear a baby crying.

"Well, at least, we know they're home," said Bill.

"This is ridiculous!" I banged on the door and yelled, "TD! Where the hell are you?"

We heard the sound of footsteps scurrying about, presumably in the kitchen. Then the kitchen door burst open. TD was slipping on his bridge coat, his combination cap was perched precariously over his left ear, and he had what appeared to be a sandwich jammed into his mouth. He mumbled something incomprehensible, but it was too much to expect that it might be an apology.

I fumed. "Do you know it's almost six o'clock? We're going to be late for *your* Quarters!"

At eight o'clock each morning, the entire ship's crew assembled for Quarters on the main deck. The lead petty officers presided over the enlisted men in their divisions, while the officers assembled on the second deck to obtain instructions from the Executive Officer. There were two ranks of officers standing at attention in front of the XO. In the first rank, were the department heads. In the second, the division officers and other officers with specialized jobs but no divisions. When the XO finished delivering his pearls of wisdom, the division officers returned to their divisions to muster (count) their men, inspect them for proper dress, and deliver instructions concerning their day's work. Without the Executive Officer, there could be no Quarters, and on this day, he was about to be late.

TD slipped into the front seat next to me. Bill Poteat sat in the back next to Harry Windon, the First Lieutenant.

Harry was never shy around TD. With a bit of edge in his tone, he asked, "What the heck is that in your mouth, XO?"

TD mumbled, "Is ah fluch nutee."

"What did you say?" Harry asked.

TD swallowed and said, "It's a *fluffernutter!*"

Now I got into the act. "What the hell's a fluffernutter?

"It's a sandwich made with Marshmallow Fluff and peanut butter. I prefer crunchy peanut butter."

"Oh, for God's sake! You mean we're going to miss Quarters because you took time to make a damn fluffernutter. Jeez up!"

"Why didn't you wait and get something from the gedunk wagon when we got there?" Harry muttered.

Personal Postscript: The word *gedunk* is a naval term referring to snack foods such as sandwiches, coffee, ice cream, crackers, candy, etc. and the places where they are sold. Since snacks were not allowed on naval vessels, gedunk wagons provided them to sailors during their breaks.

TD was not fazed. He just sat there picking his teeth with his jackknife, for crying out loud!

I jammed the gas pedal nearly to the floor.

We arrived at the ship just in the nick of time. I allowed myself to cool down and then said, "Tomorrow morning, we'll wait in your driveway for exactly 60 seconds. If that kitchen door doesn't open before that period of time expires, you'll have to find another way to get to Boston. Understood?"

TD nodded his head like a drunken woodpecker.

The next morning, TD was waiting outside, holding a paper cup and a brown paper sack that I assumed was another fluffernutter.

By 5:25 AM we were all in the car and on our way. I was relieved to be able to drive more slowly than the day before. We drove north up the length of Rhode Island and then turned east toward Boston, with TD nursing his cup of coffee all the way. After slurping the last drop from his paper cup, he crumpled it and threw it on the floor between his feet. Then he reached into his pocket for his sandwich bag.

While I'm not sure how I mustered up the nerve, I grabbed his arm and sternly said, "You're not eating that sandwich in my car."

The other two officers in the backseat were is quiet as church mice.

"But this is my breakfast!" TD said.

"You can eat it after you get out of my car."

"All right! All right! I'll eat it when we get to the ship. Geez."

"Good," I said.

That day, all hell broke loose in the forward fireroom. The yard workers discovered that several of our 1200 psi boiler-tube welds at the mud drum (lower header) were pitted. They estimated that, with remediation, these tubes would soon be added to our long string of boiler-tube failures.

I asked the foreman of the shipyard boiler gang, "Ed, what are our options here?"

"Well, while replacing all of them is a sure bet, we might try re-welding first."

"When will you be able to recommend which option we should go with?" I asked.

"I'll have a recommendation for you by this evening. I have a crew coming in at midnight. If we have your decision by then, we can get started on whatever you decide."

When I concluded that I should be available that evening, I gave Bill Poteat my car keys and asked him to call Susan when he got to Newport.

"I'll do that," said Bill. "And tomorrow I'll pick up the guys as usual. Do I have permission to forbid fluffernutters, Sir?"

I smiled and nodded.

As sometimes happened, things progressed slowly in the fireroom. It wasn't until about 4:00 am that Ed recommended that we not try to re-weld. "We should replace every tube on this side of the boiler. We'll take a close look at the other side, too."

The additional boiler work would lengthen our stay in the shipyard. When 8:00 am rolled around, I decided to attend Quarters and break the news to everyone. They would have to adjust plans. I walked up to the second deck and lined up in front of my three officers. Because I had spent the night in the dingy, dirty fireroom, I was wearing my grubbiest khaki trousers and shirt, my khaki fore-and-aft cap, and my foul-weather jacket to keep warm.

TD took one look at my outfit and announced snidely, "Please take off that foul-weather jacket. You should really be dressed in Service Dress Blues with your overcoat for Quarters, but I'll excuse your work khakis this time. Just take that jacket off!"

I unsnapped the grommet-buttons and shrugged my shoulders. The jacket fell to the deck in a great heap around the back of my shoes. I heard quiet sniggers from the men standing behind me. I simply stood at attention and stared at TD. He said nothing and continued with a long-winded discussion on the ship's lack of cleanliness. I guessed he'd never been through a shipyard overhaul, where dirt is a constant condition.

For the remainder of the overhaul, I spent hours each day in the fireroom. As the weather got colder, I kept my foul-weather jacket on at all times. Especially at Quarters.

Gemini (GT-4)

USS Blandy – Eastern Atlantic Ocean
June 1965

During the early summer of 1965, *Blandy* was one of 24 ships assigned to emergency rescue stations along the path of the low-earth orbit of the *Gemini GT-4*, a two-man spacecraft. According to plan, the GT-4 would be in orbit four days between its June 3 launch date and its June 7 splashdown. Ideally the craft would reenter the earth's atmosphere east of the central Florida coastline and make its landing in close proximity to the aircraft carrier, *USS Wasp* (CVS 15), on station at the planned landing point.

During the space craft's 48th orbit, a computer failed, making it impossible for the crew to land normally, facing upward. Since that increased the potential for injury during landing, the mission was aborted, and the GT-4 landed 43 miles short (west) of the *Wasp*. Having been informed of the GT-4's situation well before landing, the *Wasp* had dispatched a number of ships to the new touchdown point. In fact, one of the *Wasp's* helicopters arrived in time to observe the actual splashdown. Both the astronauts, James McDevitt and Edward H. White, as well as their spacecraft were declared A-Okay. The mission was historical, because it was the first American spaceflight during which one of the astronauts, namely White, performed an Extra-Vehicular Activity (EVA) outside of the spacecraft.

In anticipation of unplanned landings like this one, 24 ships were positioned across the globe along the path of the GT-4 orbit at equal intervals approximately a time-zone in length. For example, should the craft be forced to land in the Pacific Ocean, there would always be a rescue vessel in relatively close proximity. On the starboard side of each rescue ship, a powerful davit and loop of cable were installed. This rig was capable of lassoing the craft and lifting it out of the sea.

Four days of lazily circling around our assigned rescue station in the Eastern Atlantic was tedious for the *Blandy* crew, but NASA provided a brilliant way to entertain and inform our weary crewmembers. Each rescue ship was provided an informative description of every activity the two astronauts were engaged in during every minute of their four-day mission.

Having a background in radio broadcasting, I was appointed to narrate this action-packed script over the 1MC, the ship's public address system.

> *"This morning, Blandy crew, our astronauts are conducting D-8, their first experiment. Here they are using five dosimeters to measure the radiation in the spacecraft environment, paying special attention to the South American Anomaly."*

My description of the other four hundred activities was not nearly as breathtaking as this one.

As soon as the astronauts and their spacecraft were safely aboard the *Wasp*, all rescue ships were released to resume normal operations. We headed home to Norfolk, to the great relief of all members of the crew, who were sick and tired of doing nothing except making doughnut holes in the ocean, a complaint sailors often made.

This was also a common refrain after a few days of ASW exercises that involved a great deal of time executing circular search patterns to locate our American-practice submarines. Our submarine adversaries were adept at evading detection by slipping under a handy thermal layer or ducking under the wake of our aircraft carrier. When we lost contact with our target, time once again weighed heavily on our hands.

Coincidental Assignments

USS Valley Forge, USS Cony, USS Blandy
Summer 1965

As a naval officer and as a midshipman, I experienced an unusual number of *coincidental assignments*. These occurred when I served on a ship and encountered pre-Navy close friends who were also serving on that same ship. What were the odds of these chance assignments? Not great!

During this period, there were on average 700,000 officers and enlisted men in the Navy. Approximately 240 destroyers and 24 aircraft carriers were on active duty. As a midshipman, I served my 3rd Class Midshipman Cruise on the *USS Valley Forge*. Coincidentally, I also served my 1st Class Midshipman Cruise on the *USS Valley Forge*. Then as a commissioned officer, I served two-year stints aboard two different destroyers, *USS Cony* and the *USS Blandy*.

In the summer of 1965, when I was Engineering Officer on *Blandy*, we pulled into Bermuda for a liberty visit for the crew. I was concerned about obtaining a replacement part for one of the main feed pumps so we could operate the forward fireroom with two, rather than one boiler. Because we were anchored in the bay, I ordered the duty motor whaleboat to transport me to the small naval shipyard. I had been assured I could find the necessary part there. After we landed, I hopped out of the boat and walked to the parts supply department. Behind the counter was the familiar face of Ronald Worthington, a boy from my old neighborhood. We had been pals for as long as either of us could remember.

Back in the summer of 1960, during my 1st Class Mid-shipman Cruise aboard *Valley Forge*, I had experienced my first series of coincidental assignments. The ship was then anchored in Naples, Italy, and I went ashore regularly to confer with a Public Information Officer in my capacity as the editor of the ship's daily newspaper/letter. On these visits, I was transported to and from shore in motor whaleboats, which were about 26 feet long with a seven-foot beam. They were used to transport personnel or as lifeboats when needed.

A whaleboat crew consisted of two sailors. The coxswain stood on a platform in the stern and used a large wheel to steer the boat. His perch provided him with a good view of what lay ahead. The other crew member was the engineer who controlled the powerful diesel engine, installed in a large case near the center of gravity in the middle of the boat. When underway, the engineer hunched over the engine controls and faced the bow of the boat. Because the engine was extremely loud, the coxswain signaled required speed changes by clanging a brass bell. One clang for *ahead slow*, etc.

One day when I was the only passenger, I chose to sit in the rear of the boat at the feet of the coxswain. I didn't have a good view of the engineer, because his back was turned toward me. It wasn't until we'd landed at the Naples pier that he turned around. When our eyes met, we simultaneously yelled out each other's name and hugged one another. The engineer was none other than Eugene Sutton, who had lived in my old neighborhood and with whom I had walked to school each day. He had been in my kindergarten class, and we had graduated from Owosso High School together in 1957.

After discussing the amazing coincidence of bumping into each other so far from home, Eugene stunned me. "Do you know who else is on the *Valley Forge*?" he asked. Of course, since I had no clue, he answered his own question. "Wayne and Don Nesbitt. They're both Airdales." This meant that they worked in air operations or aircraft maintenance.

I knew both Wayne and Don. We had attended grade school together and had been in the same Boy Scout troop. As a matter of fact, their father had been our scoutmaster. Wayne had graduated from OHS in 1958 and Don in 1959. This meant that four of us, out of the Navy's 700,000 officers and enlisted men, had been assigned to the same aircraft carrier. And all of us had graduated from OHS between 1957 and 1959. Considering that

OHS only had about 300 students per class and more than half of them were girls, who rarely enlisted in the military in those days, this was truly an amazing coincidence.

My next coincidental assignment occurred in late December 1961 when I reported to my first destroyer, the *USS Cony*, in Norfolk. After showing my orders to the guard at the entry gate of the Destroyer-Submarine base, I parked my Karmann-Ghia alongside the pier where the *Cony* was moored. After grabbing my heavy sea bag and hanging bag, I scurried up the gangplank to the quarterdeck. The OOD directed me to the Wardroom, where the department heads were having a strategy session. My new boss, Lieutenant Rowsey, the Operations Officer, would be in that meeting.

As I walked forward on the main deck on the ship's starboard side, enticing aromas emanating from the crew's galley ahead on my left. The galley's hatch was open and slouched against the hatch frame was a sailor dressed in whites. This struck me as unusual, because it was December. I realized he was a mess cook, who also wore a white apron on which he had wiped his hands as he prepared the meal. As I approached, he saluted me.

Carrying my bags, I couldn't conveniently return his salute so I looked down to avoid making eye contact. As I came abreast of him, he said, "Gary! Is that you?" He lunged forward and hugged me, pinning my loaded arms to my sides. "Are you reporting aboard the *Cony*? Oh, boy!"

I was flabbergasted to see my old friend from Owosso High School and classmate from – you guessed it – the class of 1957. "I can't believe it! Melvin Tattersoll. How are you, Melvin?" I remembered our OHS classmates on the *Valley Forge* the previous year. I quickly told him about that experience and asked, "I don't suppose there are any more of our classmates aboard, are there?"

"No, but we do have a fella you know. Remember Tony Oswald? He used to work on your grandpa's farm. He graduated from Corunna High School in 1955, a couple years ahead of us."

"Tony! Of course, I remember him. Real nice fella. What's he up to?"

"He's a 3rd Class Gunner's Mate, and he stands quarter-deck watches too."

Corunna, a small town only three miles east of Owosso, was the seat of Shiawassee County. We lived on the eastern edge of Owosso and did a lot of our shopping in Corunna. Corunna High School was much smaller than OHS. I don't suppose there were more than 200 students in the whole school. Corunna boys used to work for nearby farmers, especially during harvest season. My grandfather's farm was nearer Corunna than Owosso, and Melvin's family had a farm not far from my grandfather's. Like many farm kids in that area, he rode a school bus into Owosso for his high-school education.

This coincidental assignment was not quite as extensive as my first on the *Valley Forge* with Eugene Sutton and crew, but there were two of us from OHS class of '57 on *Cony* now, and that was a rarity for sure. Add in Tony, and this was indeed bizarre.

I didn't have long to wait for another coincidental assignment. After my first six months aboard *Cony,* we received word that a new officer would be reporting aboard. He was a newly minted Ensign. "Does anybody know where he got his commission?" I asked.

No one knew. We didn't find out until the day he reported and walked into the Wardroom. Our eyes met and both our faces registered surprise. The new Ensign was George Taft. George had been a fellow NROTC midshipman from the class of 1962 at Michigan. Once again, the odds were strongly against this happening. By then, I was used to it.

I truly enjoyed coincidental assignments during my Navy days. They certainly kept life interesting and have provided material to write about decades later!

Three Housemates

Newport, Rhode Island and Norfolk, Virginia
Fall 1965

After leaving the shipyard overhaul, we headed to Gitmo for six weeks of Refresher Training. Then unpleasant news began to arrive. First, our homeport was changed to Norfolk. Second, shortly after our move to Norfolk, we were to be assigned to the Sixth Fleet in the Mediterranean for a sixth-month deployment.

Susan and I were depressed about having to leave the Bancroft House. Not only would we miss our apartment, we would also miss the dear friendships we had made during our time there. What's more, based on our knowledge of Norfolk, we knew it would be bland as compared with life in Newport. However, this was the Navy, and nothing lasted forever, especially for naval men and their families. I suggested that perhaps Susan should take Wendy to Highland Park and live with her parents while the ship was in the Med. Right away, I could tell my suggestion was not acceptable, so I tabled the discussion and helped her pack. With all that was occupying my attention, we agreed it would be best to place our belongings in storage in Norfolk.

While I was making preparations for the ship's Norfolk move, Susan was hatching a plan of her own. I knew only that she was busily packing and preparing for the movers to arrive and load all our possessions in the van. Then she would head south.

The Friday evening before the moving van was to arrive, I came home rather late. While I was bushed, Susan seemed in good spirits. She told me that she had made some plans with two other *Blandy* officers' wives, and they and their husbands would be coming to our house for a planning session at 2000 (8:00 pm). I was mystified, but too exhausted to resist. I simply went along with it.

Navy men are always right on time, if not early. The doorbell rang promptly at 2000, and when I opened the door, there stood Tom Jenkins, my Electrical Officer, with his wife Maxine. Standing behind them were First Lieutenant Harry Windon and his wife Eleanor. We invited them in, and the women asked the men to sit down on the couch. We glanced at each other and took our assigned seats.

Standing before us, our wives announced that they had a well-thought-out plan to share. It sounded like we were confronting a fait accompli.

- They would travel to Norfolk ahead of the moving van and find a house for Susan to rent.
- The house would have two bedrooms to accommodate Gary, Susan, and Wendy when the ship returned.
- While we men were in the Med, the three women would live in the house and share the expenses equally.
- Susan would move all our possessions into the house. Maxine and Eleanor would move in only what they needed and store the remainder.

"Well, that's about it," Susan said. "Any questions?"

"If we move only the furniture we own," I said, "we'll have to purchase additional furniture in Norfolk. For example, we don't even own this couch we're sitting on, and we only have one bed. We'll need another for the guest room."

Susan nodded "I've made a list of things to purchase to complete furnishing the house. Here it is." She handed it to me. "I figure I can cover these items with the money I've set aside from my teaching job."

I looked at Tom, who shrugged his shoulders. Harry did the same. "Ladies," I said, "looks like you have a plan. Good luck in finding a place."

The women left for Norfolk driving all three cars in a caravan. Meanwhile, we men moved onto the ship, where we really wouldn't need a car. Susan and her friends found a nice two-bedroom bungalow near the base where the Commissary and Navy Exchange were located.

While we were in the Med, our wives' letters contained glowing reports about the success of their mini-commune. Nothing but glowing reports! Months later we learned the real truth. Maxine had turned out to be a difficult roommate. She consumed more than her share of the special treats that had been acquired for everyone. Moreover, she didn't lift a finger to do housework or cooking or cleanup jobs. All in all, she had been a poor choice for a housemate. That was the bad news. The good news was that Eleanor and Susan bonded and became good friends.

Boy, I'm glad friction like that doesn't occur among us men!

Blandy's Engineering Log Room

USS Blandy – Norfolk, Virginia
Fall 1965

During my stint as *Blandy's* Engineering Officer, the Engineering Log Room was my *office*. I shared this space with my *secretary* who, in naval parlance, was called the Log Room Yeoman. In this case, my Yeoman was a young man from Milwaukee whose full name was Frank Robert Troski or Ski for short.

The Log Room was decorated in typical Navy fashion, which means that everything in the room was painted Navy gray, presumably to match the color of a destroyer's hull. Ski and I shared a long desk consisting of a double metal desk top on which Ski's typewriter was bolted down on one side and my in-and-out baskets occupied the other. Our two comfortable metal chairs slid tightly under the desk. We also had a sound-powered telephone mounted to the bulkhead. When it growled, Ski would answer, "Engineering Log Room. Ski speaking, Sir."

Our crowded Log Room contained a dozen enormous two-drawer file cabinets that contained neatly stored correspondence, schematics, blueprints, instruction books, and other documentation relating to the *Blandy's* specific engineering configuration. These documents covered such topics as shafting and bearings, propellers, pumps, condensers and air ejectors, boilers, turbines, reduction gears, piping systems, insulation, and auxiliary machinery. Reflecting naval order and discipline, these documents were meticulously marked with a printed code that followed the Navy Standard Subject Classification Group Numbering System, which was used throughout the US Navy. All subjects related to ship engineering were filed in the 9000 series, beginning with number 9000.1 and ending with 9999.9.

Even though the coding system was complex and cumbersome, after four years as a naval officer, I understood it and used it with facility. Ski was not as familiar with the system. In fact, he was intimidated and dumbfounded by its complexity. Rather than go through the painful scene of having Ski attempt to recover a document, I would find it for him. Each time I did, he thanked me profusely and heaved a huge sigh of relief.

After a month of ASW operations with Task Group Alpha, we were scheduled to pull into the Destroyer-Submarine (Des-Sub) piers in Norfolk for a three-week stay. I took advantage of the in-port time to schedule myself for a two-week course on the care and maintenance of our troublesome and unreliable 1200 psi boilers. I advised Ski to mind the shop as best he could during my absence. He trembled as we said goodbye, his self-confidence indicator reading slightly above *Very Low*.

When I returned from my training course, I stopped off at *Blandy* to spend an hour or so filing the course handouts in accordance with their Standard Classification number. I pulled out the first filing-cabinet drawer, expecting to be greeted by an organized rank of file tabs showing 9013.2 and so on. What I saw made me gasp. All the 9000 series tabs had been removed. In their place were new tabs, carrying codes like *FRT-5* and *FRT-16*. I hurriedly checked all the other file drawers and found all of them replete with shiny new FRT tabs and numbers. Naturally, I was a bit miffed. I rang up the Quarter Deck and asked the Officer of the Deck (CDO) to have Ski paged on the 1MC shipboard announcement system and ordered to report to the Engineering Log Room on the double.

Within five minutes, Ski burst into the Log Room out of breath but, for some inexplicable reason, grinning like a Cheshire Cat. I was confused by his demeanor.

I pointed to the open file drawers and barked, "Ski, what are all those FART tabs doing on our file folders?"

He smiled even more broadly and replied, "I did it, Sir. I rearranged the files so I can find everything now. Isn't that great?"

Though I was dumbfounded, I managed to sputter, "What is the meaning of those FART tabs?"

"Oh, that's me, Sir," he said. "FRT – Frank Robert Troski."

I shook my head, left the Log Room, and went straight to the DesSub Pub at the head of the pier. I needed a stiff drink.

The Welfare and Recreation Fund

USS Blandy – Naples, Italy
Christmas 1965

Aboard a smaller ship like a destroyer, officers are assigned a wide range of collateral duties in addition to their regular jobs. When I had been the Communications Officer aboard my first destroyer, my collateral duties had included ship's postal officer, medical officer, cryptosecurity officer, registered publications custodian, and the Wardroom-mess treasurer. I am sure I had additional collateral duties, but the years have blurred my recollection.

When I served as the Engineering Officer aboard my second destroyer, three commissioned officers reported to me, including my Main Propulsion Assistant, Terry Regen. One of his collateral duties was Welfare and Recreation Officer, which meant that when we were deployed to the Mediterranean Sea, he scheduled guided bus tours for crew members whenever we pulled into a port. These tours were provided by tour companies approved by the Sixth Fleet Welfare and Recreation Department.

Generally speaking, the tours were entertaining and informative visits to popular tourist attractions. In Lisbon, I took a tour to visit the Shrine of Fatima. From Naples, I took a weekend tour to visit Rome, where I witnessed the Pope blessing all of us who stood in St. Peters Square. When we were in Cannes, I signed up for a tour of a perfumery in Grasse.

The standing joke about Mediterranean tours was that no matter where the featured destination was located, the tour bus always stopped at every cathedral along the way. Having taken about a dozen tours to various places, I can recall visiting at least 25 cathedrals. According to every tour guide, each cathedral was bigger and better in some aspect than the ones we had visited before.

On Mediterranean cruises, it was customary for some officers' wives to travel to Europe and sightsee with each other before joining their husbands anytime the ship pulled into a port. This was the case with Mr. Regen and his wife Jennifer. But one visit was a near disaster and placed Mr. Regen in serious hot water. For the crew, he had booked a two-day tour of the Amalfi Coast from Naples to Positano by way of Mount Vesuvius and the Ruins of Pompeii. It promised to be a wonderful trip with splendid scenery. Accordingly the tour completely sold out.

When the tour bus pulled up to the gangway, sailors and officers were waiting on the pier, eager to board and be on their way. Since the tour-bus drivers worked on a *pay-before-we-go* basis, the quarterdeck watch dispatched the messenger to fetch Mr. Regen to pay the driver with cash from the Welfare and Recreation Fund stored securely in his stateroom safe.

After a minute or two, the messenger returned and reported, "Mr. Regen is not in his stateroom or in the Wardroom. And from the looks of it, his bed hasn't been slept in either."

Loud groans emanated from the sailors waiting on the pier. As a wave of panic swept through the group, they asked fearfully, "What will we do if he's not aboard, Mr. Slaughter? Will the tour be canceled?"

One of the sailors called to me, "I think I know where Mr. Regen is. Last night I had the evening watch, and his wife was here for dinner. Afterward, he was carrying a duffle bag when they left the ship for her hotel. I didn't hear what hotel though." The sailors waiting to board the bus swore under their breath.

By now, the discontent had escalated and the ruckus had caught the attention of the new Commanding Officer, Captain I. Nelson Franklin. He left the Wardroom and walked toward the quarterdeck. Knowing that I was the Command Duty Officer, Captain Franklin asked, "What's going on here, Mr. Slaughter?"

As I explained the situation, the Captain's face reddened. He turned to the messenger and ordered, "Go fetch the Paymaster. Tell him to report to me here and now."

The Paymaster, Ensign Hardy, was an assistant to the ship's Supply Officer and had responsibility for paying the crew in cash every payday. His safe was chock full of currency, enough to cover the payroll for the entire six-month cruise. When he joined us, the Captain quickly reviewed the situation and suggested that some of the payroll cash be used for a short-term loan. When the Paymaster firmly refused, the Captain asked, "Well, what do you suggest we do to get this show on the road?"

The Paymaster screwed up his face and rubbed his chin. Then he broke into a smile. "Captain, how would you like a sizeable chunk of advance pay?"

The Captain grinned. "You bet. How much do we need, Mr. Slaughter?"

Within ten minutes, the bus was loaded. As the driver stepped on the gas, a loud cheer erupted from the excited group. They began a rousing chorus of *For he's a jolly good fellow. For he's a jolly good fellow! For he's a jolly ...* The song faded as the bus sped northward toward the Amalfi Coast.

Before heading back to the Wardroom, the Captain told me, "When Mr. Regen returns to the ship, send him to me. In addition to a swift kick in the pants, he's going In Hack for a couple of weeks for this fiasco. Besides, he owes me a sizeable amount of money that now resides in his Welfare and Recreation safe." It was the prerogative of the Commanding Officer to put an officer In Hack, which meant being restricted to the ship and having no visitors during that time.

Mr. Regen returned later that morning. When I informed him what had happened, he slapped his forehead and uttered a short swear word. "How will I get word to my wife? Tonight's Christmas Eve! What an idiot mistake on my part."

I assured Mr. Regen that I would inform his wife of the situation and keep her company over Christmas. He thanked me profusely. That was how I came to spend my Christmas Day in Naples with Jennifer Regen. After we played Scrabble for about five hours, we celebrated by going to a wonderful Italian restaurant for a delicious Christmas dinner.

Dinner Roll Blues

USS Blandy – Naples, Italy to Lisbon, Portugal
January 1966

The *Blandy* crew spent the Christmas and New Year's holidays in Naples, Italy. However, the anticipated, festive season was marred by two incidents that caused the Wardroom morale to plummet to a depth that I had never witnessed before in all my days aboard ship. The nominal cause for pessimism stemmed from the cases of the two officers who were put In Hack for ten days each by Captain Franklin, owing to what I judged to be their incompetence and inattention to detail. Not only was Mr. Regen, the Welfare and Recreation Officer, put In Hack, but Mr. Jenkins, the Supply Officer, was too. His offense was the apparent mismanagement of the Wardroom Mess funds. When the discrepancy was discovered, the Captain pondered whether or not to convene a Court Martial for this case of malfeasance. He settled for the lesser punishment of In Hack.

Being In Hack was tough enough for these two officers. Making matters worse, their wives had flown from the states to spend the holidays with their husbands in Naples. In addition, the two guilty officers were forced to endure the wrath of two very unhappy spouses.

My fellow department heads and their division officers openly characterized the Captain as incorrect, incompetent, or vindictive. I was perhaps the only officer in the Wardroom who did not agree. I tolerated no complaining or resistance to the Captain's management style from the three officers who reported to me, and when the other department heads tried to convince me of their assessment of the new Captain, I refused to side with them. In fact, I thought it was an insulting, insubordinate, and downright disrespectful way to treat the Commanding Officer, and I made no bones about letting others know how I felt.

The Captain and I shared a level of trust that was unusual, especially so relatively early in our relationship. Of course, I think it is fair to say that I was a dependable and competent Engineering Officer. Moreover, because of my having served for several years as the lead Officer of the Deck (OOD) on the bridge of two destroyers, the Captain placed his trust in my capabilities. Instead of having me in Main Control in the forward engine room for situations involving performing challenging ship maneuvers, the Captain preferred that I be on the bridge and in charge as OOD. He assumed me to be the best choice for OOD for the Sea and Anchor Detail, taking the ship into and out of port.

The same was true for Condition 1ASW. I had a knack for seeing a submerged target in my mind and could act quickly to maneuver the ship into position to sink the target. I was also highly skilled in operating in team-like fashion with the other members of our ASW task force when conducting integrated attacks of sea and air assets against a submarine, designated as the *enemy* during an exercise.

In short, because I possessed a superior level of ability, the Captain preferred to have me in control of an exercise rather than himself or any other officer aboard *Blandy*. I was proud to have his confidence, and I was quite certain that, given my skills as OOD in every situation, I would never let him down. If I am candid, I have to admit that I didn't envy the Captain's position. He had never commanded a destroyer before and given the full capability, complexity, and power of the *Blandy*, I didn't blame him for depending on me.

My relationship with Captain Franklin and his wife Nancy was solidified when I accepted an invitation to join them for delightful New Year's Eve dinner at *La Cava*, a wonderful restaurant they had previously discovered. After a relaxed and enjoyable evening, we returned to their hotel room, where we toasted in the New Year with a bottle of mellow Italian brandy. At dawn, I walked back to the ship through streets covered with six to eight inches of firecracker-paper as well as appliances, furniture, and clothing no longer needed, which, according to Naples' New Year's tradition, were thrown out of apartment windows overlooking the street below. I managed to weave my way through the rubble back to the ship.

A couple of days later, we got underway for our next port of call, Lisbon, Portugal. We needed a bit of time at sea for tensions to cool down and an attractive new port to look forward to visiting. To take our minds off the pervasive conflict that had plagued us in Naples, the Gunnery Department Head (Gun Boss) and I decided that the crew would spend its transit time competing in a ship-wide tournament of games.

We offered four games for the competition. First, pinochle, a card game preferred by the Chief Petty Officers. Second, checkers, favored by almost everyone. Third, gin rummy, an acquired taste of many sailors. Last, team Scrabble, a favorite game among members of the Wardroom. (The Gun Boss and I were the reigning Scrabble champions.)

The Welfare and Recreation Fund would supply a prize of $50 to each winning team. The tournament ran for three full days, the length of our transit to Lisbon. On the last day, the winners were announced. I have forgotten the others, but as expected, my partner and I won the Scrabble championship going away.

The morning we were scheduled to land in Lisbon, I suggested to Captain Franklin that we employ the services of a harbor pilot. The Tagus River, which flowed with savage fury alongside the pier, was beyond even my considerable landing skills. The Captain took my advice and radioed the Pilot Boat. Before long, the boat pulled alongside, and a dapper young pilot quickly hopped aboard *Blandy*. He spritely mounted the ladder to the bridge and greeted the Captain and me. Then he immediately relieved me of the *Conn* and took full control of the ship. I must say he did a masterful job of bringing us alongside the pier, despite heavy competition from the roaring Tagus River.

After we were tied up at the pier, the crew was immediately given liberty to explore Lisbon or to take advantage of the tours lined up in advance by the Welfare and Recreation Officer, who'd plenty of time to work on this project during his ten days In Hack.

I was eager to go ashore to explore and was unexpectedly joined by Sam Jenkins, the Supply Officer. Sam told me that he respected me for being the only officer in the Wardroom who hadn't criticized him for mishandling the mess funds. I assured him that I didn't think he had intended to do anything unethical, let alone criminal. He seemed pleased by my vote of confidence and asked me to accompany him on a tour to the Shrine of Fatima.

When we arrived at the shrine, Sam and I surveyed the area from the Shrine's long, wide porch. I had just bought a new 35mm slide camera and was eager to try it out. I suggested that I take a picture of Sam looking out onto the open field in front of us. He turned to give me a profile shot. Days later, when the slides were developed, I realized that I had failed to take into account a large flagpole leaning out over the lip of the porch. Unfortunately the flag pole was positioned right behind Sam, and in a way that made it appear to be protruding out of the front of his fly. I was mortified that he would think I had framed this shot on purpose, but we both laughed at it later.

We returned to the ship just in time for dinner. Sam boasted about his special menu for our first night in Lisbon. The main course was a mild whitefish that had been lightly sautéed with fresh butter and powdered with some indescribably delicious seasoning. Then there were baskets of goose-egg size, melt-in-your-mouth dinner rolls that were the best that any of us had ever tasted.

"These are made from a secret recipe of a famous Portuguese baker," Sam proudly claimed.

Apparently, he had acquired enough of these mouth-watering rolls to treat every crewmember with two or three at each meal. Compliment after compliment came his way about this Lisbon delicacy.

Our time in Lisbon flew by with side trips here and there. We even went to an exciting bullfight. Since it was my first, I took about a hundred slides. (What was I thinking?) When it was finally time to depart, the entire crew begged the Supply Officer to stock up on the exquisite Lisbon rolls to tickle our taste buds as we headed back to Naples. To retain his reestablished reputation, he ordered ten gross of the acclaimed rolls.

The next day a huge bakery truck pulled up at the ship and unloaded bale after bale of the tasty Portuguese treat. That afternoon we got underway. The next day, we were served the infamous rolls with our meals, but this batch lacked the same intense flavor that we had previously savored. The next day, we gave our friendly rolls one more chance, but by the second day out of Lisbon, every last roll had turned to stone. You couldn't even pierce its light-brown outer layer with a steak knife. Instead of ten gross of tasty delights, we were encumbered with 9.8 gross of cobblestones.

After a somber breakfast, I accompanied poor Sam to the fantail, where his cooks and bakers dumped the hardened rolls into the blue Mediterranean. When every last dinner roll was bobbing merrily in our wake, Sam turned to me and implored, "Why me?"

Blandy Boiler Explosion

USS Blandy – Marseilles, France
January 1966

When I reported to the *USS Blandy* in 1964, Lieutenant Braxton was an officer on the staff of Destroyer Squadron 28. In theory, he was also an expert on naval engineering. Since *Blandy* was a *Forrest Sherman*-class destroyer, she was the largest ship in the squadron and the squadron flagship. The Squadron Commander and his staff, including Braxton, called *Blandy* home.

Commander George Grove, *Blandy's* Commanding Officer, did not suffer fools lightly. Before I reported aboard, Braxton had evidently proved himself to be just that in the eyes of Captain Grove. To keep Braxton from meddling in the engineering affairs of *Blandy*, Captain Grove forbade him to set foot in the *Blandy's* engineering spaces, including both engine rooms and both firerooms. Needless to say, Braxton was not pleased. And he was not happy that I *was* delighted not to have to contend with his meddling.

After we entered the shipyard for our regular overhaul, the Commodore and his staff moved from *Blandy* to another ship in the squadron. (That pleased both Grove and Braxton alike.) Captain Grove had one priority for this overhaul. He wanted major work done on the *Blandy's* extremely unreliable 1200 psi boilers. *Blandy* had set a fleet record for Casualty Reports (*CasReps*) on boilers, and Grove wanted this to stop. A CasRep was submitted when we had a critical piece of equipment out of commission. An inoperative boiler required that a CasRep be sent to the Commander-in-Chief US Atlantic Fleet with copies to every command between him and us.

During my 18 months on Blandy, we had filed 19 CasReps involving our boilers, more than half of which were filed after our overhaul in the Boston Naval Shipyard. In other words, the boiler problem was not solved during the over-haul as the Captain had demanded. As previously stated,

Captain Grove and I blamed the shipyard liaison officer, Warrant Officer Reading. The Captain had Reading relieved of his duties and followed up with a letter calling Reading a fake and imposter, or words to that effect, and copied his superiors and peers far and wide to warn them about this charlatan.

Needless to say, Reading was steaming mad with Grove and with the ship's Repair Officer and Chief Engineer, me. Before Reading left, he called me a *stoolpigeon.* And he was absolutely right. As Repair Officer, I was responsible for managing our overhaul. Part of my responsibility was to update the Captain on our progress. Every time Reading failed to do his job, especially with respect to our boilers, I informed Captain Grove. No doubt about it, Reading deserved to be relieved of his duties.

In July 1965, Captain Grove left *Blandy* for a position on the staff of ComCruDesLant in Norfolk. He was relieved by Commander I. Nelson Franklin, a true gentleman, who became a good friend during our time together on *Blandy* as well as after we both left the Navy.

Initially Captain Franklin wasn't as obsessed with fixing our boiler problems as Captain Grove had been. Regardless, as Chief Engineer, I continued to fight the battle of the boilers with my usual passion, mostly to no avail.

In early 1966, we were in the Mediterranean, operating as a component of the Sixth Fleet. On January 27, we departed from Marseilles to head back to Naples. We still had the Sea and Anchor Detail set, which meant that I was on the bridge as the Officer of the Deck. We were about to secure from the Sea and Anchor Detail and set the normal watch when white *steam* began to billow from the after smokestack, and suddenly the ship lost all power. We began gradually slowing to a stop. Obviously, something was terribly wrong in my engineering spaces.

Captain Franklin relieved me of the Conn, and I ran from the bridge to the hatch leading to the after fireroom. Superheated steam was still pouring out of the hatch. I dashed to my nearby stateroom, changed into my coveralls, grabbed a pair of gloves, and ran back to the main passageway.

As I passed sickbay, I saw that Manning, one of the men who had been on watch in the after fireroom, was badly burned. It was a sickening sight. His flesh was quite literally boiled and hanging from his bones. I wished him well, continued to the after fireroom, and descended the ladder. Even with the protection of gloves, my hands were burned. What I saw was a disaster. The after boiler had blown wide open, and its components were crushed against the after bulkhead of the fireroom. The forward boiler appeared to be intact, but its fires were no longer burning.

I returned to sickbay to ascertain the condition of my men. Two from the after fireroom, Manning and Mastripolito, were badly burned. A laundryman, who had happened to be in the passageway near the fireroom hatch, was also burned badly but not as severely. Several others had minor burns that had already been treated.

We were steaming with the aircraft carrier, the *USS America* (CVA 66), which dispatched a helicopter with medical personnel, who prepared the three critically injured men for removal from *Blandy* and subsequent transport to a hospital ashore. Sadly, Manning and Mastripolito died before they reached the hospital. The laundryman survived.

The other men on watch had not been burned as badly as the two men who died. Unlike the two dead men who ran up the ladder with the escaping steam, the more experienced Boilermen knew to dive into the bilges, avoiding the escaping steam.

We'd had the forward fireroom shut down in order to allow us to clean the firesides, which required periodic removal of soot and other deposits that built up on the boiler tubes and brickwork inside the furnace of the boiler. This was a long overdue routine, which we undertook in Marseilles but did not complete before the ship got underway. When the firesides were clean, the forward boilers were lighted, and we headed for Malta, where a British shipyard was located.

Two of our tenders, repair ships, were also located there, the *USS Cadmus* (AR14) and the *USS Everglades* (AD24). They would attempt to repair Boiler #2a. Boiler #2b was deemed to be beyond repair. Special technical assistance, including an engineer and a chemist from the Naval Boiler and Tube Laboratory (NBTL) in Philadelphia, were flown to Malta to oversee the repairs. All repair equipment and replacement tubes were air-freighted to Malta as well.

Meanwhile, Boards of Inquiry had been convened to make recommendations to Admiral Rucker, the Type Commander (ComCruDesLant), and to Admiral Moorer, the Commander-in-Chief of the Atlantic Fleet (CincLantFlt). The Inquiry Board at ComCruDesLant included technical members, Warrant Officer Reading and Lieutenant Braxton, avowed enemies of both Captain Grove and me. Greatly influenced by its technical members, the Board strongly recommended that Captain Franklin, the current *Blandy* Commanding Officer, receive a Letter of Instruction, a non-judicial instrument that theoretically meant to instruct an *ignorant person*. This letter was not placed in the recipient's personnel file.

The technical members also strongly recommended that I receive a Letter of Reprimand, a judicial punishment that does go into your personnel file. Unless the Letter of Reprimand is appealed and overturned, your Navy career is over.

Captain Grove, who now was on the ComCruDesLant staff, was familiar with the situation on *Blandy*. Moreover, he proved to be a great admirer of mine, as you shall see from his rebuttal to the recommendations of the technical members of the Board.

The following are selected excerpts from Captain Grove's five-page letter to Admiral Rucker, the Type Commander of CruDesLant.

> *I feel very strongly that our proposed action in the case of the Chief Engineer is ill-advised. There are so many reasons that it is hard to list them in an orderly manner.*
>
> *I wrote numerous letters to the Force Personnel Officer and visited him frequently on the subject of our Boilerman (BT) shortages and on their skills, knowledge, and experience. Here is a brief description of the situation:*

1. *A shortage of BTs qualified in 1200 psi steam plants. There are only two aboard* Blandy.
2. *Large loss of BTs due to normal attrition aggravated by change of homeport and abnormally high stress levels during Refresher Training at Guantanamo Bay.*

If we want to do the unusual, we had to have unusually well-qualified people to do it. Despite the personnel shortages, the Chief Engineer recommended and I concurred that four of the Chief Engineer's petty officers be restricted from standing watch because they are a danger to the ship.

Even under these conditions, the highest grades in Refresher Training in Gitmo were in Engineering. In our Admin and Material Inspection in late FY65, Engineering received grades of EXCELLENT. In fact, two weeks before the casualty, the Engineering Department received a mark of 96.6 in the annual Admin Inspection, the highest marks received on the ship.

Lieutenant Slaughter is a good Chief Engineer. His record before, during, and after Destroyer School on Blandy *was such that he was recommended for post-graduate training, was considered for an Aide's position and for duty on our (CruDesLant) staff. He was and is a career officer of high potential.*

We propose to reprimand an officer for the insufficient training of his men and unauthorized set up of his plant when this plant had been set up similarly and safely many times before and when he had done everything possible to train what men he had, remove those who could not be trained, and asked repeatedly for more men!

Isn't it tragic that as a result of the casualty a Senior Chief BT and a Master Chief BT reported aboard two and six weeks thereafter. Must our distribution inequities be corrected in this manner?

Lieutenant Slaughter should be completely exonerated from responsibility for this accident. In view of this memo, should consideration be given to Letter of Instruction, my objections would be the same. What instruction could be given him?

1. *Train your men - He has trained them. All written reports and inspections indicate he had.*
2. *Administer your Department properly - No mark lower than Excellent in a year prior to the accident.*
3. *Insure qualification of your watch standers - He had removed the incompetent from the watch list.*
4. *Insure adequate personnel to safely run the plant - He had repeatedly requested additional personnel. They arrived later as a direct result of the death of two men.*

Finally the responsibility lies on the shoulders of the Commanding Officer where the ultimate responsibility always lies. Specifically, he must have exerted tremendous pressure on the Chief Engineer to reverse a position he had held for over six months under my command and put unqualified people on watch. The CO could have personally ordered that it be done in contravention to the clear and unmistakable and documented evidence that these same personnel were incompetent.

Captain Grove was obviously trying to ensure that my career was not injured by this unfortunate tragedy. If I had discussed this letter with him before he wrote it, I might have added a few items to help him make his point even more forcefully:

1. My lead BT was a First Class Petty Officer who had never been on a ship propelled by steam until he reported to *Blandy* three years before the casualty.
2. Manning, one of the dead men, had never been in a fireroom before *Blandy*. He had been a Steward's Mate and had spent the three years before *Blandy* in charge of a golf course at Lakehurst.
3. He was correct in his assumption that Captain Franklin forced me to put the four men, including Manning, back on watch, despite my insistence that they were dangerous and could not handle the plant.

Now all we could do was wait to see what action the Boards recommended and what the Admirals in charge would decide to accept or reject. Still we had a tremendous amount of work to do, and I didn't have time to worry about what would be decided. For the next 30 days, I worked no fewer than 20 hours a day overseeing the repairs on Boiler #2a. Even with the able assistance of the two technicians from NBTL, I felt it was my responsibility to oversee the repairs. These men worked in ten-hour shifts. My shifts averaged twice that long. It was a terribly stressful experience. Thankfully the Chief Hospital Corpsman was willing to provide me with some magical pills to help me sustain this pace. By the time I returned home, I had lost over 30 pounds and none of my uniforms fit.

Wrist Alarm

Board of Inspection and Survey – Arlington, Virginia
Summer 1966

When I was in the Navy, officers' salaries were very low. As a newly commissioned Ensign my base pay was $222.30 per month plus a Basic Allowance for Subsistence (BAS) of $47.50. I left the Navy as a full Lieutenant with seven years of service, yet my salary had never reached five figures. During the first five of those seven years, I attended naval schools or served on Navy ships where I never needed civilian office attire. While I wore only naval uniforms, I had to pay for them personally.

I spent my last two years in Washington, DC serving as Aide and Office Administrator to the President of the Navy Board of Inspection and Survey, headquartered in the Navy Annex to the Pentagon. As an Admiral's Aide, I assumed I would be required to wear naval uniforms, which was not the case in Washington. There were so many military personnel stationed there that, if they all wore uniforms, visitors would think America was a military dictatorship.

Clothing-wise, I was totally unprepared for Washington. When I arrived, my formal civilian office attire consisted of one plaid madras sport coat, a pair of tan slacks, and an olive drab cord suit that I had purchased in college some seven years earlier. This suit was so old that the cords on the right knee had worn away, revealing the white lining inside.

On the day I reported for duty, Rear Admiral Harry L. Reiter, Jr., my new boss, was traveling and due back the next day. Rose, the Admiral's secretary, informed me that he loved to travel, and inspecting Navy ships all over the world gave him his chance. Captain Woodard, the Admiral's deputy, also preferred traveling and inspecting to sitting behind his desk in the office. Thus my job was to manage the Board of Inspection and Survey in the absence of the Admiral and his deputy. Rose also informed me that military personnel in the organization wore civilian clothing at the office, news that hit me right in the wallet. All I could think of was my ratty cord suit. Then she delivered more bad news. Admiral Reiter and his wife would like Susan and me to pay our obligatory social call on them at 5:00 pm the following day, which was a Friday.

As a newly reporting naval officer, I and my wife were expected to pay a formal social call on my new commanding officer and his wife at their home. In theory, although not always in practice, the social call was to last 15 to 20 minutes. On our departure, Susan and I were expected to place the correct number of calling cards in a silver tray located on a hall table near the front door. We both carried engraved social cards formatted in the official naval manner. By protocol, I was to leave one card each for the Admiral and his wife. If there were another lady in the house over 18 years old, I would leave another card for her. However, I was not to leave more than three cards in total. My wife was to leave a card for the Admiral's wife and for another lady in the house over 18 years old, but no card for the Admiral.

Friday evening, I wore my old cord suit. As we sat in a circle of chairs, chatting, I rested my right hand on my knee and I held a saucer and a cup of coffee with my left hand. When I took a sip of coffee, I rested the saucer on my right knee and lifted the cup with my right hand. I don't know whether I succeeded at concealing my secret or not. I never asked.

That evening, I called Mr. Rowsey, my former department head on *Cony*, who now worked at the Navy Bureau of Personnel whose offices were also in the Navy Annex. I told him about my civilian-clothing crisis.

Mr. Rowsey instantly provided the solution. "Tomorrow morning, hop in your car and drive to T.I. Swartz and Sons in Baltimore. They tailor men's suits to order and sell them at wholesale prices. You can't beat the quality or the price. Buy at least four suits. You'll need 'em." I heard him put down the phone to retrieve the address. When he picked up again, he said, "Their warehouse's located at the corner of South Pulaski and Eager Streets in downtown Baltimore." He gave me the directions and then assured me, "When you get to Baltimore, everybody knows where Swartz is located. Ask anybody for directions. Arrive before 10:00 am. They'll alter the suits for you so you can take them home with you in the early afternoon."

Mr. Rowsey was right on all counts. By six o'clock on Saturday evening, Susan and I were back home in Arlington with four fine suits, perfectly tailored. The cost was just under $150, which we paid for in traveler's checks that we had purchased for an emergency, which this certainly was.

The following Monday, Admiral Reiter and I met to review what he expected of me. He emphasized how much he'd count on me during his and his deputy's absences. He was candid about the failure of my predecessor to assume this level of responsibility. I didn't take his words as a threat by any means but understood that he was imploring me to run the organization effectively.

"We have Sub-Boards – offices – in every major naval base in America, including Hawaii. The officers who manage the Sub-Boards are all four-stripers who are experienced and competent or they wouldn't be in their jobs. However, you're going to know many things they won't know, simply because you'll be my liaison with every major naval command in this city. In my absence, they'll depend on you to answer their questions.

"Furthermore, you'll oversee the preparation of the final reports of our findings from Acceptance Trials for new ships and aircraft and from periodic Materiel Inspections for the same. You'll learn the difference between deficiencies that are critical and must be remedied immediately and those that we safely grant waivers for a time. You'll get calls from fleet and type commanders who'll try to intimidate you into granting waivers that shouldn't be granted. Not only will you have to know the difference, you'll need the backbone to say no to those requests. Or perhaps I should say demands."

I began to feel the weight of my new job on my shoulders. "That sounds like a lot of responsibility, Admiral. I hope I can live up to your expectations."

"Gary, let me be candid. I checked your qualifications for this job very thoroughly. All of the people who know you and have worked with you convinced me that you are more than qualified for this job. As a matter of fact, given the positions you've held and the schooling you've had in your short time in this man's Navy, you'd make a darned good inspector for this Main Board – an inspector of communications, electronics, boilers, or anything having to do with being a fine OOD. Am I right?"

I was both flattered and proud. "Well, Admiral," I began. Just then my wrist-watch alarm sounded with a loud buzz.

"What was that?" the startled Admiral yelped. "Did you do that to avoid answering my question?" Then he laughed.

"No, Sir. It was to remind me that I have a conference call at 9:30 with a number of people at the Bureau of Ships. But I'll answer your question before they call. I'm confident that I won't let you down."

"I knew you'd say that. Thank you. When you're finished with your call, I'd like to talk to you about something else."

"Yes, Sir."

When I finished the conference call, I returned to the Admiral's office.

"Gary, I want to mention two things. First, your job, as we discussed earlier, will not give you time to perform the tasks that are normally demanded of an Admiral's Aide. When you are with me in the office or out, I will not refer to you as my Aide. My assistant perhaps, but not my Aide. If you bought an epaulette for your shoulder, have the uniform store refund your money. Understood?"

"Yes, Sir. Yes, Sir, indeed!" I replied with a broad grin.

"The second item is this. I have a meeting at the Pentagon in an hour. I have a car coming to pick me up at 10:30. I'd like to try something using that wrist alarm of yours."

When we arrived at the Pentagon, the Admiral turned to me and asked, "Can you set that alarm to go off at 11:45?"

I nodded and reset my wrist alarm.

The meeting started late and dragged on and on. I could see why the Admiral wanted an excuse to escape. At precisely

11:45, my alarm sounded. Everyone in the room stared at me as though I'd fired a gun.

The Admiral asked, "Mr. Slaughter, do we have to depart?"

"Yes, Sir. We'll just make it back in time for our lunch meeting."

When we arrived back at the Navy Annex, the Admiral winked at me. "We can't miss that lunch meeting." Heading for the cafeteria, he added, "This lunch is on me."

Sports and the Navy

Board of Inspection and Survey – Arlington, Virginia
Fall 1966

The Board of Inspection and Survey's offices were in the Navy Annex of the Pentagon in Arlington, Virginia. The Annex was also home to the Bureau of Naval Personnel and to the Commandant of the United States Marine Corps. Because the Annex was located on a hill and miles from the Pentagon, the Navy and the Marine Corps had built recreational facilities on the property for the benefit of the personnel stationed there. These facilities included a swimming pool and an outdoor volleyball court, as well as a gymnasium with a basketball court, weight-lifting area, and exercise equipment. The gymnasium also included a large locker room to enable those working at the Annex to change from office attire into athletic clothing. In addition, there was a small Navy Exchange that carried a limited inventory of groceries and household supplies.

When Admiral Reiter was not traveling on inspection trips, he and I ate lunch together in the Navy Annex cafeteria. However, since the Admiral traveled most of the time, I spent my lunch hour in the gymnasium. Each day as I walked down the hill to the gym, I passed the volleyball court, where a dozen or so men were playing aggressive but skilled volleyball.

On one occasion after my workout, I was dressing in the locker room when the volleyball players entered. After a quick shower, one of them sat down next to me. "I notice that you work out by yourself," he said. "Would you be interested in playing volleyball? We can always use another player."

To be honest, I had never thought about joining them. Because they wore uniforms before and after their games, I knew they were all Marine Warrant Officers. Since I hardly ever wore my uniform to the office, they had no reason to know that I was a Navy Lieutenant and, as such, superior in rank to them. So I hid my identity as an officer to join their volleyball team.

"I've not played much volleyball," I admitted, "and what I have played has been kid's stuff compared to your level of play. But if you indulge me until I get the hang of it, I'd like to join you. The way you fellows play, I'm sure it would be a good workout as well."

"Great! We try to start about 11:15 and go for about an hour or a little less. That's Monday through Friday." Then as an afterthought, he said, "My name's Joe."

"Mine's Gary," I said shaking his hand.

Without exception, the volleyball players were welcoming and encouraging, especially in the beginning when I muffed more than my share of plays. Their number of players differed each day, ranging from 13 down to eight or so, and they rotated team captains so that each day the new captains chose members for their teams. In about a month, my game was in shape, and the captains started selecting me over some of the other regulars, which made me feel good. I also learned that they did not consider weather as a relevant variable. I began playing with them in September 1966 and played until my resignation from the Navy in August 1967, and all that time, we never missed a game, regardless of rain, ice, or snow.

On my last day, my teammates presented me with a going-away present, a brand-new volleyball addressed to *Lieutenant Gary Slaughter, USN.* They all signed their names and ranks. Without exception, each was a Warrant Officer. I wondered how long they had known my rank. On the other hand, it had made no difference to me or to them, and I hated saying good-bye.

Ever since I can remember, I've been a sports enthusiast, both as a fan and as a player. When I entered the Navy, that enthusiasm continued unabated. My hometown of Owosso, Michigan was located close to two major cities, Flint and Lansing, where It was difficult not to be a fan and player of softball. Flint had a professional softball team that always ranked near the top of its league. Because of Owosso's city-wide interest in softball, the recreation department built Bennett Field, a superb softball facility close to my home on the west side of town. During the summers, we grade-schoolers were organized into leagues according to age. Physical education teachers from the Owosso school system spent their summers officiating our games which were played during the day at Bennett Field. In addition, there were two adult leagues, one comprising teams sponsored by the city's churches and the other sponsored by the city's businesses. These games were played in the evenings at Bennett Field and were well attended by Owosso softball fans.

When I first picked up a bat and attempted to hit the ball, I wasn't very successful. Like every other right-handed kid I knew, I was a right-handed batter. However, a knowledgeable neighbor, after observing my swing, advised, "Gary, you're batting cross-handed. You've got a good swing there. Here, try doing it this way. Keep your hands on the bat just as they are now." He took me by the shoulders and turned me around so I was swinging the bat as a left-handed batter. I hit the next pitch out of the ballpark, so to speak. From that day forward, I batted left-handed and my batting average soared. Thank you, Mr. Delcamp.

From the time I was in fifth grade until I left for the Navy, I was always a permanent member of at least one softball team, either in Owosso or at Michigan. During the summer months, between midshipman cruises and college, I continued to play softball. After I was commissioned and home on leave, I was invited to play for my old church-league team. Since I had a knack for throwing strikes, I was always the pitcher. During my midshipman years at Michigan, I also pitched for SAE's winning softball team.

Then there was football. East Lansing was the home of Michigan State College and the Spartans football team. Who can forget Don McAuliffe, the captain and star halfback on MSC's 1952 consensus national championship team? And I'll never forget the colorful MSC football coach, Biggie Munn. On leave in 1965, I visited some friends who lived in Sarasota, Florida. For lunch one day, we went to a restaurant on Sarasota's main street. The owner had covered the huge glass entrance door with a life-sized poster of Don McAuliffe dressed in his green and white Spartan uniform. The interior of the restaurant had also been decorated with those same school colors. By then, of course, the school's name had changed to Michigan State University.

We started early in Owosso as Spartan fans. Our Boy Scout troops were assigned as ushers in Spartan Stadium. We sat on the end of each row of bleachers and did not always have the best views. Near the end of the season, when the winter winds swept through the stadium, we loyally manned our posts, even if the fans with seats in our section were home by the fire. It was a bone-chilling and rather lonely experience.

During my Boy Scout years, I also played tackle football in 7th and 8th grades at Central School. We had two teams, the Light Weights and the Heavy Weights. I was on the Heavy Weights, because I had yet to shed my baby fat. Even though on sandlot football I played quarterback, my junior-high coach thought I would make a better guard. While I was insulted, I accepted the assignment, because I wanted to be on the team.

SAE Championship Touch Football Team (1960)

Over the course of my 11 years as a midshipman and commissioned officer, I still managed to find time to play on a dozen or more softball and touch-football teams. My proudest football experience took place during my NROTC midshipman years, when I played on the *Sigma Alpha Epsilon* (SAE) touch-football team. Normally, I would have played quarterback, but Jack Moak, the captain and star pitcher of Michigan's varsity baseball team, had a far better arm than I. Instead I played wide receiver and, believe it or not, defensive end. I was quick enough to evade the heavy-weight blocking backs and tag the opposing quarterback with ease. During those years, our team won an astounding four consecutive championships of the Michigan Interfraternity Touch-Football League, comprising the 43 fraternities at Michigan. That record has never been broken.

Recently, to reacquaint myself with the rules of touch football, I visited the website of the Recreational Sports Department at Michigan. There I discovered a document that laid down the rules for Flag Football. Apparently touch football has been retired because it involves physical contact between players. The Flag Football Rulebook comprises 17 pages of detailed *Do's and Don'ts*. Just the presence of such a document makes me happy to have been in college several decades ago and not today. What a sign of the times.

Back then, during each academic year, the Michigan Interfraternity Council ranked its 43 members on their success rates and participation percentages in about two dozen categories, most of which were athletic in nature. SAE was named top fraternity in the system all four years that I was an SAE member.

While I was at Michigan, I played quarterback on two other teams. The first was for Winchell House, my dormitory during my first year at Michigan. I also played quarterback on the NROTC touch-football team for four years as well. We only had two opponents in that league, the Army and Air Force ROTC teams, and we played each of them twice during the season. We never had a losing record, because we could always count on winning both Air Force games and at least one of two Army games.

In addition, I am very proud to say that for a few days, I was almost a Wolverine on the University of Michigan's varsity football team. It happened by pure luck. Winchell House, where I lived during my freshman year, was called a *jock house*, because a great proportion of the Winchell House residents attended Michigan on athletic scholarships. On our floor of about 35 students, there were at least 15 scholarship-holders in various sports. One of them, John Zanglin, became a good friend. Not only did we enjoy each other's company, we also loved to toss a football to each other, challenging one another to catch the ball on the run. John, a Michigan running back, claimed that our sessions allowed him to sharpen his catching skills. Although John was clearly a gifted football player, he wasn't a huge fellow. In fact, he was about 5'6" and weighed less than 160 pounds. Like me, he was a fast and evasive runner.

One day after our football tossing session, John said, "Gary, you're as good a football player as I am, and I won a Michigan football scholarship. I think you should try out for the team, too." I was shocked. He continued, "I've talked to my running-back coach about how good you are. He's agreed to give you a tryout tomorrow after classes. Is that okay with you?"

My mind was a blur, but I agreed to meet him at the football practice field at 4:00 pm the next day.

"Just wear what you normally wear when you're playing touch football, and don't forget your spikes."

The next day, John observed my tryout and felt that I had done very well. The coach told him that I was a good prospect and that he would make his decision in a few days.

The following week, John and I continued our daily sessions, and I didn't ask about the coach's decision. Finally, one evening after his practice, with obvious trepidation, John confessed that the coach had decided not to ask me to join the team, but he felt that I could make it at a smaller college. I reminded John that I was at Michigan on a NROTC scholarship.

John said, "Well, some guys choose the Navy and other guys choose football." How could I disagree?

On our 3rd Class Midshipman Cruise on the *Valley Forge*, one of the Missouri midshipmen who shared our compartment was John Upthegrove. While he and I were not particularly close during that cruise, we became friends when we were both stationed at Great Lakes. While I was attending the Electronics Officers School, he was an outpatient at the Great Lakes Naval Hospital.

John had chosen the naval aviation option after his commissioning in June of 1961. While in basic training, a physical examination had revealed a minor medical problem related to his heart. He never told me what it was. Apparently, his outpatient status allowed doctors to observe him over a period of time before releasing him to return to flight training. But he was not restricted from any form of physical activity at Great Lakes. (Incidentally, years later, we saw each other again. He was wearing the wings of a naval aviator.)

When John and I were leaving the Officers Mess one evening, we observed an enormous swath of light in the clouds not far away. We went to see what caused it and discovered that the light was created by four brightly lighted football fields, where eight teams were playing flag football. We learned from a spectator that the teams were made up of naval enlisted men stationed at Great Lakes and that many of the teams needed players.

On our way back to the BOQ, I confided in John that September always brought out a desire to play football. John admitted that he suffered from the same affliction. While John and I had both played a lot of touch football, neither of us had played flag football. Still we plotted a way to join one of the teams.

The next week, dressed in our midshipman dungarees and plain tee shirts, John and I returned to the football field, pretending to be enlisted men. After we ran through a brief set of drills, we were recruited by one of the better teams. We played once a week for the next six weeks, and during that period I learned two things. First, John Upthegrove was one hell of a football player. Second, Great Lakes flag football was one tough sport. If you were carrying the ball, it was not unusual to be roughly knocked to the ground before your opponent yanked the flag from your belt. However, it was football, and we loved it.

When I served as Chief Engineer on the *USS Blandy*, I was the pitcher for our ship's destroyer squadron championship softball team. Oddly enough, there were four officers on that team, and two of them worked for me. My Main Propulsion Assistant was my catcher, and my Damage Control Assistant played first base. Our short stop was Captain George Grove, *Blandy's* Commanding Officer. Even in his early forties, he was a topnotch infielder and a good hitter.

Incidentally, during that championship season, my batting average was .666, the league's highest. Over the years, I continued to play softball whenever I had the opportunity, but that *Blandy* season was the jewel in my softball crown!

The Admirals' Decisions

Board of Inspection and Survey – Arlington, Virginia
November 1966

Commander George Grove had been *Blandy's* Commanding Officer immediately before he was relieved by Commander I. Nelson Franklin. Grove sent a five-page letter regarding the *Blandy* boiler explosion to his Commanding Officer, Admiral Rucker, Commander Cruiser-Destroyer Force US Atlantic Fleet. The letter outlined the history of boiler maintenance and personnel issues (shortages) and, most important, the reasons why I should be exonerated from any and all accusations of incompetence in the case. The letter was dated November 5, 1966.

Admiral Rucker, ignoring Grove's advice, wrote a *Letter of Instruction* to me on November 23, 1966. Because of its nature, technically nothing went into my record to impede my further promotions and success as a Naval Officer.

Admiral Moorer, Commander-in-Chief US Atlantic Fleet, wrote a *Letter of Reprimand* to Commander I. Nelson Franklin. The *Letter* was dated April 6, 1967, over five months after my *Letter of Instruction*. Since the *Letter* was an official judicial punishment, it was appealable, so Franklin appealed and won. The *Letter of Reprimand* was set aside and cancelled by Admiral Moorer himself on June 16, 1967, and nothing went into Franklin's record.

Because my *Letter of Instruction* was not a judicial punishment, it was not appealable. Still I strenuously objected to its content. This was exactly what Captain Grove had advised Admiral Rucker to avoid. It did not instruct me how to improve my performance, because I was already doing everything that the letter said I should be doing. It appeared that Admiral Rucker hadn't bothered to read Captain Grove's letter or the testimony of witnesses from the *Cony*, including myself.

The day I received the *Letter of Instruction*, I wrote my letter resigning from the Navy. With this act, the Navy lost a highly valuable young naval officer in which American taxpayers had a huge investment in training and education. During my undergraduate four years at Michigan, I had attended more NROTC classroom instruction than any other subject. For 120 weeks (four years), I had attended five hours of NROTC training per week for a total of 600 hours, not counting the training I received during my three summer cruises. In all the courses I took during my undergraduate years, I spent approximately 1,800 hours in the classroom. That number is derived from multiplying 120 (four years) weeks by 15 class hours per week. NROTC training amounted to one-third of that number.

Over the course of my seven years of active duty, I had also received a great amount of training, including the following 40 hours per week training courses that I attended:

- US Naval Communications Officers Course (8 weeks)
- US Naval Electronics Officers Course (12 weeks)
- Electronic Countermeasures Officers School (1 week)
- Electronic Intelligence Officers School (1 week)
- AN/WLR-1 (Electronic Countermeasures Equipment) (1 week)
- ASW Air Controller School (3 weeks)
- Damage Control School (1 week)
- Crypto Operators School (2 weeks)
- US Naval Destroyer School (26 weeks)
- ASW Air Controller Refresher Course (1 week)
- Gunfire Support School (1 week)
- US Naval 1200 psi Boiler Inspection School (1 week)
- Maintenance Data Control Supervisors' School (1 week)

This total of 59 weeks at 40 hours per week equals 2,360 classroom hours. Adding the 600 hours of NROTC classroom hours, the grand total is 2,960 hours. Comparing this number to the 1,800 hours needed to earn a four-year college degree reveals how well-trained naval officers were in the late 1950's through 1967 when I was in the Navy.

I shared my letter of resignation with Admiral Reiter, for whom I had worked diligently for some time. "Gary, this is the Old Army Game. Things have changed radically in the Navy since I was your age. If you were my son, sadly, I would recommend you do exactly what you've done. Thank you for your service to our country and the Navy. Above all, thank you for serving me so capably and faithfully over these past two years."

My letter of resignation was dated November 22, 1966. However, there was one small problem. With the rapid build-up of forces in Vietnam, the Navy wasn't accepting resignations from Regular naval officers like me. It would take another ten months before my resignation was finally accepted.

Valetta, Malta

Board of Inspection and Survey – Valetta, Malta
Summer 1967

Malta is a stunning archipelago in the Mediterranean Sea south of Italy and east of Sardinia. Because of its strategic location and importance as a naval base, over the centuries Malta has been occupied by the Phoenicians, Romans, Moors, Normans, Sicilians, Spanish, French, and most recently the British. The British valued the Maltese Islands, because after the Suez Canal was completed, the islands were halfway between the British Isles and India. In 1814, Malta became a part of the British Empire and remained so until 1964 when Malta gained its independence. During World War II, Malta remained in British hands. Both the British forces and the Maltese people suffered heavy casualties from intense bombing by Nazi Germany. Though Germany was eager to occupy this valuable naval base, it was never able to defeat Malta.

Today the Republic of Malta is a part of the European Union, and its population is less than a half-million people. About 6,000 people lived in Valetta, the historical capital, located on the main island of Malta. Valetta has the distinction of being the southernmost capital in Europe and, in my opinion, is one of the most beautiful cities in the world. In addition, Valetta is one of the most desirable naval bases. Both British and American ships, conducting exercises in the Mediterranean, laid over in Valetta to replenish fuel and other supplies and to allow their crews to enjoy liberty in Valetta.

Having spent two long cruises in the Mediterranean, I can't remember exactly how many times I have visited Valetta. Still I do have vivid recollections of two visits there. One was extremely positive, and the other was just the opposite. The unpleasant experience was the 30 days I spent in the British shipyard in Valetta overseeing the replacement of the tubes in

Boiler #2a after the boiler explosion. The only brief respite for me was a softball game between the chiefs and officers from *Blandy* and the chiefs and officers from the *Cadmus*, the repair ship providing support during the boiler repairs. As usual, I pitched for *Blandy,* and we won by a score of 4 to 3.

The positive Valetta experience occurred when I was Aide to the President of the Board of Inspection and Survey (INSURV). My sole responsibility was to manage the INSURV headquarters in Arlington, which enabled Admiral Reiter to do what he enjoyed most, traveling around the world on inspection trips.

On one occasion, I scheduled an ambitious, six-week series of Material Inspections of about two dozen ships attached to the Sixth Fleet in the Mediterranean. These ships ranged in size from aircraft carriers to tugboats. Accomplishing these inspections required the expertise of each and every inspector on the Main INSURV Board, approximately 30 highly trained specialists plus Admiral Reiter himself. While inspections were scheduled in three Mediterranean ports, including Cannes, Naples, and Valetta, most inspections were conducted in Valetta. I had made the flight arrangements, and the board was scheduled to depart on the last Sunday in October 1966. But on Thursday evening, our only boiler inspector suffered an acute attack of appendicitis and was admitted to the Bethesda Naval Hospital for observation and possible surgery.

On Friday morning, I broke the bad news to Admiral Reiter. He immediately ordered me to find a qualified replacement. I went back to my desk pondering whom I could possibly call to obtain a last minute replacement. I made calls to my three best contacts in the Bureau of Ships and in the office of the Chief of Naval Operations. I struck out three times, and I didn't want to deliver more bad news to the Admiral. Then it occurred to me. I'm a Certified Fleet High-Pressure Boiler Inspector. Why not me?

When I suggested the idea to the Admiral, he nearly fainted. "Why hadn't I thought of that?" he lamented.

"I can help out in the communications and electronics areas as well," I suggested. "I bet the operations inspectors will be delighted to have some help."

The Admiral called the chief inspectors for Engineering and Operations to his office and introduced them to their new inspector, me. They were delighted that I was willing to help out on such short notice.

"There's just one more person who has to know about this. My wife."

Susan was more than supportive. She declared that she was proud of me for saving the day.

Without going in all the detail about the inspections, there was one memorable occasion on the trip. The Senior British Naval Officer in Malta invited Admiral Reiter to dinner at the British Officers Club in Valetta. His host suggested that the Admiral bring along four of his officers, and I was one of the lucky ones. Each of us was provided with a dinner partner. Mine was by far the most attractive, a beautiful young woman whose husband was an engineering officer on a British frigate. He was in London at the time, and she was available that evening. The dinner was delightful, with one exception. I wasn't aware of how untrained my ears were to British-spoken English.

After dinner, we danced to lovely music provided by the Officers Club orchestra. I learned that Admiral Reiter was a talented dancer, and, based on the reaction of my dance partner, I was rather accomplished myself.

I learned that my companion lived on the base in officers' housing. As the evening drew to a close, I asked her if she would like me to escort her home.

"I would be delighted!" she exclaimed.

When we reached her quarters, she thanked me profusely and shook my hand. Then, much to my surprise, she kissed me quickly on the cheek. I was so startled, I couldn't speak. As I walked back to the club to join the others for the ride to our hotel, my cheek was burning. After all these years, I've never mentioned that kiss to anyone. The evening had completely neutralized the negative experience that I had suffered putting my broken boiler back together on my previous visit to Valetta. Boy did it ever!

Crossroads

When I had first reported to Admiral Reiter, he was in his fifth year as a Rear Admiral. At the end of the fifth year, the Admiral Selection Board in the Navy Bureau of Personnel would decide which of the fifth-year Rear Admirals deserved to be continued, i.e., allowed to remain on active duty for another five years or more, and which would be retired. Over time, I began to sense that the Admiral didn't expect to be continued. Furthermore, I don't think he was overly concerned about this possibility. I base my opinion on two primary factors.

First, the Admiral was seldom in the office. He loved to travel to exotic ports, where he justified his destination by the presence of a ship or two that needed a Materiel Inspection. He would gather his top inspectors and headed for the Mediterranean Sea or another attractive destination. Sometimes he was gone for weeks on end. Captain Woodard, the Admiral's deputy, who looked forward to retiring soon with 30 years' service, followed the Admiral's example and headed to his own exotic destinations with his team of inspectors.

I didn't consider this to be irresponsible behavior. Both men had had long and distinguished naval careers and had been highly decorated during World War II and the Korean War. They deserved to have a plum job. Besides, it was hard not to like or respect Admiral Reiter and Captain Woodard. They were both gentlemen who treated everyone with dignity, respect, and friendship.

In addition, both men were comfortable with turning over complete responsibility for running the Board to me. I may have been a mere Lieutenant with only five years of service under my belt, still I was experienced and trustworthy. Most of the people I dealt with in other organizations outranked me by three or four levels, but a great portion of my time was spent turning down requests for waivers on inspection deficiencies. Often I had to break this *bad* news to extremely difficult individuals. Among the most cantankerous was Admiral Hyman Rickover, with whom Admiral Reiter didn't care to speak. Therefore, I had to handle the dear, sweet man myself.

This was a critical year for me for several reasons. First, because I had gone to Michigan on the Regular NROTC scholarship, I held a Regular (as opposed to a Reserve) Commission. Second, in 1967 the Vietnam War dramatically increased the need for military manpower, especially young officers with my experience. In fact, the Navy had stopped accepting resignations from Regular officers like me. In short, I was in for the duration until the Vietnam situation straightened itself out. In the Navy, each officer was assigned a Detailer, who worked in the Navy Bureau of Personnel. My Detailer advised me that my next duty station was likely to be Commanding Officer of a Motor Gun Boat (PGM) in the Mekong Delta.

I had technically been at sea for five years and was enjoying my first shore assignment. What's more, by this time, I had a wife and one-and-a-half children. I wasn't prepared to be separated from them just yet. Then there was my dream of the future. Before leaving the University of Michigan, I had successfully completed the acceptance testing to earn deferred admission into both the Michigan Law School and Michigan's MBA program. If I had chosen the MBA option, I would have been most interested in majoring in International Marketing.

Since there was a real possibility that I would be in the Navy indefinitely, I started to research the available higher education options that the Navy offered. I stumbled on a perfect one. Each year, the Navy paid for a limited number of naval officers to earn Masters Degrees at Princeton's School of International Relations. I talked to my Detailer and learned the application process. He explained that an ad hoc selection board would be formed to review the candidates and select the lucky scholarship winners. He also reminded me that each year of graduate school came with the requirement to remain on active duty for two additional years. But given my tenuous situation, this was not an issue with me.

I submitted my application and waited for the board's selection, making a mental note to call my Detailer for a status report. Before I could call him, he called me. The board had met and made their selections, but my application hadn't been selected. In fact, he said, sounding irritated, "It wasn't even considered."

"Not considered! Why not?" I asked angrily.

"I'm sorry to have to tell you this. Somehow your application was lost."

"Lost? Can I resubmit it for consideration?"

"No, the board has been dissolved. You're sunk, I'm afraid."

"What next?" I moaned.

"Well, would you like some good news?"

I thought he was joking. "I suppose you're going to tell me I got command of that PGM."

"No. Better than that. If you act today, you can resign your commission."

"You mean that?"

"Come on over and we'll fill out the paper work. You're heading for civilian life in – I'd guess within about six months. Can you wait that long?"

"You bet I can. I'll be right over. Be prepared to be bear hugged."

When I arrived in my Detailer's office, he helped me fill out my resignation application, which I signed and handed to him. As a formality, the application had to be approved by the head of his department. Once that was done, he'd notify my commanding officer by sending him a copy of the order.

"I'd like to break the news to Admiral Reiter first. Could you give me a call as soon as you have the approval?"

The next day, my Detailer phoned to say everything was complete. The order called for my last day of active duty to be August 31, 1967.

"My wife is due to deliver our second child on August 24," I told him. "I hope her doctor's right."

When I entered Admiral Reiter's office, I didn't know whether to display sadness or joy.

"Admiral, I have some news to share with you." I told him about the selection board losing my Princeton application. Then I broke the real news. "But the Bureau has accepted my resignation. I'll be leaving the Navy in about six months."

Admiral Reiter looked sad. Then he said, "You know, Gary, I think you've made the right decision. The Navy isn't what is used to be, but you'll be successful in whatever you choose to do in life. You can bet on that." As an afterthought, he asked, "Has your wife heard the news yet?"

"No, Sir. I wanted you to know first."

"I appreciate that very much, Gary. Now, I have a little news, too. I wasn't continued. You'll soon have a new boss. I'm sure you know of him. Rear Admiral John Bulkeley. He'll be reporting next week, and I will leave immediately after he arrives."

I was speechless, caught completely off guard.

He added, "Please don't say anything to the other staff members. I'd like to tell them myself – when I build up my courage. I'm not good at goodbyes."

Who is? I thought to myself.

My Hero

During World War II, General MacArthur and his family were evacuated from the Philippines by a PT boat commanded by Lieutenant John Bulkeley. This heroic story was depicted in John Ford's 1945 movie based on William White's best-selling book, *They Were Expendable*. The part of Bulkeley was played by Robert Montgomery, and his Executive Officer, Robert Kelley, was played by John Wayne. For his brave acts, Lieutenant Bulkeley was awarded the Medal of Honor. He was to become one of the three most highly decorated heroes of World War II. His only peers were Army infantryman and future movie star, Audie Murphy, and Marine General, Lewis B. "Chesty" Puller.

During the Cuban Missile Crisis, Admiral Bulkeley commanded the Naval Operating Base at Guantanamo Bay, where he gained worldwide fame for his dramatic face-down of Fidel Castro when the Cuban dictator threatened to cut off drinking water to the base. For this act of defiance, he became a hero in the eyes of Cuban emigrants to America, who often sought him out to back their plans to overthrow Castro. I personally witnessed a number of these exchanges.

Before his distinguished naval career ended, Vice Admiral John D. Bulkeley's awards included the Medal of Honor, the Navy Cross, two Distinguished Service Crosses, three Distinguished Service Medals, the Silver Star, the Legion of Merit with the "V" for valor, two Bronze Stars, the French Croix de Guerre, and the Purple Heart. Of all his awards, honors, and war mementoes, the one he held dearest was a dollar bill covered with the autographs of fellow war heroes, world leaders, and movie stars. He kept it hidden deep in his wallet and showed it only to a few privileged people. I was honored to have been one of those.

In 1967, Bulkeley was appointed President of the Naval Board of Inspection and Survey, a critically important organization of naval officers and civilian engineers responsible for conducting Acceptance Trials and Materiel Inspections of all naval ships, submarines, and aircraft. Thanks to a special act of Congress, he served as Board President well beyond the normal retirement age. In 1987, he retired with fifty-five years of naval service. After his death in 1996, he was honored by the commissioning of the *USS Bulkeley* (DDG 84), an Arleigh Burke destroyer.

On my last assignment as a naval officer, I had the honor of serving as Vice Admiral Bulkeley's personal aide and administrative officer for a short period of time. He was one of the most unforgettable people I've ever known. He had a reputation of being a tough, no-nonsense officer. During my stints at the Guantanamo Naval Base, we occasionally caught a glimpse of him from afar. Once I saw him having dinner with his staff at the Officers Club. Another time, he passed me in a jeep driven by a spit-and-polished Marine. I saluted, and he saluted back. What a thrill!

Admiral Bulkeley had become a personal hero of mine. Now he was here to take Admiral Reiter's place, with me as his personal aide and administrative officer. I was honored. The day he arrived at the Board of Inspection and Survey, Admiral Reiter gave him a full tour, introducing him to every member of our Washington office, about 40 people in all. The last to be introduced were Rose, the Admiral's secretary, and me, since our desks were right outside the Admiral's office near the front entrance.

Bulkeley and Reiter disappeared inside the Admiral's office and talked for about two hours. The secretary and I looked at each other and shrugged our shoulders. We didn't know quite what to do with ourselves.

Finally Admiral Reiter, briefcase in hand, came out of his office and said goodbye to Rose and me. Then he walked briskly out the door and down the hall toward the elevator to the garage. I thought Rose was going to cry. If she had, I was in trouble.

"Lieutenant Slaughter, would you please step into my office?" Admiral Bulkeley's tone was warm and friendly. I was optimistic for the first time since I had heard he'd be our new boss, though I was a bit surprised that he wanted to talk to me before he spoke to his new deputy, Captain Woodard.

When I entered the Admiral's office, he asked me to join him at the conference table in the center of the room. His first words nearly knocked me off my chair. "Lieutenant, or if you wouldn't mind, Gary, I've done my homework on you, and I want you to know that from all I hear, you've been doing a whale of a job. The point is that I don't want you to change a thing. Keep answering that phone. Keep saying *No* to those bullies. And I don't need an aide any more than Admiral Reiter did. I want you to continue as administrative officer of this entire organization, worldwide. For a period, I'll be traveling to meet the staffs of the other offices, but I'll travel there by myself. I need you here to see that things run smoothly in my absence. Any questions?"

"No, Sir. I'll be honored to serve you to the best of my ability. And, if I may say so, I am delighted that you approve of how I've been doing things. It makes me proud to hear you say that, Sir."

"You deserve it, Son. Believe me, you do. Now there are two more things. First, I know you've submitted your resignation and will leave the Navy the last of August. That won't make a nickel's worth of difference to me. We'll work together until the day we say goodbye, and I'll be wishing you good luck in whatever you choose to do with your life."

"Thank you, Sir. I sincerely appreciate that. I won't let you down."

"By the way, Gary, keep that wrist alarm of yours in fine working order. We'll need to use that thing quite often if we're going to get anything done in this town."

"Yes, Sir. I will, Sir."

Admiral Bulkeley kept his word, and I never let him down. When I applied for admission to the College of William and Mary's MBA program, I asked the Admiral to write me a letter of recommendation. The letter that follows explains, in part, why he is *My Hero.*

18 August 1967

Head, Department of Business Administration
College of William and Mary
Williamsburg, Virginia 23185

Dear Sir:

Lieutenant Gary Slaughter has requested that I submit to you a letter of recommendation summing up his personal character, professional abilities, and ability as a scholar from my personal observation of him during the past six months.

Lieutenant Slaughter has served as my personal aide and the Administrator of the Office of the Board of Inspection and Survey for the Navy Department. I am the President of the Board. The purpose of the Board is to administer the trials of all ships and crafts, aircraft, and submarines for acceptance for the Secretary of the Navy. In addition, each ship of the Navy is given a Materiel Inspection once every three years. All inspections are thorough, delving into every phase of the materiel condition (electronics, propulsion, operations, and weaponry).

To schedule inspections, administer the office force which must maintain, record, print, and summarize reports, and also being capable of inspecting at least one area himself requires an officer of exceptional administrative and management ability. It further requires integrity, responsibility, tact, and a keen and astute mind.

Lieutenant Slaughter has been handling my office for me for the past six months. I find no fault whatsoever in his handling of a multitude of details, and I can only praise him for his work and management ability.

His military character is beyond reproach. His personal character is outstanding insofar as I know. He is a family man, drinks in most modest amounts, is a gentleman, possesses moral courage, and is sincere and tactful in everything he does. His wife is charming and acceptable anywhere. This officer will be a success anywhere he goes and in most any field of endeavor.

As for scholarly ability, I am attaching his record for your information. I note that he graduated fifth out of 232 in high school, and in the upper 10% at the University of Michigan. In Destroyer School of the Navy which is a professional school, he stood eighth out of a class of 52 outstanding young officers.

I must admit that he is a far better scholar than myself.

If there are any further questions, do please let me know, and I shall be more than happy to answer them. I consider that the Navy is losing an officer of great potential.

Most sincerely,

JOHN D. BULKELEY
Rear Admiral, US Navy
President of the Board of Inspection and Survey

Delayed Discharge and Beyond

Arlington, Virginia
Fall 1967

Because Admiral Bulkeley knew I was a short-timer, he brought my replacement aboard early so I could train him to do my complex job and introduce him to the dozens of contacts I had developed throughout the Navy to make my job easier. Despite the Admiral telling me not to change the way I did business, he needed his new aide to be a traditional Admiral's Aide, not his office manager.

With my relief on board months before I was discharged, I had time to prepare for my separation. I interviewed and was offered three jobs from businesses and was accepted by three excellent post-graduate programs. Two were MBA programs at the University of Michigan and at William and Mary College. The third was early admission to Michigan's School of Law, for which I had been accepted before I was commissioned.

During my tenure with the Board of Inspection and Survey, I initiated the mustering out process for several naval officers who were retiring or had resigned to pursue civilian employment. The process involved scheduling a separation physical and arranging for transporting the officer, his family, and their household goods to the officer's Home of Record, which was usually the town where the officer had been inducted into the Navy. Because this process could take a number of weeks, I generally cut the officer a set of temporary duty orders to Naval Air Station (NAS) Anacostia.

In early August, I was informed that my resignation was being processed for a discharge on August 31, 1967. I immediately cut myself a set of orders to Anacostia. This gave me more time to focus on my next step and on the birth of our second daughter, Jennifer Mitchell Slaughter. As luck would have it, she was born in Bethesda Naval Hospital only seven days before my discharge. Another $8.00 baby!

As I look back, resigning from the Navy was the very best decision I've ever made. If I had known what the future held for me in terms of happiness and success in the business world, I would have resigned years earlier. I accepted an attractive position working at Newport News Shipbuilding and Dry Dock Company in Newport News, Virginia, where I would be part of a team creating the specification for a new marine helicopter assault ship called a *Landing Platform Helicopter* (LPH). Because of my background in shipboard communications, electronics, and engineering, I would play a key role establishing Assurance Engineering Standards involving reliability and maintainability of the new ship's equipment. I found it rather strange that among the 40-person design group, I was the only one who had ever served on a Navy ship. Team members constantly appeared at my office door with what, to me, were ridiculously naïve questions for naval engineers to ask, like "Gary, what's a feed pump?"

In the evenings, I enjoyed taking graduate business courses at William and Mary. Quite honestly, neither Susan nor I particularly enjoyed living in Newport News. We were homesick for Washington. So when the first phase of the design ended, I volunteered to take a severance pay from the shipyard.

We returned to Arlington, Virginia, where I interviewed for jobs, including one for AT&T's Initial Management Development Program (IMDP). The evening before the interview, our house guests, Susan's sorority sister and her husband, arrived far later than expected. After dinner, we settled in for an extremely long session of bridge. Early the next morning, I arrived for my AT&T interview, feeling the effects of little sleep.

Moreover, I was unaware of and unprepared for the lengthy interview process, similar to the 1957 Fort Wayne agenda: AT&T's Scholastic Aptitude Test, a thorough physical examination, and multiple interviews with top managers of the AT&T staff from the Eastern Area, a six-state region headquartered in Washington, DC.

My last interview with the Vice President of the Eastern Area was off to a fine start until I said, "I'm honored to be considered for the IBM Management Development Program."

The gentleman took my error in stride, stating that IBM also offered some fine opportunities for bright fellows like me. To make his point, he revealed that I had scored the highest on the AT&T SAT in the history of the IMDP. This was remarkable news, indeed, for a future IMDP member, still suffering lack of sleep.

Because of my successful interview and my communications and electronics schooling and job experience in the Navy, I was the highest paid member in the history of IMDP. My area of responsibility covered all AT&T outside plant equipment, including underground cable and microwave towers in Maryland and the District of Columbia, as well as parts of Virginia, Delaware, Pennsylvania, and West Virginia. AT&T provided me with a company car equipped with a mobile telephone and a maintenance radio so I could communicate with my technicians in the field. Frankly, it was the most interesting and varied job I have ever had in my life.

To stay on my career path in the IMDP program, my initial assignment was Outside Plant Manager in Baltimore and would last no more than one year. Since I had been given approval to design and implement an innovative method of restructuring the way work was performed in order to improve productivity, I stayed a full 18 months. It was a terrific opportunity for me and AT&T to have a work-restructuring model that was effective in the field. I loved the Navy and am proud of the job I did as a naval officer. But, surprisingly, I didn't miss the Navy a bit after I resigned.

My next AT&T assignment put me back in Washington, where I was the company's National Account Manager for one of their largest customers, Martin-Marietta, the aerospace giant. However, compared to my previous jobs in the Navy and in business, this one was boring. In addition, top management wanted me to stay in that position for at least two years.

With some reluctance, I left AT&T to start several information technology businesses, selling each when it became successful. I have never been as happy or as proud of my successes as I was in the decades following the Navy.

And, isn't it strange that, in business, no one ever issued me a *Letter of Instruction*. In fact, I spent almost all of my time *instructing* corporate managers on how to utilize computers and computer people more effectively. That subject area ultimately became my area of expertise, and I carried out new my profession with pride and perfection.

Enduring Navy Friendships

Nashville, Tennessee
Fall 2016

Both *Cony* and *Blandy* have long since been decommissioned and have met their fates. In 1970, *Cony* was sunk as a target and now is a rusty habitat for sea life off the Virginia coast. For the past 40 years, on the wall in my home office, I have displayed a series of three photographs depicting the stages of *Cony's* sinking. *Blandy's* disposal was less noble. In 1992, she was sold for scrap. I also have photographs showing these two ships in all their glory, slashing boldly across the waves with their colors flying.

The sinking of the *USS Cony*

I am particularly fond of the colored photo of *Blandy* which is inscribed:

> *To Lieutenant Gary Slaughter, US Navy with my thanks for doing such a tremendous job under the most difficult circumstances. Best wishes for the future – light brown haze and full steam!*
>
> *George S. Grove,*
> *Commander US Navy, Commanding*
> *July 30, 1965*

One of the unexpected benefits of serving on two naval destroyers during my active-duty years was building enduring friendships with many of my fellow officers.

Soon after the demise of *Cony* and *Blandy*, their former crew members formed associations that continue to meet in locations across the country. Association members are predominately former enlisted men. Officers are always welcome, and many, including myself, attend these meetings. As I write this book, I look forward to attending the *Cony Association* reunion to be held here in Nashville, Tennessee in April 2016 and the *Blandy Association* in Pensacola, Florida in November 2016.

In the late 1970s, Susan and I lived in Bethesda, Maryland. Having regularly received updated address lists of former crew members from both ships, I noticed that many former *Cony* and *Blandy* officers lived in the nearby Washington, DC and Norfolk, Virginia areas. So I decided to invite those with whom I had served to our house for a reunion. Much to my surprise, 15 of the possible 25 joined us with their spouses.

Among those attending, only one officer was from *Blandy*: Bill Poteat, my former Damage Control Assistant (DCA) and a fine officer. After the Navy, Bill and I worked together in the IT consulting business. Sharing many business successes, our friendship lasted for many years after we served on *Blandy* together. When I decided to leave the IT business and become a novelist, our business relationship ended. Bill was a loyal friend and an extremely gifted IT professional. Most important, he was the finest Naval Officer who ever worked for me.

All other friends who attended were former *Cony* officers. In fact, the *Cony* turnout was complete. Every *Cony* man invited came, including Captain Morgan, who had retired from the Navy and was selling real estate in the Virginia suburbs. He brought a set of original photos of the *Cony*'s sinking, which later I had copied and sent to all of the *Cony* officers with whom I had served.

I have thought about why the *Cony* turnout was so much larger than that of the *Blandy*. I've concluded that serving on *Cony* was an extremely positive experience. We were a proud and proficient crew, who accomplished our mission effectively, especially during the Cuban Missile Crisis. As you have read from Captain Grove's inscription above, *Blandy* was indeed fraught with *difficult circumstances*. The *Blandy* experience was not as positive for me, and I suspect for some of my *Blandy* shipmates.

To relive the positive associations with old *Cony* Wardroom friends, I organized another reunion of *Cony* officers, as a subset of the *Cony* Association's Annual Reunion held in 2007 in Pigeon Forge, Tennessee. Ten of us attended with our spouses. We officers reserved a private dining room, where we chatted about the old *Cony* days and brought each other up to date on what was happening in our lives. At this reunion I gave each officer and enlisted man a copy of my first novel, *Cottonwood Summer*. While I inscribed the books, we spent hours reliving our successes together on *Cony*.

Cony's Operations Officer, Jim Rowsey, attended the Pigeon Forge officer's reunion. He had been my stateroom mate as well as my boss. Back then, we shared a cordial but formal relationship. I addressed him as either *Mr. Rowsey* or *Lieutenant Rowsey*. That formality has melted away with the years. Since Pigeon Forge, we have communicated regularly by telephone and e-mail on a first-name basis.

Two other *Cony* officer reunions have been held in Washington, neither of which I have been able to attend. From a full report from my old friends, I know the practice of getting back together is a good one. The most recent officers' reunion, in

October 2015, received glowing reviews. I was disappointed to miss it, because two of the attendees were men I hadn't seen since the early 1960's when we served together on *Cony*. Since *Cony* was my first ship and my first love you might say, I have stayed in touch with about 15 fellow *Cony* officers over these 55 years or so.

Another *Cony* officer, Andy Bradick, who was ASW officer during the Cuban Missile Crisis, was interviewed with me by Bedlam Productions during the filming of their documentary, *The Man Who Saved the World.* Our interviews were filmed aboard the *USS Barry* (DD 933) which was on exhibit in the Washington Navy Yard in Washington, DC. In October 2012, the documentary was broadcast on PBS stations nationwide to celebrate the 50th anniversary of the *Cony-B59* confrontation during the Cuban Missile Crisis. The *Barry* was a *Forrest Sherman* class destroyer, the same class as *Blandy.*

Coincidentally, Andy, a career man, served as Executive Officer on the *Barry*. Andy also served in Viet Nam and in the Middle East. In short, his career was very diverse. He is the only officer I know who initially resigned his commission after his first tour of duty. A short time later, he rejoined the Navy and put in a full career. Because of my respect for him, after he retired from the Navy, I offered him a position as CEO of Gary Slaughter Corporation. Unfortunately, he decided to go into business for himself. We shook hands and remained friends.

The officer with whom I have had the most interaction since we served together on *Blandy* is Les Westerman. Les graduated with an engineering degree from Purdue University. After graduation, he worked at Underwriters Laboratory in Chicago before attending Officers Candidate School in Newport. Les was the ASW Officer and a fine OOD. We served together for two years until I was ordered to be the Aide to the President of the Board of Inspection and Survey. Les and I lost track of each other until my wife and I moved from Naples, Florida to Nashville in 1999. Les lived in Pensacola, Florida, where he owned and operated a marina for many years. Since living in Nashville, we have returned to Southern Florida on two-week vacations about twice a year. On our return trip to Nashville, we've visited

Les and his wife Bobbie in Pensacola. Les still has family in his hometown of Chicago and often returns there by traveling through Nashville. On a number of occasions, he and his wife have occupied our guest quarters.

I've mentioned Chuck Nuechterlein's name at least 20 times. Since our first meeting in the fall of 1957, Chuck and I attended NROTC classes together for four years, participated in two midshipman summer cruises, pledged the same fraternity, and were college roommates for three years. He and I also lived in Naples, Florida. Obviously, Chuck is a shoo-in for the Most Enduring Navy Friend. I can't overestimate the value of our loyal relationship over all these decades.

My shipmates have proved to be the most constant and reliable friendships of my life. One more reason for my love of the United States Navy!

Remnants from My Navy Service

Nashville, Tennessee
Fall 2016

Since I spent 11 years in the Navy, it might seem that I would have many possessions to remind me of those days. However, I have amazingly few. While some of the items I've retained might seem insignificant, they mean a lot to me.

At the height of my commissioned service, I had at least two sets of the four different uniforms that I was required to wear as a naval officer: Service Dress Blue, Service Dress Khaki, Tropical White, and Service Dress White. In addition, I had a supply of accessories. Combination caps with three different colored covers and fore-and-aft hats. Pairs of black, brown, and white shoes. Shoulder boards and collar pins signifying my rank. A dark blue woolen overcoat, a tan raincoat, and a foul-weather jacket.

The only component from my uniform clothing that I retained was my dark-blue woolen overcoat, but it didn't last long. Back in the 1970's, a good friend, Dave Kartalia, was a hippie of sorts. He happened to see my overcoat hanging in our front-hall closet, and he fell in love with it. All he had to do was remove the shoulder boards, he told me, and he would have the perfect hippie winter coat. I couldn't deny him the pleasure. Besides I hadn't worn the coat once in the seven years since I'd left the Navy. I gave it to Dave, and he wore it every day, even in summer as I recall.

I do still have my formal Navy sword and scabbard as well as my service ribbons and the medals they represent. Recently, I purchased new medals and ribbons, because the originals had turned green from exposure to salt air. I have willed my sword to my oldest grandson Josh and the ribbons and medals to his younger brother Tim. I told them this when they were young boys. Now that they are in their twenties, I wonder if they remember. If not, they'll be that much more surprised when I transcend.

During the summer of 1960, when I was on my 1st Class Midshipman Cruise in the Mediterranean on the *USS Valley Forge,* I purchased my first 30mm camera from the ship's store. That summer, I took hundreds of pictures, which I dutifully converted into slides. I accumulated about a dozen carousels of slides and only watched them once. After 40 years or so, my projector gave up the ghost, so a few years ago, I purchased a device that converts old slides into computer images. This conversion took me about a week. I culled my slide collection down to a reasonable size. Among other excesses, I discovered that I had taken close to a 100 pictures of a bull fight in Lisbon. I guess I was suffering from a severe case of new camera syndrome.

I have also mentioned the memorable photographs of the *USS Cony, USS Blandy*, and *ASW Task Group Alpha* that hang in my home office. When I want to make a copy of one of them, I have to copy the photo through the glass, because the pictures are impossible to remove from their frames without damaging them.

I still have my old draft card, and I did have my two dog tags on chains. However, long ago, my young daughters, Wendy and Jennifer, raided the attic for interesting items. My dog tags were fatalities of this raid, traded away for some toy or another, I presume.

My last three relics are my favorites. First, I kept my old Navy sea bag that I have had since the fall of 1957. My name is stenciled on it along with the initials KWN, belonging to Karl William "Chuck" Nuechterlein, my fraternity brother, roommate, and fellow NROTC scholarship holder. Second, my old set of white INSURV coveralls with *Lieutenant Gary L. Slaughter, USN* marked above the left chest pocket. I am happy to report that I can still fit into them while doing chores around the house.

Finally, my dear old sea chest. That huge heavy plywood box with a hasp for a hefty padlock was built by the tender. There I stored all my gear when I left *Blandy* for shore duty at the INSURV Board. The sea chest sets in my garage, providing a comfortable place to sit while I change into my work shoes in preparation for helping my wife in her beautiful flower gardens.

While these items are not much in the way of physical remnants, I still have a great fondness for them. But I suppose the most important remnants to me today are these vignettes that I have written from memory and comprise this book. These are everlasting, and I don't anticipate any of them being traded by my grandchildren for toys!

About the Author

Gary Slaughter was born and raised in Owosso, Michigan. After graduating from the University of Michigan, he served seven years, during the Cold War, as a naval officer primarily on anti-submarine destroyers.

Following his distinguished Navy service, he became an expert on managing corporate information technology. He traveled extensively, lecturing and consulting to clients in the United States and abroad. In 2002, he put this career on hold and began to write the *Cottonwood* series, five award-winning novels, depicting life on the World War II home front.

In *Sea Stories: A Memoir of a Naval Officer*, he reveals an incident that occurred on October 27, 1962 during the height of the Cuban Missile Crisis. This incident was the closest that the Soviet Union and the United States ever came to having an exchange of nuclear weapons. However, the incident was classified as *Top Secret* under the terms of an agreement between Premier Khrushchev and President Kennedy that ended the crisis. After 40 years of keeping his secret, even from his family, the event was finally declassified when his story was revealed in Peter Huchthausen's 2002 book, *October Fury*.

Since then, four documentary filmmakers sought his participation in developing a film to celebrate the 50th anniversary of the Cuban Missile Crisis. He selected Bedlam Productions, whose movie, *The King's Speech*, won the 2010 Best Picture Academy Award. Fittingly, the Bedlam documentary was entitled *The Man Who Saved the World.* He was also interviewed and filmed for the BBC documentary, *The Silent War.*

After having written and lectured extensively about the Cuban Missile Crisis for a dozen years, the author shares the fascinating details of his entire naval career in 60 vignettes comprising *Sea Stories*.